Making
Heirloom Toys

Making
Heirloom Toys

Jim Makowicki

The Taunton Press

Cover photo: Boyd Hagen

© 1996 by The Taunton Press, Inc.
All rights reserved.

First printing: 1996
Printed in the United States of America

A Fine Woodworking Book

Fine Woodworking® is a trademark of the Taunton Press, Inc.,
registered in the U.S. Patent and Trademark Office.

The Taunton Press, 63 South Main Street, Box 5506, Newtown,
CT 06470-5506

Library of Congress Cataloging-in-Publication Data

Makowicki, Jim.
    Making heirloom toys / Jim Makowicki.
        p.   cm.
    "A Fine Woodworking book"—T.p. verso.
    ISBN 1-56158-112-7
    1. Wooden toy making.   I. Title.
TT174.5.W6M348   1996
745.592—dc20   96-17860
                                                                     CIP

About Your Safety

Working wood is inherently dangerous. Using hand or power tools improperly or ignoring standard safety practices can lead to permanent injury or even death. Don't try to perform operations you learn about here (or elsewhere) unless you're certain they are safe for you. If something about an operation doesn't feel right, don't do it. Look for another way. We want you to enjoy the craft, so please keep safety foremost in your mind whenever you're in the shop.

This book is dedicated to Priscilla, my wife and lifelong friend, for helping me cut several miles of lumber to a workable size and tolerating all the mountains of sawdust.

Contents

Acknowledgments

Opportunity is a wonderful gift, and I must first thank Helen Albert of The Taunton Press for making this book possible. Her professional marketing advice over the many months of this book's development has been invaluable. I'm also grateful to Charley Robinson for all his help with the preliminary drafts of this book.

Communication is a primary function of any book, and for his help in making the book flow I'd like to thank my editor, Peter Chapman. I'd also like to thank Christopher Casey (book designer), Susan Kahn and Boyd Hagen (photographers), Joanne Renna (publishing coordinator) and all the other folks at The Taunton Press who've had a part in the creation of this book.

Finally, a special thanks to Chrystene Makowicki for helping me articulate my thoughts and for typing the various drafts of the manuscript.

Introduction

As an avid woodworker and father of three children, I've been making wooden toys for more years than I care to remember. My early toys were a little crude, but as my woodworking skills and design sense developed three of my toys were accepted for a limited production run. One of the three won a Parents' Choice Award, given by a publication dedicated to the promotion of toys that have high educational value. But the toy that really launched my toymaking career was the grasshopper, which is featured as the first project in this book. The exaggerated features, big colorful eyes and floppy antennae of this playful little critter caught the attention of some friends at a Connecticut library, who suggested that I start teaching toymaking to children. The classes were a great success with the kids, and ultimately brought the folks at *Fine Woodworking* magazine to my door. In essence, the grasshopper made this book possible.

Toys worth making are worth making well. What distinguishes the toys in this book from the run-of-the-mill offerings you'll find at all too many toy stores is the high standard of craftsmanship and the quality of the materials used. In many cases, commercial toys are made with construction-grade lumber and painted in garish colors. My toys are made with select hardwoods and quality finishing materials that enhance the natural beauty of the wood (I use paint only sparingly to highlight the details). They're beautiful toys, but don't be fooled into thinking that they belong only on the display shelf. These are durable toys that are designed to be played with—put any one of them in the hands of a child and you'll quickly see that they have that irresistible, "play-with-me" appeal.

Although the projects in this book may appear simple because of their size, some of them can take as long to build as a piece of furniture. Many of the toys have over 50 pieces; the ferry boat (with its vehicles) has well over 100 parts. For the most part, I've organized the projects from simple to complex, though I've also tried to group the toys by type.

The projects represent various levels of difficulty, but all require strict attention to safety. Cutting and drilling small pieces can present serious safety hazards, and throughout the book I've stressed the importance of using jigs, fixtures and safe practices to minimize the risk of injury.

BUILDING SAFE TOYS

The safety of the toymaker is only one side of the story. The other side is the safety of the child playing with the toy. Safety should be the primary consideration when designing and building any toy for a child. To minimize the risk of injury, potentially hazardous hardware such as hooks should be avoided where possible; if you have to use them, don't conceal them, and try to position them so that they won't inflict any harm. For example, if you're using a hook and eyebolt to connect two train carriages, turn the hook portion downward. Similarly, on toys that will be played with by young children, round over sharp corners to reduce the risk of injury.

If you're making toys for young children, you can almost guarantee that the toy will find its way to the mouth at some point, so it's important that the finish you use is safe. I use non-toxic finishes only—which is not only safer for the child but also friendlier to the environment (and to your lungs).

Check toys periodically for loose parts. This safety precaution is especially important if the toys are for children under the age of three. Legislative safety regulations help us make wise decisions when developing toys for young children, but ultimately it's the parents' obligation to teach safe play.

Toymaking Techniques

Toymaking presents a special woodworking challenge because of the small scale at which you have to work—many of the parts you'll be cutting and shaping are no more than 6 in. long. Working with small parts demands exacting tolerances and accurate measurements. It also requires that you be particularly vigilant about safety.

Working in $1/32$-in. increments is no easy task, so I've developed jigs, fixtures and techniques that let me accurately and reliably perform repeat operations without having to squint at those blurry little hatch marks along the bottom edge of my rule. I've also acquired some tools and developed processes and procedures that promote safe, accurate and tearout-free work.

General Guidelines

Accurate work requires accurate layouts, which in turn require accurate reference surfaces. Before beginning a project, I check to make sure that the stock I'm using is straight, square and flat. To avoid the hassles of layouts, though, I use full-size patterns whenever possible, particularly for complicated pieces. With this in mind, I've included a few full-size drawings for the more difficult, non-geometric-shaped pieces in these projects. (For those patterns that are too big to fit in the book at full scale, I've included scale drawings that can be enlarged on a copier to make full-size plans.)

TRANSFERRING PATTERNS

Transferring patterns to wood presents another challenge. Some toymakers like to use carbon paper, but I find it too messy. The easiest way to transfer a pattern is to photo-copy it from the book, lay the photo-copy face down on the stock and then run a hot iron over the back side of the photo-copy. The heat-set ink from the photo-copy will be magically transferred to the stock. The only problem with this technique is that it yields a mirror image of the pattern.

For non-concentric patterns that can't be reversed, I trace the pattern onto tracing paper with a soft black pencil. Then I turn the paper over and redraw the pattern on the back side, following the lines that show through the paper. Next I lay the tracing paper on the stock, back side down, and go over the lines on the front of the paper one more time. Pencil pressure on the front of the paper transfers the lines on the back to the stock just like carbon paper, but without all the mess.

WORKING FROM THE CENTER OUT

Once I have the pattern laid out, I work from the center of the stock out whenever possible. Working from the center out means making any internal cuts or drilling before shaping the perimeter of a piece (I usually start with stock that's slightly thicker than the finished thickness). The center-out procedure leaves reliably square surfaces for measuring from and for referencing against fences, stops and tables for accurate work. In many cases, the subsequent shaping of the perimeter will clean up tearout or splintering that may have occurred during the internal operations.

USING THE PARTS LIST

Each project in this book includes a detailed list of parts, with a description of the part, the quantity needed, dimensions and suggested material. All dimensions are in inches and indicate the overall finished size, with the third dimension as the preferred grain direction, except as noted. As explained above, in some cases you'll need to cut the blank oversize and then trim to final size after completing internal cutting and drilling operations.

USING COMMERCIAL PARTS

Some of the parts for the toys in this book, such as wheels, smokestacks and people, are easier to buy than to make (for sources, see Sources of Supply on p. 151). Just remember to buy the parts before you begin a project to be sure they'll fit as planned. You may have to adjust some dimensions to accommodate the mass-produced parts.

TOOLS

To build the toys in this book, you'll need the usual complement of hand tools and stationary machines—table saw, drill press, bandsaw, high-speed router, lathe and scrollsaw. There are also a few specialty tools that I've found to be invaluable aides to accurate work (see the photo below). These include a center finder, a set of metal-cutting countersinks, a set of radius gauges and a full set of drill bits.

The center finder I use is called a "Wiggler," made by General Hardware (item # S-389-4) and available from most industrial supply stores. It consists of an arbor with a ball-joint needle pointer. To use the Wiggler, chuck it in your drill press and then turn on the machine. To align the pointer with the exact center of the drill-press chuck, simply apply a little pressure against the side of the needle until it appears not to be turning (see the photo on the facing page). Now align the workpiece with the needle point and clamp it in place, remove the Wiggler without disturbing the alignment and replace it with the desired drill bit to drill the hole.

I use metal-cutting countersinks rather than regular wood-cutting countersinks because I find that they don't leave chatter marks around the hole. Radius gauges are the best tools for drawing rounded corners on small toy parts. And it's handy to have a complete set of drill bits for boring accurate holes (necessary primarily because dowels aren't true to size). I'd recommend a set that includes all the letter sizes, number sizes and fractional sizes, from 1/16 in. to 1/2 in. graduated in 1/64-in. increments.

Specialty tools that come in handy for toymaking include (clockwise from top) a full set of drill bits, a set of metal-cutting countersinks, a set of radius gauges and a center finder. Also shown are a small machinist's square (foreground) and a right-angle steel block (left).

MATERIALS

When deciding what type of wood to use for my toys, I always consider durability and coloration. My first choice is usually poplar, a dependable hardwood at a reasonable price. I also use a lot of birch, as well as Baltic birch plywood, which is a good choice for wings, thin walls and other long, flat surfaces. I use contrasting woods such as maple, cherry and walnut to create interesting effects and highlights. Woods to avoid are those that are toxic—remember, young children will put anything into their mouths.

When making toy parts, I always cut extra pieces—some so I can experiment with different designs, and some to use for machine setups. I always check my machine setups with scrap stock or with one of the extra parts before committing good wood to the process.

Use a center finder to line up the workpiece under the exact center of the drill-press chuck.

Designing Toys

One of the biggest problems when designing toys is remembering that they are toys, not models. Some craftsmen get so wrapped up in the process that they forget this basic distinction and find themselves with highly detailed pieces that aren't at all suitable for children to play with.

Trying to find just the right balance between authenticity and over-complication can be a challenge. When designing a toy, I start with research, leafing through old catalogs, magazines and books; Dover Publications (see Sources of Supply, p. 151) has a wonderful line of reprinted books, chock-full of antiques and collectibles, that are a great source of inspiration for the nostalgic toys that I favor. In the initial research stage of development, I determine how much detail I can incorporate without sacrificing the intended playful image of the toy.

When developing the design, I give a lot of thought not only to the blocks of wood that make up the toy but also to the space that surrounds and, in many cases, penetrates it. This "negative" space adds character and visual interest to any toy. My favorite example of the use of

negative space is the Trolley Car (see pp. 102-105), where the combination of the positive and negative spaces of the seven evenly spaced rows of seats gives this toy its unique charm.

Combining these design principles and my research, I create some preliminary drawings, modifying them until I come up with what I think is just the right balance of detail and utility. The fun begins when I actually try to build the toy as I've drawn it. With experience, I've gotten better at not designing parts that are next to impossible to make or that are so fragile they wouldn't last a day. But it's not until you get into the shop that you'll discover the shortcomings of your design. Many of my toys have been designed and built a half-dozen times before I'm satisfied. At this point, I'll develop my final drawings. And even then, each time I make that toy, I'm as likely as not to try yet one more variation.

Even more important than a toy's visual appeal is the safety of the toy. So, my designs always take into consideration the age of the child who will be playing with the toy. The same toy can be made appropriate for children of different ages just by varying the degree of detailing.

For example, the Sports Car is quite suitable for toddlers as presented (see pp. 57-59), but adding a few details, such as headlights, taillights, exhaust pipes and rear-view mirrors, will make it more interesting to older children. But the same small parts that grab the older child's attention could become a choking hazard for the toddler. In addition to these more obvious hazards, I also try to avoid hidden safety hazards, such as the finishes (see p. 15).

Design is a matter of choice. These choices are made to satisfy the toymaker's interest, based on his level of craftsmanship and his sensibilities. Design isn't something that can be taught, but it can be motivated. One of my objectives in this book is to stimulate the creative process. Keep in mind that designing is a dynamic process that usually achieves success through evolution. Experiment—don't be afraid to try different approaches to the same problem. But always keep in mind the ultimate purpose—you're making a toy, something that's meant to be handled and played with. Don't overdesign and overdevelop the piece beyond a child's imagination.

Safe Work Habits

Always use a push stick when ripping small parts on the table saw. For added safety, fasten the workpiece to an auxiliary block with double-sided tape.

Toymaking involves shaping and cutting a lot of small parts, which can be extremely dangerous if you try to hold the parts by hand. For safety (and accuracy), always use a jig, a fixture or a clamp to hold the workpiece and to keep your fingers away from sawblades and other high-speed cutters.

PUSH STICKS

I always use a push stick when ripping small parts on the table saw. For particularly narrow rip cuts, I use a 10-in. long, flat metal bar, $1/16$ in. thick by $7/8$ in. wide, that's been cut to a point to push stock through the saw, as shown in the photo at left. Because this bar is so thin, it can ride between the fence and the blade on all but the thinnest of cuts without danger of hitting the blade. And the flexibility of the thin bar helps hold the workpiece against the fence. The pointed tip gives it a good grip, but on finished pieces I tape a small piece of scrap pine to the stock to keep from marring the surface.

DOUBLE-SIDED TAPE

One "tool" that I've come to rely on heavily is double-sided carpet tape. I use it so often for so many different operations that I don't know how I ever got along without it. A toy part that's too small to hold can be fastened to a larger piece of stock with double-sided tape and safely sawn, drilled or routed without your fingers ever getting close to the cutters (make sure to use plenty of tape so the workpiece won't slip). Double-sided tape is also handy for holding parts in jigs or for keeping parts in place while trial-fitting an assembly. It's important to use top-quality tape and to experiment with it before working on finished pieces.

GENERAL SAFETY PRECAUTIONS

Even though you're working on a small scale, you still need to be sure to wear the appropriate protective items (safety glasses, ear protection, respirators, etc.) for the operations you're performing. Avoid loose clothing and long sleeves, especially when working with power tools. And if you feel at all uncomfortable about performing any of the operations in this book, take the time to evaluate each step, and if necessary use an alternate method that you feel more comfortable with.

Using Spacer Blocks

Many of the projects in this book call for incrementally stepped operations, such as drilling rows of equally spaced holes or making a series of repeat cuts (see, for example, the Crane Truck, the Jet Plane, the Trolley Car and the Cable Car). One technique that I've found to be very accurate is to use a stop block and a set of spacer blocks, as shown in the photo on the facing page. The spacer-block technique requires a relatively simple setup and can be used with a variety of tools. To illustrate the procedure, I'll first describe the steps necessary to drill a set of evenly spaced holes on the drill press, and then I'll explain how to make repeat cuts on the table saw.

DRILL-PRESS SETUP

To use the spacer-block technique on the drill press, you'll need an auxiliary fence and a stop block. You can simply use a board clamped to the drill-press table for the fence and a small block clamped to the fence for the stop block, but a fence and stop block are so handy on a drill press that I've added them and an auxiliary table to mine permanently, as shown in the drawing on the facing page. To make the spacer blocks, rip a strip of wood to the desired width (the on-center distance between the holes) on the table saw, and then cut the strip into the number of pieces required. You'll need one fewer spacer blocks than the number of holes to be drilled.

Start by using a center finder to position the first hole on the right end of the stock under the chuck. With the stock clamped in place against the fence, butt the stop block against the left end of the stock. Clamp the stop block to the fence (my auxiliary fence has an adjustable stop block with a built-in locking mechanism). Remove the center finder, replace it with the appropriate drill bit and drill the first hole. Now slide the stock to the right and insert the appropriate-sized spacer block between the stop block and the stock. Drill the second hole. Repeat this procedure to complete the series of holes.

You can also work the spacer-block technique in the opposite direction, removing blocks instead of adding them. Start with all the spacer blocks in place, drill the first hole, remove a spacer, drill the second hole, and so on. The technique is different, but the result's the same.

If I'm making two identical pieces with a mating set of evenly spaced holes (such as the ladder for the Fire Truck, see pp. 114-120), I'll tape the pieces together back-to-back, drill the first hole in the first ladder rail, and then flip the two pieces over and drill the first hole in the second rail. Next, I slide the rails to the right, add a spacer block and drill the second holes in both rails, and so on until the holes are complete. If the series of holes needs to be centered on the stock, lay out the holes and make the setup as above with the center finder, but before changing to the drill bit, measure from the needle point to the right end of the stock. Then, slide the stock to the right, insert all the spacers you'll be using to drill the series of holes between the stop block and the stock, and then measure the distance from the needle point to the left end of the stock. It should be the same as the distance at the right end. If not, make the required adjustment on the stop block and re-check.

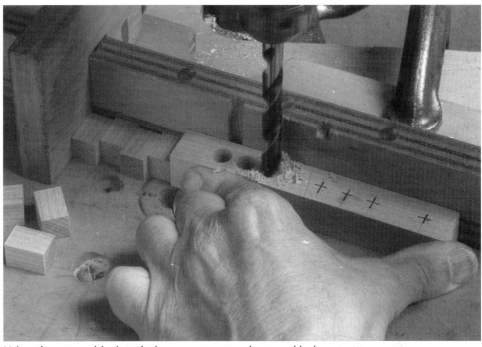

Using the spacer-block technique ensures evenly spaced holes or cuts.

Spacer-Block Setup on Drill Press

A fence, a stop block and some spacer blocks are all you need to drill sets of evenly spaced holes without measuring.

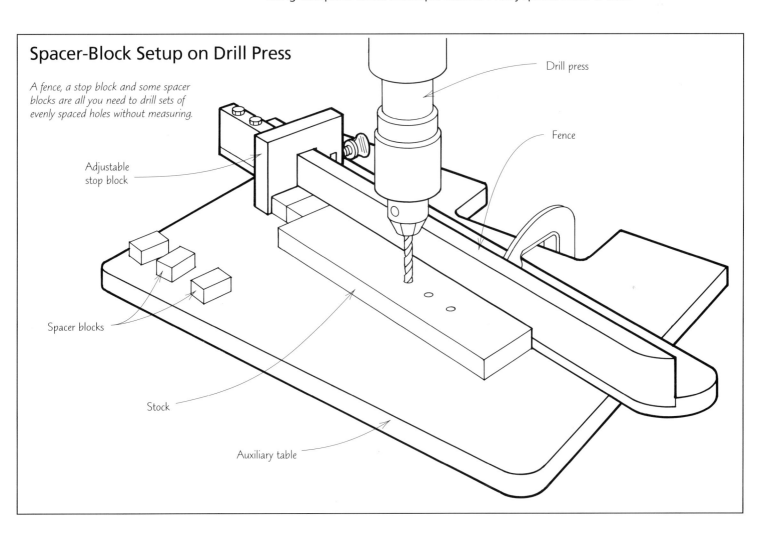

Adjustable stop block

Spacer blocks

Stock

Auxiliary table

Drill press

Fence

To make repeat cuts on the table saw, set the rip-fence position with the appropriate number of spacer blocks. Remove one spacer and reset the fence for subsequent cuts.

TABLE-SAW SETUP

The spacer-block technique can be used on the table saw with either the miter gauge for crosscuts or the rip fence for rip cuts. For crosscuts, you'll need to attach an auxiliary fence and a stop block to the miter gauge, as on the drill press (see the photos on p. 103). I find it easiest to align the sawblade from the back side of the saw when initially positioning the stop block. Otherwise, the procedure is the same.

To space rip cuts, I use the rip-fence stop shown in the photo and drawing at left. The stop, which locks onto a steel bar that rides in the table saw's miter-gauge slot, works just like the stop block on the drill-press fence. Begin by setting the rip fence for the first cut along the edge of the stock farthest away from the fence. Place the appropriate number and size spacer blocks on the saw table butted against the fence, and then slide the rip-fence stop against the spacer blocks and lock it in place by tightening the wing nut on top. Make your first cut, remove one spacer block and slide the rip fence to the left so it butts up against the remaining spacer blocks. Lock the rip fence in place and make the next cut. Repeat this procedure for the remaining cuts.

Rip-Fence Stop

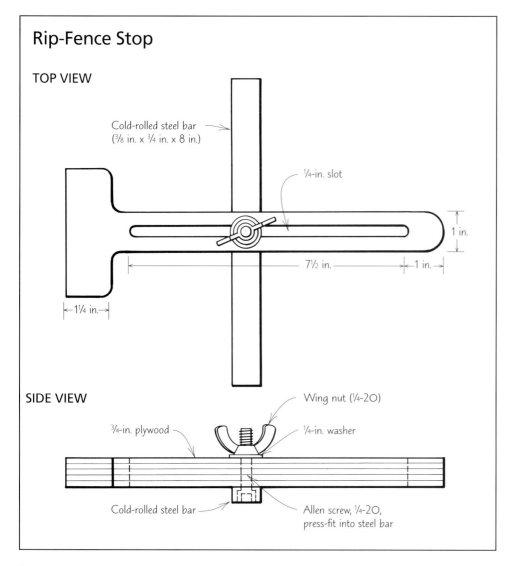

TOP VIEW

Cold-rolled steel bar
(3/8 in. x 3/4 in. x 8 in.)

1/4-in. slot

1 in.

7 1/2 in.

1 in.

1 1/4 in.

SIDE VIEW

Wing nut (1/4-20)

3/4-in. plywood

1/4-in. washer

Cold-rolled steel bar

Allen screw, 1/4-20, press-fit into steel bar

Angle-Cutting Strategies

One feature that helps distinguish my toys from the usual chunky blocks scrollsawn from standard construction lumber is the variety of angles that each model incorporates. Unless these angles are accurately cut, however, they can detract from the quality image you're striving for. To develop most of these angles and tapers, I use a simple jig cut from a piece of ¾-in. thick plywood. The jig has a straight edge that rides along the table-saw fence and a notch cut into the opposite edge that holds the blank at the desired angle to the blade (see the photo at right).

I make the angle cuts before I do any other perimeter shaping so I'll have straight and square edges for references. The real key to cutting angles with jigs successfully is making the cuts in the right order so that you maintain straight reference surfaces (the right order is particularly important in shaping the Life Star Helicopter; see pp. 63-68).

Another jig that I've found helpful is a tenoning jig, as shown in the drawing below. I use this jig for cutting tenons and rabbets on small parts, but by simply tilting the blade it also works for cutting bevels and tapers, as shown in the photo at right on p. 28. In addition to the shopmade jig, I also use a commercial tenoning jig for larger pieces (as shown in the photo at left on p. 97).

Using a simple jig made of ¾-in. plywood makes it easy to cut accurate angles.

Tenoning Jig

Position the stock in the jig with one edge butted against the clamping block. Push the sliding block against the opposite edge and tighten the screw to lock the sliding block in place. Tighten the bolt in the clamping block to secure the stock in the jig.

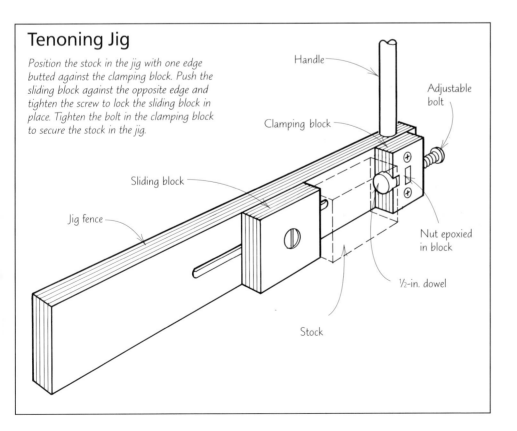

Handle

Adjustable bolt

Clamping block

Sliding block

Jig fence

Nut epoxied in block

½-in. dowel

Stock

Drilling Techniques

A drilling operation of one sort or another is common to every one of the projects in this book, from drilling simple axle or smokestack holes to making a complex series of holes that create a major design element of the piece. Although drilling a hole may seem like a simple enough task, poor drilling techniques can lead to splintered holes, torn wood fibers or poorly fitting parts. The jigs, fixtures and tips featured in this section will make drilling operations easy.

ELIMINATING TEAROUT ON CLOSELY SPACED HOLES

The biggest problem with drilling a series of closely spaced holes, as in the Jet Plane (see pp. 73-76), is that the drill bit exiting the back side of the stock invariably tears out large chunks of wood between the holes. I solve this problem by leaving the stock about ¼ in. thicker than I actually need and then drilling just until the point of the drill breaks through the back side of the piece. Then I saw the extra ¼ in. off the back side to expose the holes, leaving perfectly clean holes on both sides of the stock.

DRILLING ANGLED HOLES

Some drill presses have tilting tables for drilling angled holes; you can also build a special tilting auxiliary table for this purpose. But with either method I've always had trouble with the drill bit drifting slightly as it's presented to the angled piece of wood. As a result, the hole ends up being a little sloppy or slightly out of position. To counter this problem, I use the angled drilling jig shown in the drawing below. The jig, which is custom-made for a specific workpiece, holds the stock at the proper angle and prevents the drill bit from wandering as it contacts the stock. (For a photo of the jig in use, see p. 38.)

DRILLING DOWELS

After making the Ferry Boat or the Walk the Ball project, you'll be convinced that the dowel-drilling jig, shown in the top drawing on the facing page, is well worth the few minutes it takes to make. The jig is simply a block of wood with two holes drilled in it. The larger horizontal hole drilled into the end holds the dowel, while the vertical top hole guides the bit. Clamp the block to the auxiliary fence with the guide hole centered under the drill bit. Insert the dowel stock into the horizontal hole and drill through the guide hole into the dowel. Hold the dowel firmly so that it doesn't turn. The only critical aspect of making this jig is to be sure the guide hole is centered over the dowel hole. (For a photo of the jig in use, see p. 61.)

DRILLING ROUND STOCK

When you're drilling wheels and other round pieces, it can be difficult to line up the stock. Also, the stock tends to spin because there's only one small contact area between the wheel and the fence. Adding a stop block may help with the alignment problem, but it doesn't do much to eliminate the spinning. The V-shaped jig, shown in the bottom drawing on the facing page, overcomes both these problems. Once positioned and clamped to the drill-press auxiliary fence, the jig quickly and consistently aligns the stock, and the rubber facing (made from a wide elastic band) provides a good grip to prevent spinning. (For a photo of the jig in use, see p. 20.)

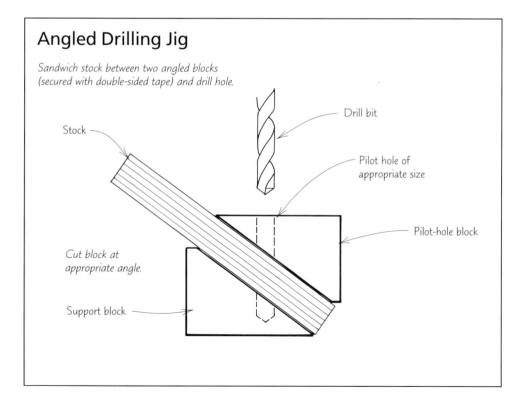

Angled Drilling Jig

Sandwich stock between two angled blocks (secured with double-sided tape) and drill hole.

Stock

Drill bit

Pilot hole of appropriate size

Cut block at appropriate angle.

Pilot-hole block

Support block

Dowel-Drilling Jig

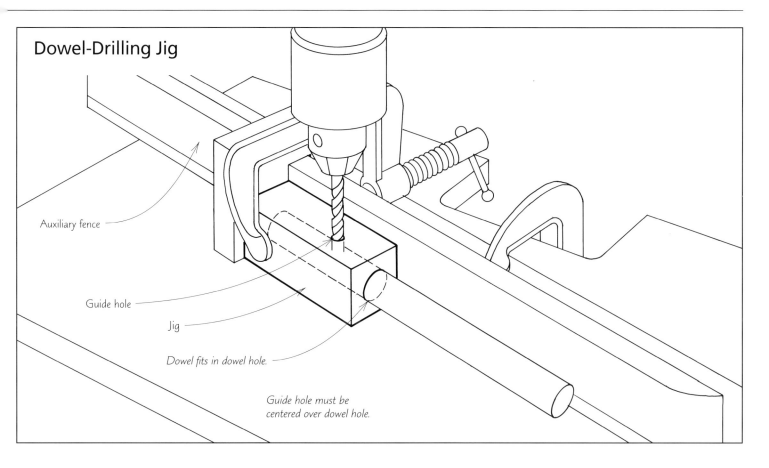

Auxiliary fence

Guide hole

Jig

Dowel fits in dowel hole.

*Guide hole must be
centered over dowel hole.*

V-Jig for Drilling
Round Stock

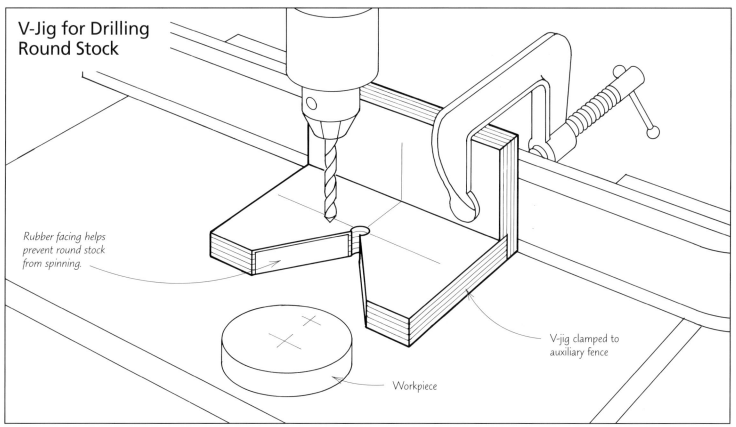

*Rubber facing helps
prevent round stock
from spinning.*

V-jig clamped to
auxiliary fence

Workpiece

Wheels and Axles

You've probably already noticed that many of the toys in this book are transportation toys—cars, trucks, trains, planes, and so forth. This means that, for most of them, you'll have to attach one or more pairs of wheels.

DRILLING AXLE BLOCKS

Some of the vehicles in this book use an axle block to mount the wheels (see the Dump Truck, for example). The hole for the axle has to be drilled through a block that measures only about ⅝ in. by ¾ in. by 2⅛ in. End-drilling this piece of hard maple would present quite a challenge without the aid of the drilling jig shown in the drawing below. For the initial setup, I clamp an axle blank into the jig and then butt the jig to the auxiliary fence on the drill press, aligning the center of the hole with the center finder mounted in the drill's chuck. Once the jig is positioned, I clamp it to the auxiliary fence. The jig supports the piece vertically and, once clamped in position, makes it easy to drill subsequent blocks without needing to line each one up. You simply unclamp the drilled block, put a new blank into the jig and clamp it in place. Drill the hole in steps to minimize heat buildup and potential drifting. I drill the hole with a ¼-in.-dia. bit first, and then redrill with a 9/32-in.-dia. bit to provide sufficient clearance for easy axle rotation. Also, reaming out 1/32 in. in a final pass leaves a much cleaner and more accurate hole. (For a photo of the jig in use see p. 28.)

CUTTING AXLES TO LENGTH

To make sure I get the axle length just right, I cut the axles long and then dry-assemble the wheels, axles and spacer washers to the vehicle and mark the axle's length. I disassemble the unit, trim the axles to length and then crimp glue grooves in the axle ends with a pair of Channelock slide-jaw pliers. (I prefer slide-jaw pliers because they have sharper, better defined teeth and press in better glue grooves than ordinary pliers.)

DRILLING WHEELWELLS

Some of the projects, such as the Sports Car, involve cutting a wheelwell with a Forstner-type bit. However, the wheelwell is only a partial hole, and the actual center of the bit may fall below the bottom of the chassis. To give the bit's center some stock to drill into and to prevent tearout along the bottom edge of the vehicle, I clamp a scrap block to the bottom of the chassis, as shown in the photo at left on the facing page.

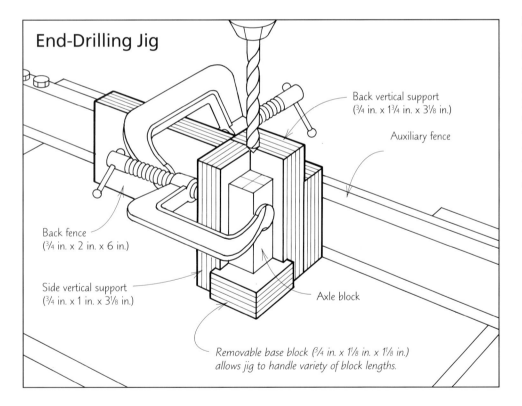

End-Drilling Jig

Back vertical support
(¾ in. x 1¾ in. x 3⅛ in.)

Auxiliary fence

Back fence
(¾ in. x 2 in. x 6 in.)

Side vertical support
(¾ in. x 1 in. x 3⅛ in.)

Axle block

Removable base block (¾ in. x 1⅛ in. x 1⅛ in.) allows jig to handle variety of block lengths.

When cutting wheelwells, clamp a scrap block to the bottom of the workpiece to give the bit's center some stock to drill into and to prevent tearout along the bottom edge of the vehicle.

When cutting a series of wheels, align the perimeter of the hole saw with the kerf of the previous wheel.

CUTTING WHEELS WITH A HOLE SAW

Although I tend to buy more wheels than I make these days, there are occasions when the wheels available commercially either aren't the right size or the right wood species. On these occasions, I cut my own wheels with a hole saw and then touch them up on the lathe to get just the right size, finish and detail. To make the wheel blanks easy to remove from the hole saw, I drill about 80% of the way through the stock from one side with the pilot bit penetrating the backside of the stock. Then I flip the workpiece over, align the pilot drill with the center hole and finish up the cut. When drilling several wheels, I align the outer perimeter of the hole saw with the kerf of the wheel that's just been cut, as shown in the top photo at right. Working this way allows sawdust to escape, speeds up the drilling process and helps reduce heat buildup. Be careful, however, not to create little islands of waste stock between the wheels, which could break loose and become airborne.

After cutting the wheels, true them up on the lathe.

Details Make the Difference

Use a jig with an adjustable pivot pin to sand a smooth radius on the belt sander.

Little things can make a big difference in the way your toys are perceived. I've found that spending a little extra time to get the details right makes for toys I can be proud of and toys that my customers are proud to own or give as presents.

VEHICLE LIGHTS

Lights are an optional detail on toy vehicles and can be added to or taken away from any project in this book to suit the builder or the user of the toy. For toys for small children, leave them off; for display pieces, lights add interesting detail.

The lights I use on most of my vehicles are pieces of dowel cut about ¾ in. long. I either countersink a studded pearl button in the end of the dowel or paint the end (white for headlights, red for taillights, yellow for turn signals). On some vehicles, I glue the dowels into corresponding holes in the body; on others, I mount them on top of the fenders. For fender-mounted lights, I round off the back end on a lathe, using a press-fit wooden collet (as shown in the photo on p. 133).

SANDING A SMOOTH RADIUS

Another nice detail is a smooth radius on the the end of a toy part. To speed up the process of smoothing the leg ends on my popular grasshopper toy (see pp. 19-23), I developed a jig for use on the belt sander. The adjustable jig allows me to pivot the legs against the belt for a fair and even curve, as shown in the photo at left. This jig also works well for sanding wheels and other curves.

Jigs

Sometimes we forget that jigs are just a means to an end. Although you'll see photos of jigs in this book that I've spent some time developing, building and finishing, there are lots of jigs that are cut from scrap, used for the intended purpose and then thrown away.

Not every jig has to be a shining jewel; in fact, it's best to build a crude jig, try it out and then modify it until it's just right before you build the fancy version (which should be finished with sanding sealer to help control wood movement). Only build the fancy version if it's a particularly useful jig that you'll use often, such as the tenoning jig on p. 9. You'll get more productive work done, and you'll be more likely to take a few extra minutes to make the jig that just might save some fingers on a dangerous operation. And don't forget, fastening smaller pieces to a larger board with double-sided tape is probably one of the quickest and easiest ways to keep your fingers away from the blade.

Finishing

The difference between an heirloom toy and one that gets banged around and thrown away is very often the finish. A toy with a nice finish commands respect, whether it's at a craft-market sales booth, on the shelf of a collector or in the hands of a happy child. A quality finish lets people know that the toy is special—one to be enjoyed, but also to be handled with care.

By sealing the pores, a quality finish helps protect the wood from the normal dust and dirt encountered in use and in storage. The finish also creates a harder, more durable surface that helps the wood endure the abuse that children will surely inflict on any toy designed to be played with (as all of the toys presented in this book are). During the course of hard play, the finish may eventually wear away, but it's easily renewed with a few quick brush strokes.

Safe Finishes

The most important factor when selecting a finish for a toy is that the finish is safe. I use any durable oil-based polyurethane that the manufacturer claims is non-toxic when fully cured. Be sure to read the label on the can to find out how long it takes for the finish to cure—some will cure quickly, but others can take up to 30 days. I always allow a few extra days just to be on the safe side. Although a finish may be non-toxic when dry, it doesn't mean it is also non-toxic in the can. Check the label for any safety precautions necessary while applying the finish, apply finishes only in an area with adequate ventilation and always keep young children and pregnant women away from the finishing area.

Some specific safe finishing options that you may want to experiment with include a line of citrus-based finishes from Livos Plantchemistry, a company that specializes in non-toxic and environmentally safe products (see Sources of Supply on p. 151). The Peterson Chemical Corp. offers a clear epoxy finish that has been approved by the Food and Drug Administration for use on utensils. And, long a favorite with woodturners for finishing food implements, Behlen's Salad Bowl Finishes are available from Garrett Wade.

Other low-toxicity finishes to consider are, starting with the least toxic, shellac (dissolve-it-yourself flakes are better than premixed shellacs), *pure* tung oil (Danish oils, which are a tung-oil mixture, may contain metallic driers and should be avoided), water-based latex paints (whites and light pastels are generally safer) and certain water-based polyurethanes (check the can for toxicity rating or ask the manufacturer). I generally avoid vegetable-oil-type finishes, such as olive, peanut or castor oil. Although these oils are non-toxic, they are also non-drying and can leave a sticky surface or turn rancid.

The Finishing Process

Because of the many small parts involved in building toys, I like to finish as many of the pieces as possible before assembly. Sanding and finishing before assembly make it possible to get to surfaces that will be inaccessible in the completed toy and eliminate the need to work inside small, tight places. Working with pre-assembled pieces allows long, sweeping brush strokes and avoids the problem of the buildup of finish in corners, thereby yielding a better-looking toy.

SANDING

To prepare parts for finishing, I first sand them to 120 grit, apply a coat of sanding sealer (for a smoother surface) and then lightly sand again with 220-grit paper. After each sanding, I vacuum the pieces and wipe them with a tack cloth. To avoid sucking the pieces into the vacuum, I tape a piece of window screening over the vacuum nozzle. Cloth-type screening works better than wire screening because it is easier to wrap around the nozzle (and it won't scratch the workpiece).

For sanding flat pieces, I've designed some sanding blocks that really come in handy (see the drawing at left). I size the blocks to accept quarter, half and whole sheets of paper. One side of the block is padded (with cork or foam rubber) and the other is hard to suit a variety of sanding needs. Changing paper is simple. You just pull out the wedge in the side of the block, discard the old paper, wrap a new piece around the block and reinsert the wedge to hold the paper firmly in place. The blocks are so simple to make that I have several in all sizes so I'm always ready to sand with whatever grit and size are needed.

A common problem when sanding dowels is that the sandpaper can slip in your hand. A trick I've found that helps is to roll a couple of strips of masking tape into a tube with the adhesive side out and apply them diagonally across the back of the sandpaper, as shown in the top photo on the facing page. (You can also use double-sided tape, though it's more expensive than masking tape.) The tape sticks to the palm of your hand so you can wrap the paper around the dowel and sand without slipping.

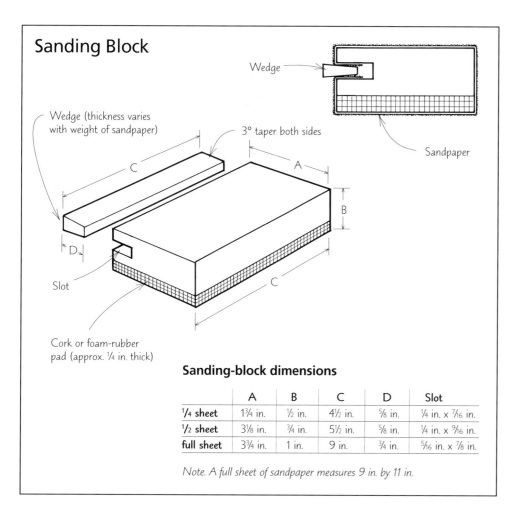

Sanding Block

Wedge

Wedge (thickness varies with weight of sandpaper)

3° taper both sides

Sandpaper

C

A

B

C

D

Slot

Cork or foam-rubber pad (approx. ¼ in. thick)

Sanding-block dimensions

	A	B	C	D	Slot
¼ sheet	1¾ in.	½ in.	4½ in.	⅝ in.	¼ in. x 7⁄16 in.
½ sheet	3⅛ in.	¾ in.	5½ in.	⅝ in.	¼ in. x 9⁄16 in.
full sheet	3¾ in.	1 in.	9 in.	¾ in.	5⁄16 in. x ⅞ in.

Note. A full sheet of sandpaper measures 9 in. by 11 in.

APPLYING THE FINISH

Woodworkers with large shops may have the luxury of a separate finishing room, but most of us have to cut, sand and finish in the same space. After sanding and wiping off all the parts, I clean up the shop, dusting and vacuuming everything within the area designated for finishing. Then I go do something else for a couple of hours to let all the dust that I've stirred up settle out of the air. When I return to the shop, I wipe the pieces with a tack cloth one last time and begin brushing on the finish. I leave finishing for the last task of the day. That way, the wet pieces can dry overnight before I start to stir up any more dust.

For toys that will be played with, I prefer to use a high-gloss polyurethane because it dries harder and is more durable than a satin (semi-gloss) or flat finish. For display toys or showpieces, I use a semi-gloss urethane because it's more consistent with an heirloom image than the sheen of a high-gloss finish. And semi-gloss urethane still offers plenty of protection from the handling that these toys naturally invite.

I apply the finish with an artist's brush made of red sable or camel hair. Because most of the pieces are small, a 1-in. wide brush is plenty big enough. You can expect to pay $10 to $20 for a good artist's brush, but as long as it's taken care of properly it should last a lifetime. When done with a brush, I clean it in the appropriate thinner, switch to a fresh batch of thinner and then wash the brush out with detergent and hot water. I comb the bristles back into shape and then return the brush to its original package or wrap it in clean paper to protect the bristles and hold its shape.

I brush the finish on in long sweeping strokes to minimize brush marks. If the piece is large enough, I'll hold it in my hand, applying finish to all sides except the bottom. Then I place the piece on a rain-gutter screen to dry, as shown in the photo at right. The screen holds the piece away from the work surface so it can dry without sticking. For smaller pieces, and to finish off the top of each of the larger pieces, I lightly hold the piece right on the screen with a divider point while applying the final brush strokes.

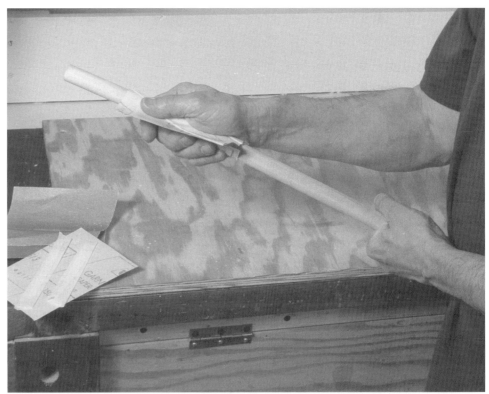

For a firm grip when sanding dowels, apply rolled strips of masking tape (sticky side out) or double-sided tape to the back of the sandpaper.

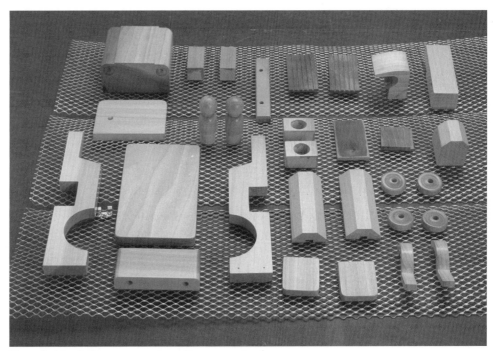

Place finished pieces on a rain-gutter screen to dry.

Once the first coat has dried, I sand the entire surface with 220-grit production-grade sandpaper, making sure to sand off any drips or runs that might have worked their way to the bottom surface. After vacuuming and wiping the piece with a tack cloth, I flip it over and finish the bottom. A second coat, applied in the same manner finishes the job.

One problem with finishing pieces before assembly is that glue doesn't bond well to the finish. So to get good glue joints, I don't apply finish to areas that will be joined. To control the finish, I'll either mask off the area or score a line across a piece, as shown in the photo at left. The scored line acts as a dam that helps keep the finish from flowing into the joint area.

PAINTING

It's the small details, like the T-roof pattern on the Sports Car or the windows on the Fire Truck (see the photo on pp. 42-43), that make wooden toys special. To get the crisp, clean lines on these details, I apply a coat of oil-based sanding sealer first and then lightly sand with 220-grit paper. Next I mask off the entire area where the paint will be applied and draw the detail onto the masking tape. Then, using a sharp X-Acto knife and a straight-edge guide, I cut out the pattern and peel away the tape from the area to be painted. Cutting through the tape helps seal the edges and minimizes paint bleed under the tape. The score mark also creates a dam to further inhibit the paint from bleeding, resulting in clean paint lines. I spray on two or three light coats to avoid runs and sags, and then, when the paint is dry, top it off with a coat of clear polyurethane.

To prevent finish from flowing into glue-joint areas, score a line across the workpiece. The scored line acts as a dam.

Grasshopper

The grasshopper was the toy that launched my toymaking career, so it seems only appropriate to begin with this engaging little critter. Although the 'hopper has evolved with age, its bright eyes, floppy antennae and rapid-action legs have ensured that it has remained one of my most popular toys over the years. Kids just can't resist picking the grasshopper up and playing with it. It's a fairly simple toy to build, though you do have to be careful with the glue so that it doesn't interfere with the free movement of the legs and wheels.

Parts Preparation

BODY

1. Cut the body block slightly oversize, and then transfer the profile and hole layouts from the pattern on p. 23.

2. For accurate references and easier drilling, drill all body holes while the block is still rectangular (see p. 4). A center-punch mark helps keep the bit from drifting on the angled holes for the antennae.

Drill an ⅛-in.-dia. hole through the body to locate the eyes. After the finish has been applied to the body, enlarge the eye holes to 1-in.-dia. by ⅛-in.-deep sockets. When drilling the 1-in. eye holes, drill a test hole in scrap wood to ensure that the dowel will fit. If necessary, use an adjustable bit to compensate for oversized or undersized dowel stock.

3. Turn the eyes into a half-round section from a piece of 1-in.-dia. dowel on the lathe. The finished length is ⅝ in., but for ease of handling don't part it off until you've sealed it with sanding sealer and painted the eye.

4. After all holes are drilled, cut the body to shape and radius the edges with a ³⁄₁₆-in. roundover bit in a router table or an overhead or hand-held router.

LEGS AND WHEELS

The two legs are made up of four identical pieces, as shown in the drawing on p. 23.

1. Drill the holes in the legs—through holes for the inside leg sections, and one through hole and one stopped hole (⅜ in. deep) for the outside legs.

2. Radius the ends of the legs. Although you can do this freehand, I prefer to use a special sanding fixture to ensure a uniform, professional appearance (see the photo on p. 14).

3. Cut the front and back wheels using the hole-saw and lathe technique discussed on p. 13. Redrill the axle hole in each wheel to fit the ⁵⁄₁₆-in.-dia. axle dowels. Drill the offset leg-peg hole in each back wheel with the wheel held in a V-jig (see the photo at right).

ANTENNAE

Each antenna is a ⅝-in.-dia. wood bead glued on the end of a 3-in.-long piece of #12 gauge, stranded wire covered with black vinyl insulation. You'll probably have to get this wire from an industrial or electrical supply house. Make sure the wire is stranded, not solid-core; otherwise the antennae won't have the right action. Roughen up the insulation on each end of the wire with sandpaper for a better glue bond.

Parts List*

Quantity	Description	Finished Dimensions	Material
BODY			
1	Body	1¼ x 2½ x 9	Birch
2	Eyes	1 in. dia. by ⅝ in. long	Birch
LEGS AND WHEELS			
4	Leg sections	½ x ⁹⁄₁₆ x 4½	Birch
6	Leg pegs	³⁄₁₆-in.-dia. pegs by 1 in. long	Birch
2	Leg spacer washers	³⁄₁₆ in.	Steel
2	Front wheels	½ in. thick by 2 in. dia.	Birch
2	Back wheels	½ in. thick by 1¾ in. dia.	Birch
2	Axles	⁵⁄₁₆-in.-dia. dowel by 2⅜ in.	Birch
4	Wheel spacer washers	⁵⁄₁₆ in.	Steel
ANTENNAE			
2	Antennae	3 in. of #12 stranded wire with black insulation	Steel
2	Antenna knobs	⅝-in.-dia. beads	Birch
PULL HANDLE			
1	Pull handle	¾-in.-dia. dowel by 1⅜ in.	Birch
1	Braided string	Approx. 32 in. long	Nylon

*All dimensions are in inches and indicate the overall finished size (thickness x width x length), with the third dimension as the preferred grain direction, except as noted.

Drill the offset leg-peg hole in each back wheel using a V-jig.

Assembly

Finish all parts as described on pp. 16-18. Refer to the drawings on p. 22 for correct orientation of the parts during assembly.

1. Dry-assemble the front wheels with washers between the body and the wheels, and then mark the axle for correct length. Disassemble and trim the axle to length. Crimp the axle ends with a pair of slide-jaw pliers to create glue pockets for better adhesion (see p. 12). Glue one wheel to the end of the axle, slip a washer over the axle and insert the axle into the body. Glue the other wheel to the other end of the axle, with a washer between the wheel and the body.

2. Assemble the inside and outside leg sections with a leg peg and just a dab of glue in the stopped hole in the outside leg. Don't get any glue on the inside leg section. Secure the assembled leg to the body with a leg peg, again being sure not to get glue on the inside leg. The peg between the two leg sections should face in. (Note that if you switch the position of the inside and outside leg sections, this leg peg can face out; the photo in the gallery on p. 56 shows both design options.)

3. Glue one back wheel to the back axle with the leg-peg hole facing out and let it dry. Then insert the axle through the body, with a washer between the wheel and the body, and dry-fit the second wheel (no glue yet and be sure the leg-peg hole is facing out). Insert the leg pegs in each wheel and rotate the unglued wheel so the pegs are aligned, as shown in the top photo at right. Now remove the free wheel, apply glue, and slide the wheel and a washer back onto the axle, making sure the leg pegs are still aligned. Remove the leg pegs from the wheels, assemble the leg sections on either side, add a drop of glue to each wheel hole and reinsert the pegs. Check for free movement of the wheels and legs.

4. Using a slow-setting epoxy, glue the antennae into the body and the beads on the ends of the antennae.

5. Install the pull string as discussed in the sidebar at right.

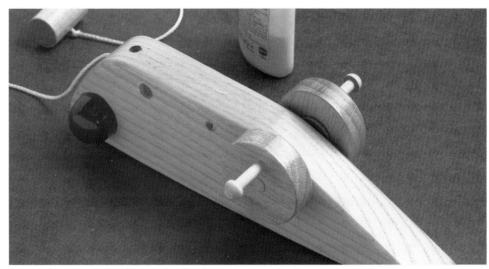

When dry-assembling the back wheels, make sure the leg pegs are aligned.

Installing Pull Strings

Pull strings can be added to almost any toy with wheels. Strings are often attached with small screw eyes, but I don't like to use them because they can cause injury if a child falls on them or create a choking hazard if they come loose. To avoid screw eyes, I use a neat little trick that involves drilling a couple of holes and pulling a piece of nylon string through the holes with a hot paper clip. First the holes. One hole ($^3/_{32}$ in. dia.) is drilled from the front of the toy; the second hole ($^3/_{16}$ in. dia.) is drilled from the bottom of the toy to intersect the first hole.

Now comes the tricky part. With the toy upside-down, insert the string into the front hole. Then heat a straightened paper clip and insert it into the bottom hole (see the photo at left below). The hot paper clip will fuse itself to the nylon string (it may take several attempts). Gently pull the string out of the bottom hole (see the photo at right below), tie an oversized knot and fuse it with a match to prevent unraveling. Then pull the string from the front while pushing the knot back into the bottom hole. Proceed with caution, because hot nylon will stick to your skin and burn.

When adding the handle to the end of the string, tie a large knot on both sides of the handle so that it won't slide down on the string. Fuse the outer knot.

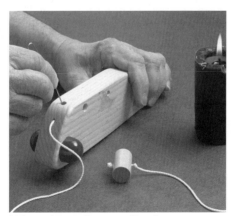

Using a heated paper clip allows you to pull the string through the body of the grasshopper.

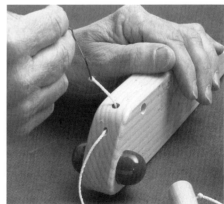

The hot clip fuses itself to the nylon string.

Grasshopper

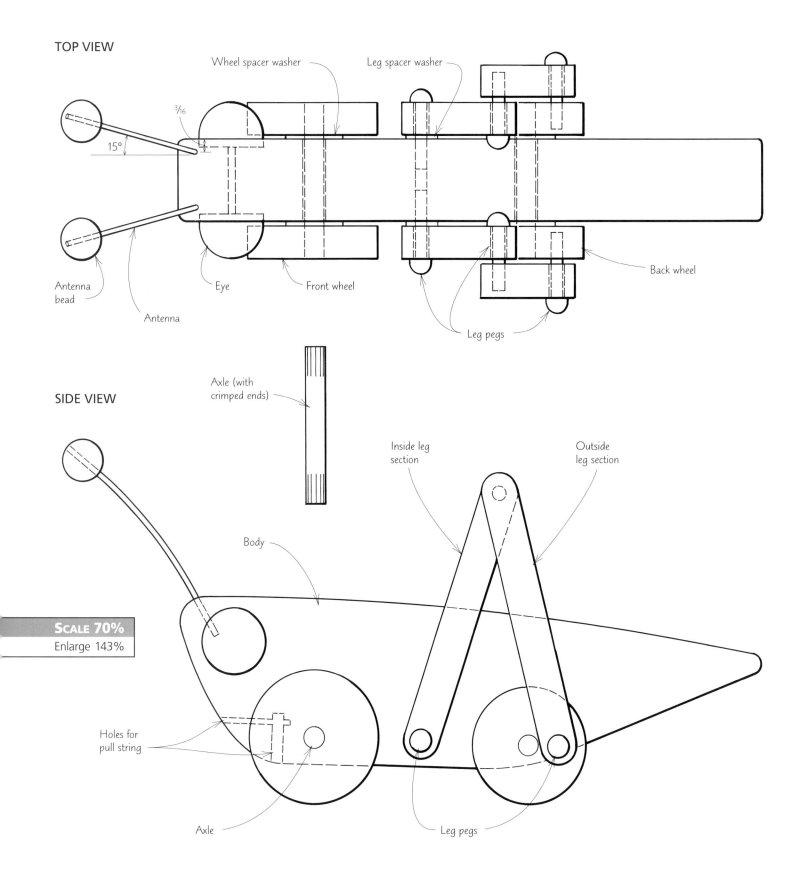

Wheel spacer washer

Leg spacer washer

3/16

15°

Antenna
bead

Antenna

Eye

Front wheel

Back wheel

Leg pegs

SIDE VIEW

Axle (with
crimped ends)

Inside leg
section

Outside
leg section

Body

SCALE 70%
Enlarge 143%

Holes for
pull string

Axle

Leg pegs

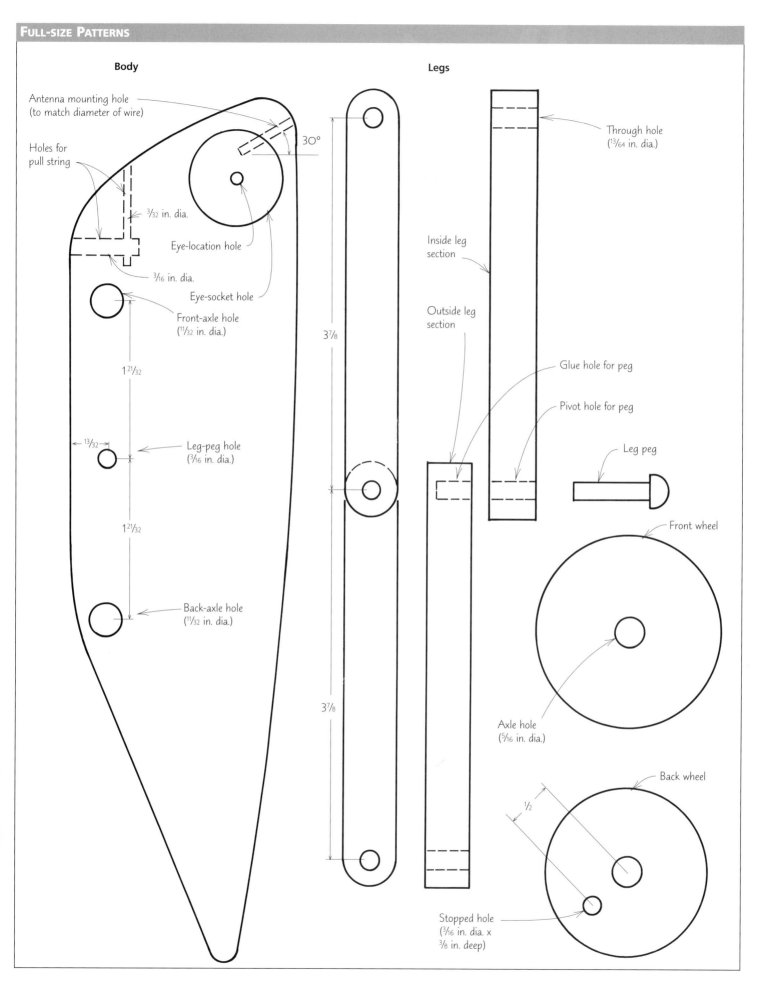

Body

Antenna mounting hole
(to match diameter of wire)

Holes for
pull string

³⁄₃₂ in. dia.

³⁄₁₆ in. dia.

Eye-location hole

30°

Eye-socket hole

Front-axle hole
(¹¹⁄₃₂ in. dia.)

1²¹⁄₃₂

¹³⁄₃₂

Leg-peg hole
(³⁄₁₆ in. dia.)

1²¹⁄₃₂

Back-axle hole
(¹¹⁄₃₂ in. dia.)

Legs

3⁷⁄₈

3⁷⁄₈

Through hole
(¹³⁄₆₄ in. dia.)

Inside leg
section

Outside leg
section

Glue hole for peg

Pivot hole for peg

Leg peg

Front wheel

Axle hole
(⁵⁄₁₆ in. dia.)

Back wheel

½

Stopped hole
(³⁄₁₆ in. dia. x
³⁄₈ in. deep)

Grasshopper 23

Tug Boat

It's hard to imagine a more perfect subject for a toy than a tug boat. Working tug boats look just like toys as they tow long barges or push huge commercial liners into moorings. My design has exaggerated features—a chunky hull and oversized cabin and smokestack—and is painted in bright colors to accentuate the playful image. Tug boats were always a highlight of my childhood visits to Staten Island, New York. Now they can be the highlight of your 3-year-old's visits to the bathtub.

Parts Preparation

HULL

I use hardwood for most of my toys, but to improve buoyancy for the tug boat I recommend pine for the hull and cabin. After all, we're making a boat—not a submarine.

1. To make the hull, start with an oversized blank that's slightly wider and about 2 in. longer than the finished dimensions. This extra material leaves room for attaching the routing template for cutting the recessed area into the deck, as shown in the photo below. To rout the recess, I nailed a ¼-in.-thick masonite template to the workpiece and used a ¼-in.-dia. straight bit with a guide collar.

2. Cut the perimeter of the hull to shape on the bandsaw, with the table tilted to a 10° angle. Drill the ³⁄₁₆-in.-dia. hole for the back post.

3. Sand the hull and apply two coats of an oil-based sanding sealer, sanding lightly between coats. Leave some unfinished wood in the recessed area for gluing in the deck cabin and pilot's cabin later. Mask off the top of the hull and spray the sides and bottom with at least two coats of your favorite color paint.

4. Remove the masking tape and round off the top edge of the hull with a ³⁄₁₆-in. roundover bit in a table-mounted router. Finish the top of the hull and the border of the recessed area with two coats of an oil-based high-gloss urethane.

CABINS

1. Cut the blanks for the deck cabin and the pilot's cabin and glue them together with epoxy. (Don't use water-based glue or water-based finishes on toys that will get a lot of exposure to water.)

2. Drill the ½-in.-dia. portholes, and then round off the front of the cabin assembly (as explained on p. 14).

3. Apply sanding sealer and two coats of high-gloss urethane to the cabin assembly, leaving the top and bottom unfinished for later glue-up.

4. Cut the cabin roof to shape, round the front end and finish with sanding sealer and paint, leaving a section of the underside unfinished for gluing to the cabin.

Parts List

Quantity	Description	Finished Dimensions	Material
HULL			
1	Hull	1 x 3¹⁄₁₆ x 7½	Pine
1	Back post	³⁄₁₆-in.-dia. peg, ¾ in. long with ⁵⁄₁₆-in.-dia. head	Birch
CABINS			
1	Deck cabin	¾ x 1³⁄₈ x 3¾	Pine
1	Pilot's cabin	¾ x 1³⁄₈ x 1⁵⁄₈	Pine
1	Cabin roof	¼ x 1⁵⁄₈ x 1¾	Birch
1	Smokestack	¾-in.-dia. dowel by 1⁵⁄₈ in. long	Birch
1	Main mast	¼-in.-dia. peg, 2½ in. long with ⁵⁄₈-in.-dia. head	Birch
1	Short mast	¼-in.-dia. peg, 1¼ in. long with ³⁄₈-in.-dia. head	Birch

Assembly

Refer to the drawings on p. 26 for correct orientation of the parts.

1. Glue the cabin roof onto the cabin assembly with epoxy.

2. Locate and drill the holes for the smokestack and masts.

3. Epoxy the main deck to the hull, and glue the masts, smokestack and back post into place. For the smaller post and masts, it's safer to use commercial pegs with large rounded heads rather than cut-off dowels (see Sources of Supply on p. 151).

4. Finish the remaining parts with two coats of urethane.

Check this toy from time to time to see if water exposure has caused any of the parts to come loose.

Use a template to rout the recessed area for the deck in the hull. Shown on the bench are the oversized hull blank (marked for routing) and the finished hull.

FULL SIZE

SIDE VIEW

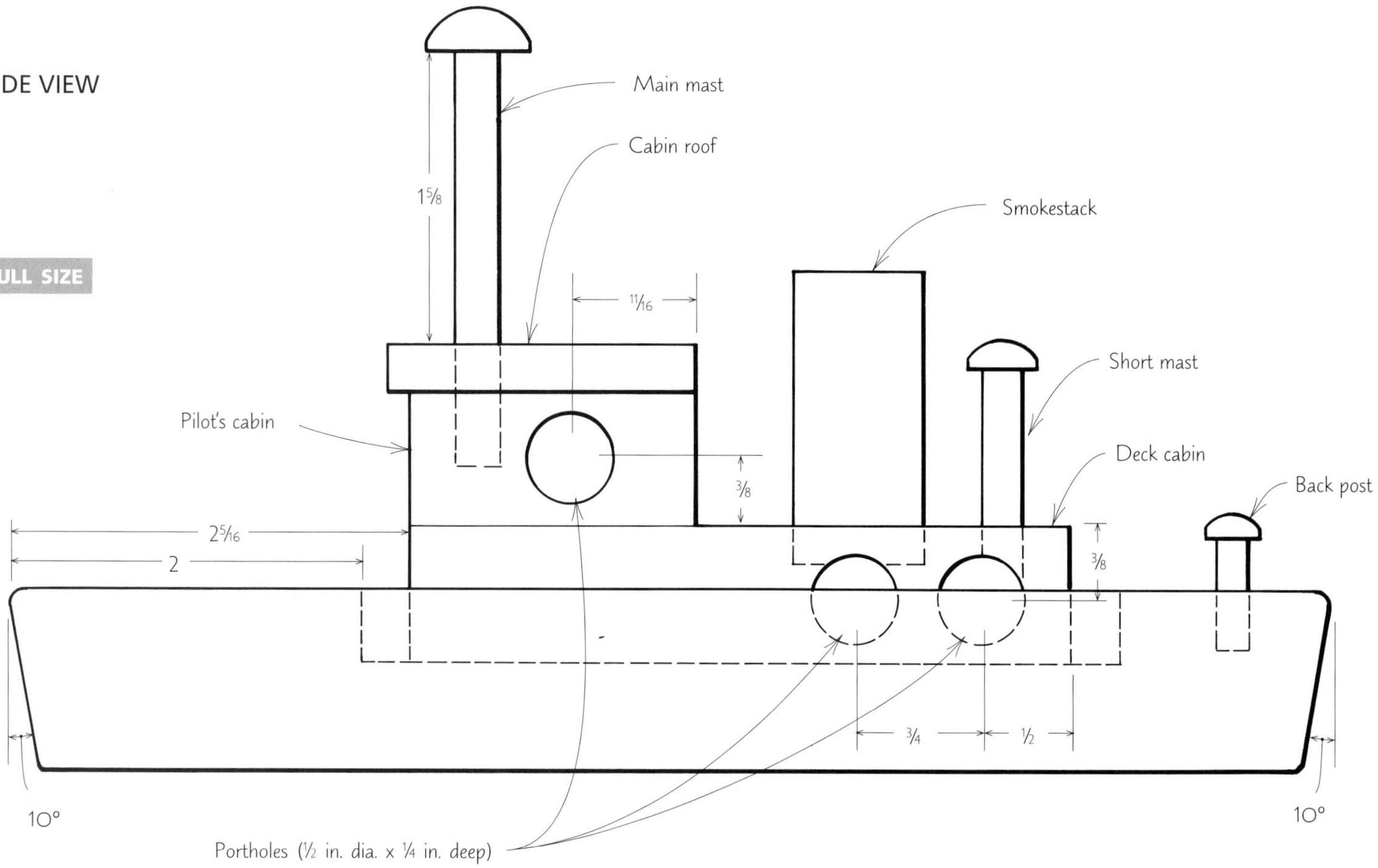
Main mast
Cabin roof
1⅝
Smokestack
11/16
Short mast
Pilot's cabin
Deck cabin
3/8
Back post
2 5/16
2
3/8
3/4
1/2
10°
10°
Portholes (1/2 in. dia. x 1/4 in. deep)

TOP VIEW

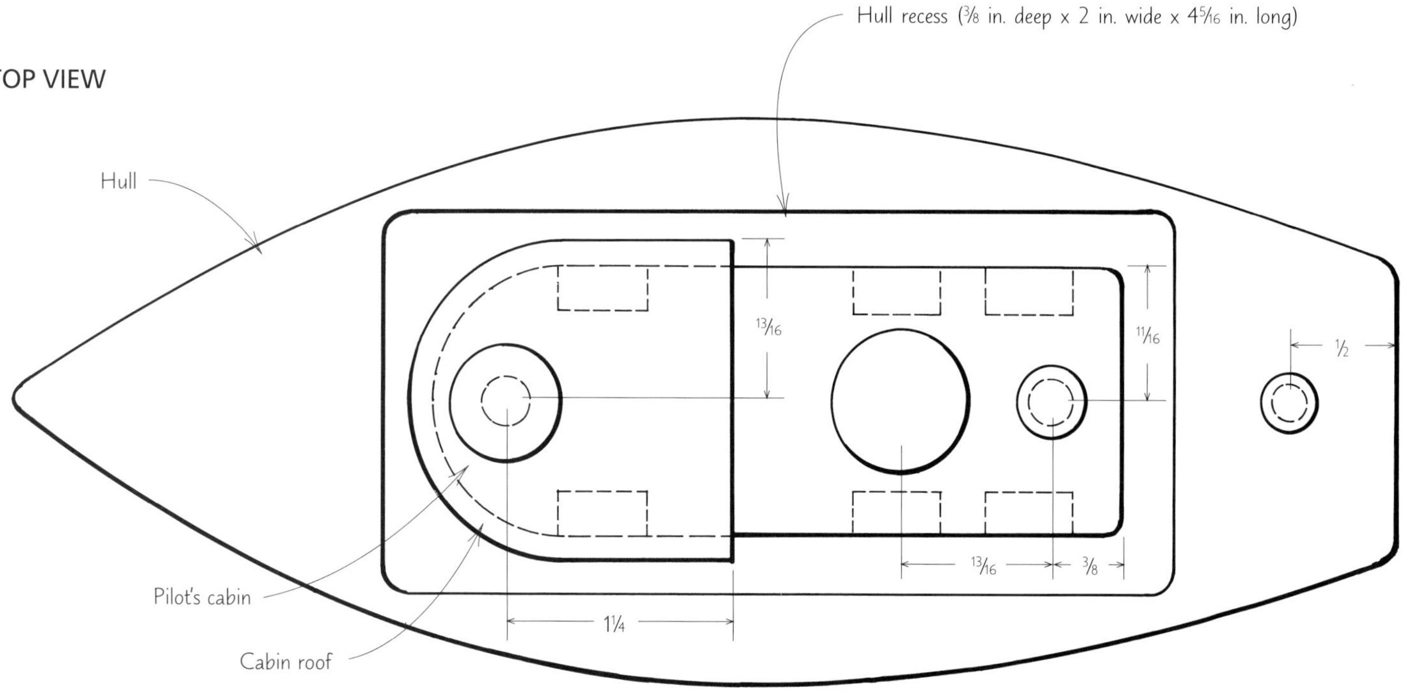
Hull recess (3/8 in. deep x 2 in. wide x 4 5/16 in. long)
Hull
13/16
11/16
1/2
13/16
3/8
Pilot's cabin
1¼
Cabin roof

Dump Truck

The key feature of this rugged, ready-for-action dump truck is the tilting bed, which is hinged to the chassis with a brass hinge. The truck is made with contrasting woods to highlight certain features. It shares many similar components with the crane truck in Project 4—bumper, headlights, hood, cab, axle blocks and wheels. With all these similar parts, it would be easy to knock out a whole fleet of construction vehicles.

Parts Preparation

TRUCK CHASSIS

1. Cut the chassis block to size, and then score the bottom of the block to prevent finish from flowing into the area where the axle block will be glued (see p. 18).

2. Cut the axle blocks a little long, and then trim to the correct length during final assembly. Drill the axle blocks for the axles, as discussed on p. 12 and shown in the photo at left below.

3. Drill holes for headlights into the front bumper.

4. Make the headlights, as explained on p. 14.

5. Cut the wheels using a hole saw, as discussed on p. 13.

CAB ASSEMBLY

1. Cut the sides of the hood at 17°, as shown in the middle photo below. Refer to p. 9 for the angle-cutting jig used in this operation.

2. Lay out the window while the cab is still in block form, and then drill the holes for the window (see the drawing on the facing page).

3. Using a tenoning jig, cut the front of the cab at 30° to end at the hood (see the photo at right below and the drawing on p. 30).

DUMP ASSEMBLY

1. Cut the bed, side walls and end wall to size. The side walls are mirror images of each other; taping the blanks together with double-sided tape will ensure identical parts.

2. Cut $\frac{1}{8}$-in. by $\frac{1}{4}$-in. rabbets for the dump bed along the bottom inside edge of both side walls and the end wall and also along the front inside edges of the side walls.

3. Drill a $\frac{1}{4}$-in.-dia. hole in the side walls for the tailgate pivot pin. Separate the side walls.

4. Cut the tailgate and tailgate hinge block to size.

5. Drill the tailgate hinge block to receive the pivot pin, using the same technique as for the axle blocks.

Parts List

Quantity	Description	Finished Dimensions	Material
TRUCK CHASSIS			
1	Chassis	$2\frac{1}{8}$ x $\frac{1}{2}$ x $6\frac{1}{8}$	Maple
1	Front bumper	$\frac{11}{16}$ x $\frac{5}{16}$ x $2\frac{7}{8}$	Walnut
2	Headlights	$\frac{5}{16}$-in.-dia. dowel by $\frac{3}{4}$ in. long	Birch
2	Axle blocks	$\frac{5}{8}$ x $\frac{3}{4}$ x $2\frac{1}{8}$	Maple
2	Axles	$\frac{1}{4}$-in.-dia. dowel by $3\frac{3}{8}$ in. long	Birch
4	Wheels	$1\frac{5}{16}$ in. dia. by $\frac{1}{2}$ in. thick	Maple
4	Spacer washers	$\frac{1}{4}$ in.	Steel
CAB ASSEMBLY			
1	Hood	$1\frac{7}{8}$ x 1 x $1\frac{3}{4}$	Walnut
1	Cab	$2\frac{1}{8}$ x $1\frac{1}{4}$ x 2	Walnut
DUMP ASSEMBLY			
1	Dump bed	$\frac{1}{4}$ x $2\frac{3}{8}$ x $3\frac{5}{8}$	Maple
1	End wall	$\frac{1}{4}$ x $2\frac{1}{8}$ x $2\frac{3}{8}$	Maple
2	Side walls	$\frac{1}{4}$ x $2\frac{1}{8}$ x $3\frac{3}{4}$	Maple
1	Tailgate	$\frac{1}{4}$ x $2\frac{1}{8}$ x $1\frac{13}{16}$	Maple
1	Tailgate hinge block	$\frac{1}{2}$ x $\frac{3}{4}$ x $2\frac{1}{8}$	Maple
1	Tailgate pivot pin	$\frac{1}{4}$-in.-dia. dowel by $2\frac{3}{4}$ in. long	Birch
1	Dump hinge block	$\frac{1}{2}$ x $\frac{9}{16}$ x $2\frac{1}{8}$	Maple
1	Butt hinge	1 in. by 2 in.	Brass

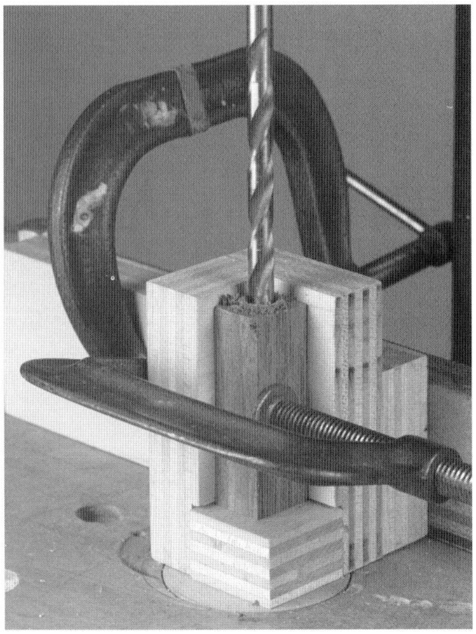

Use a jig to hold the axle block on end while drilling the hole for the axle.

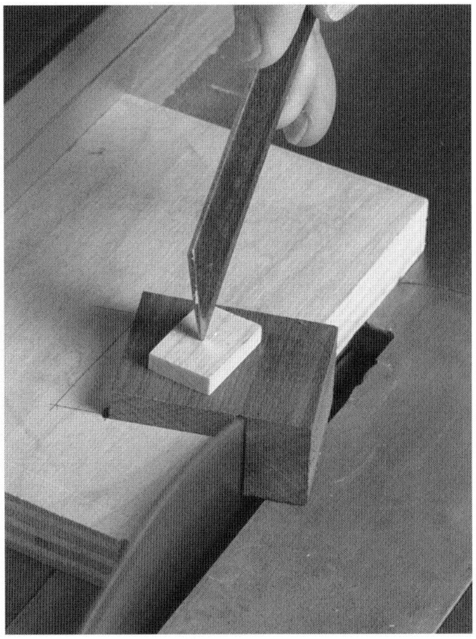

Use an angle jig to cut the sides of the hood at 17°. The small pine scrap (secured to the workpiece with double-sided tape) prevents damage from the push stick.

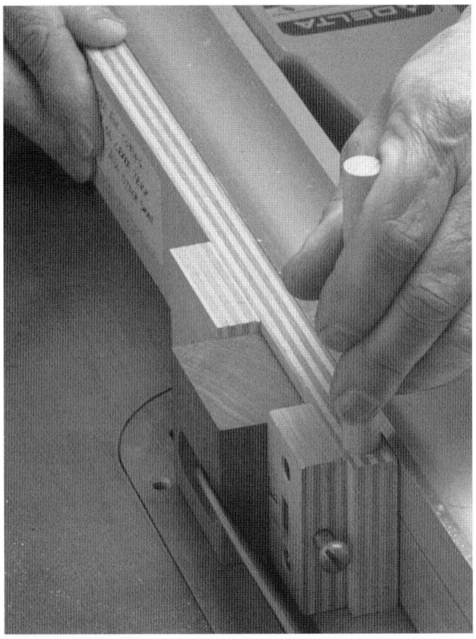

Use a tenoning jig to cut the angled front of the cab.

Assembly

Finish all parts as described on pp. 16-18. Refer to the drawings on p. 30 for correct orientation of the parts during assembly.

TRUCK CHASSIS AND CAB ASSEMBLY

1. Glue the front bumper, centered in all directions, on the front end of the chassis.

2. To install the headlights, secure the chassis to a right-angle steel block on the drill press, as shown in the photo at right, and drill into the chassis through the holes in the bumper. The holes should be deep enough that the headlight dowels protrude approximately ⅛ in.

3. Glue the cab assembly and axle blocks (but not the wheels) to the chassis.

DUMP ASSEMBLY

1. Assemble the tailgate and tailgate hinge block.

2. Assemble the end wall and side walls to the dump bed.

3. Align the tailgate hinge block between the side walls, and glue in the tailgate pivot pin. Make sure not to get glue between the tailgate hinge block and the pivot pin.

4. Fasten the dump assembly to the dump hinge block with double-sided tape to check for proper movement. If everything checks out, glue the dump assembly to the dump hinge block, and then connect the dump assembly to the chassis with a 1-in. by 2-in. brass butt hinge.

5. Assemble the wheels and axles, using ¼-in. spacer washers between the wheels and axle blocks.

With the chassis clamped to a right-angle block for vertical support, drill holes for the headlights through the holes in the bumper into the chassis.

FULL-SIZE DETAIL

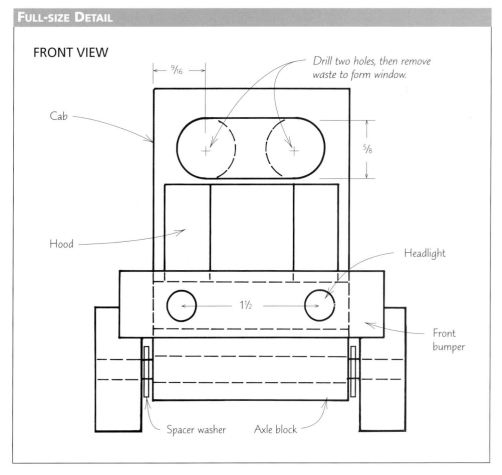

FRONT VIEW

Cab

Drill two holes, then remove waste to form window.

⁹⁄₁₆

⁵⁄₈

Hood

Headlight

1½

Front bumper

Spacer washer   Axle block

Dump Truck

SCALE 80%
Enlarge 125%

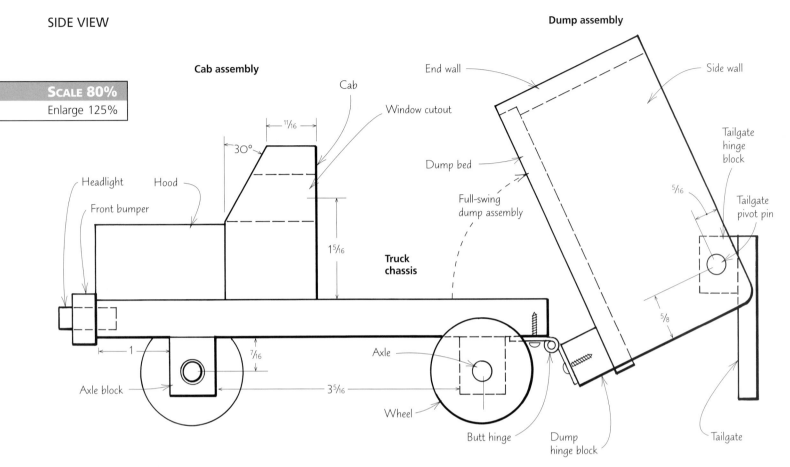

Cab assembly

Cab

Window cutout

End wall

Dump assembly

Side wall

Tailgate hinge block

$^5/_{16}$

Tailgate pivot pin

Dump bed

Full-swing dump assembly

Truck chassis

$^{11}/_{16}$

30°

Headlight

Hood

Front bumper

$1^5/_{16}$

Axle

$^5/_8$

Tailgate

Axle block

$^7/_{16}$

1

$3^5/_{16}$

Wheel

Butt hinge

Dump hinge block

TOP VIEW

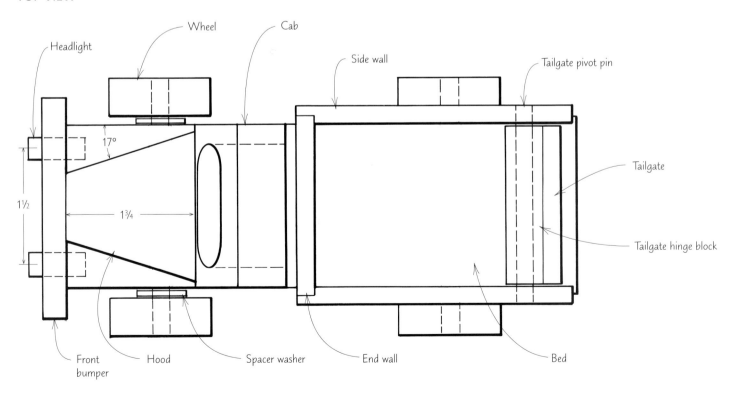

Wheel

Cab

Side wall

Tailgate pivot pin

Headlight

17°

Tailgate

$1^1/_2$

$1^3/_4$

Tailgate hinge block

Front bumper

Hood

Spacer washer

End wall

Bed

Crane Truck and Trailer

The crane on the back of this truck is equipped with a magnet to pick up cargo drums (dowels with a steel washer on one end) from the separate trailer. It's great fun to play with by itself or with the truck detailed in Project 3 or the freight train described in Project 12. Between the truck and the trailer, there are 75 pieces (including some commercial parts), yet this project requires only basic woodworking skills and tools. It is important that the parts go together in the proper order, though, especially the moving parts in the crane housing.

Parts Preparation

TRUCK CHASSIS

1. Cut the chassis block to size, and then score the bottom of the block to prevent finish from flowing into the area where the axle block will be glued (see p. 18).

2. Drill ⅜-in.-deep holes for the ¼-in. trailer hook-up peg and the crane pivot pin. Cut and drill the chassis pivot disc.

3. Cut the axle blocks a little long, and then trim to the correct length during final assembly. Drill the axle blocks for the axles, as discussed on p. 12.

4. Drill holes for headlights into the front bumper.

5. Make the headlights, as explained on p. 14.

6. Cut the wheels using a hole saw, as discussed on p. 13.

CAB ASSEMBLY

The crane-truck cab assembly is identical to the dump-truck cab. See p. 28 for cutting details.

CRANE HOUSING

To drill the crane side walls accurately and ensure that both sides are identical, use double-sided tape to hold the blanks together.

1. Lay out and drill the crank-axle hole through the first side wall and about ⅜ in. into the second side wall. Locate and drill stopped holes for the boom pivot pin.

2. Rabbet along the inside bottom edges of both side walls, and then cut the boom end of the side walls at 17° (see the full-size detail on p. 35).

3. Trim the back edge of the floor panel to the same angle as the boom end of the side walls. Lay out and drill a hole in the floor panel for the crane pivot pin, which is a commercially made piece (see Sources of Supply on p. 151).

4. Drill the crank-axle hole through the length of the wind-up reel dowel. (I do this on a lathe, wrapping a piece of flexible plastic around the dowel to prevent jaw marks.) Drill a ¹⁄₁₆-in.-dia. hole in from the side of the wind-up reel to meet the axle hole for mounting the string.

5. Finish the reel with a single coat of urethane (see p. 17), and then use epoxy to glue the string into the reel. (Alternatively, you can glue the string into the reel after the crane housing is assembled, as shown in the accompanying photos.) Push the string in to meet the axle hole, and, once the epoxy sets, redrill the axle hole to clean out extra string and dried epoxy.

CRANE-ARM ASSEMBLY

Leave the boom stock ¼ in. thicker than specified in the parts list to prevent tearout when drilling the series of closely spaced holes along the boom.

1. Use the spacer-block technique (see pp. 6-7) to drill the seven, evenly spaced holes in the boom. Then drill the pivot pin hole at the end of the boom.

2. Cut the boom to the correct thickness, and drill the end for the mini-screw eye.

3. Radius both ends of the boom.

4. Drill a ¹⁄₁₆-in.-dia. hole in the pick-up head to receive the end of the braided nylon string.

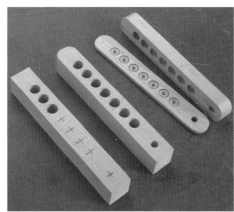

This photo shows the sequence of operations (from left to right) for drilling and cutting the crane arm.

TRAILER

1. Rabbet the bottom inside edge of both the side and end walls. Also rabbet both ends of the end walls.

2. Prepare axle blocks, axles and wheels as for the truck chassis.

3. Drill the trailer hitch for the hook-up peg and round the end.

Assembly

Finish all parts as described on pp. 16-18. Unlike most projects in this book, I used a satin-finish urethane to enhance the natural beauty of the walnut components. However, if this toy is going to see a lot of play, I'd recommend using a high-gloss oil-based polyurethane, which dries harder for a more durable finish.

Refer to the drawings on pp. 34-35 for correct orientation of the parts during assembly.

TRUCK CHASSIS AND CAB ASSEMBLY

1. Assemble all parts of the chassis and cab except the wheel assembly. The front bumper should be centered in all directions on the front end of the chassis.

2. To install the headlights, secure the chassis assembly to a vertical block on the drill press (see the photo on p. 29) and drill into the chassis through the holes in the bumper until the headlight dowels protrude approximately ⅛ in.

CRANE HOUSING AND CRANE-ARM ASSEMBLY

Now comes the tricky part—assembling the housing and arm assembly without getting glue into the moving parts.

1. Glue the crane floor panel into the rabbet on the left side wall (the one with no through holes); see the photo below. Insert the crane pivot pin.

2. Slide the wind-up reel onto the crank axle,

Glue the crane-floor panel into the rabbet on the side wall.

and insert the axle into the top hole in the left side wall (see the photo below).

3. Slide the right side wall into its assembled position and center the wind-up reel. Without disturbing the reel, remove the right side wall and mark the axle on both sides of the reel.

4. With the wind-up reel removed, crimp the axle with slide-jaw pliers to create depressions between the marks. The depressions create glue pockets for better adhesion to the wind-up reel. Lightly apply glue between the marks, slide the wind-up reel into position and carefully remove all excess glue. Any glue left behind may prevent the crank from turning.

5. Re-insert the crank axle with wind-up reel and insert the boom pivot pin into the lower hole on the left side wall. Slide the second wall into assembled position to check the alignment of both axles.

6. Remove the right side wall, glue the boom pivot pin in the left side wall only, then re-assemble the right side wall (dry) for alignment purposes. When the glue is dry, remove the right side wall and wind-up reel with axle.

7. Slide a rubber washer made from a bicycle tube or a faucet washer onto the boom pivot pin, slide the boom into position and then add another rubber washer (see the top photo on p. 36). Press and hold the right side wall back in position to check for a friction fit of the crane arm. The objective is to have the boom stay in position at any angle. Add additional rubber washers if necessary.

Insert the crank axle with wind-up reel into the top hole in the side wall.

Parts List

Quantity	Description	Finished Dimensions	Material
TRUCK CHASSIS			
1	Chassis	2⅛ x ½ x 6¾	Maple
1	Front bumper	¹¹⁄₁₆ x ⁵⁄₁₆ x 2⅞	Walnut
2	Headlights	⁵⁄₁₆-in.-dia. dowel by ¾ in. long	Birch
3	Axle blocks	⅝ x ¾ x 2⅛	Maple
3	Axles	¼-in.-dia. dowel by 3⅜ in. long	Birch
6	Wheels	1⁵⁄₁₆ in. dia. by ½ in. thick	Maple
6	Spacer washers	¼ in.	Steel
1	Trailer hook-up peg	¼-in.-dia. dowel by ¾ in. long	Birch
1	Chassis pivot disc	1½ in. dia. by ⁷⁄₁₆ in. thick	Walnut
CAB ASSEMBLY			
1	Hood	1⅞ x 1 x 1¾	Walnut
1	Cab	2⅛ x 1¼ x 2	Walnut
CRANE HOUSING			
1	Floor panel	⅞ x ½ x 2½	Maple
2	Side walls	1¾ x ½ x 2½	Cherry
1	Crane pivot pin	¼ in. dia. by 1⅛ in. long with ⅝-in.-dia. head	Birch
1	Crank arm	¾ x ¼ x 1¾	Maple
1	Crank handle	¼-in.-dia. dowel by 1⅛ in. long	Birch
1	Crank axle	¼-in.-dia. dowel by 1¾ in. long	Birch
1	Wind-up reel	⅝-in.-dia. dowel by ⅝ in. long	Birch
CRANE-ARM ASSEMBLY			
1	Boom	¾ x ½ x 5⅜	Maple
1	Boom pivot pin	¼-in.-dia. dowel by 1½ in. long	Birch
1	Pick-up head	⅝-in.-dia. dowel by ¾ in. long	Walnut
1	Pick-up magnet	½ in. dia. by ¼ in. thick	
1	Braided string	Approx. 12 in. long	Nylon
1	Screw eye	Mini (smallest size available)	Steel
2	Washers	¼ in.	Rubber
TRAILER			
1	Floor board	1¾ x ¼ x 3⅜	Maple
2	Axle blocks	⅝ x ¾ x 2⅛	Maple
2	Axles	¼-in.-dia. dowel by 3⅜ in. long	Birch
4	Wheels	1⁵⁄₁₆ in. dia. x ½ in. thick	Maple
4	Spacer washers	¼ in.	Steel
2	Side walls	1¼ x ¼ x 3⅜	Walnut
2	End walls	1¼ x ¼ x 2³⁄₁₆	Walnut
1	Trailer hitch	⅝ x ¼ x 2⅝	Walnut
1	Flat-head wood screw	Optional (for hitch)	Brass
CARGO			
8	Drums	¾-in.-dia. dowels by 1⅜ in. long	Birch
8	Washers	⅝ in. dia.	Steel

Crane Truck and Trailer

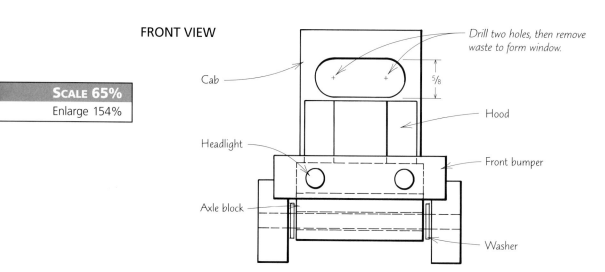

FRONT VIEW

Cab

Drill two holes, then remove waste to form window.

⁵/₈

Hood

Headlight

Front bumper

Axle block

Washer

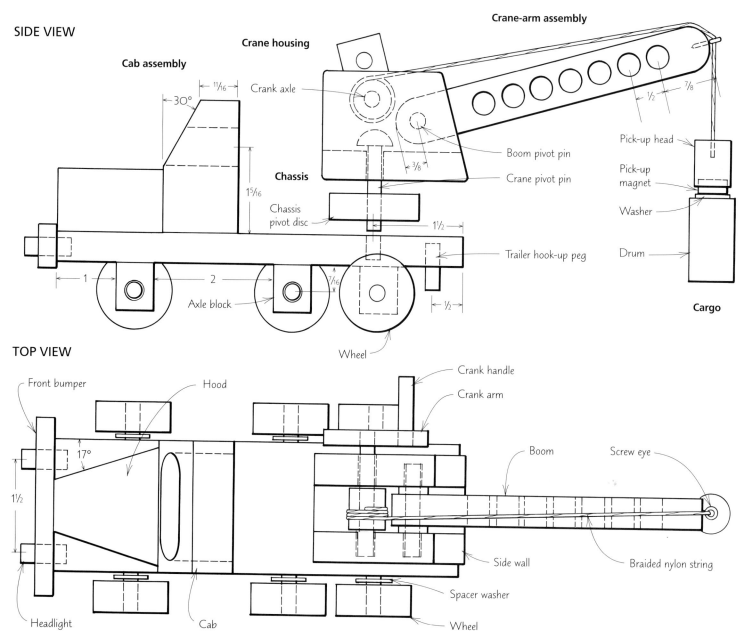

SIDE VIEW

Cab assembly

Crane housing

Crane-arm assembly

30°

¹¹/₁₆

Crank axle

1⁵/₁₆

Chassis

Boom pivot pin

³/₈

Crane pivot pin

½   ⁷/₈

Pick-up head

Pick-up magnet

Washer

Chassis pivot disc

1½

Drum

Trailer hook-up peg

1

2

⁷/₁₆

Axle block

½

Cargo

Wheel

TOP VIEW

Front bumper

Hood

Crank handle

Crank arm

17°

Boom

Screw eye

1½

Side wall

Braided nylon string

Headlight

Cab

Spacer washer

Wheel

REAR VIEW — Crane housing

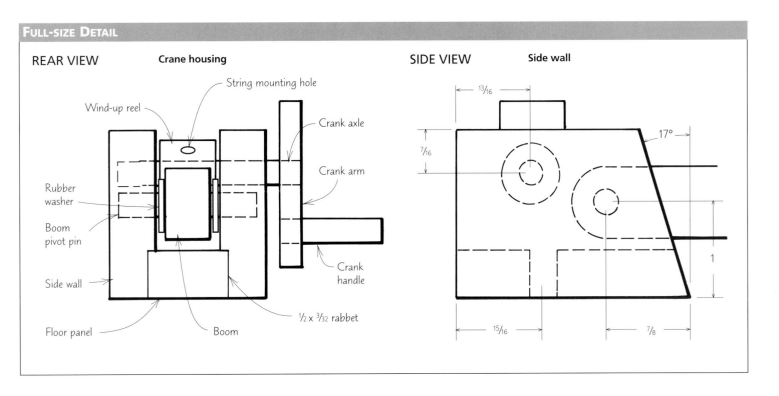

- String mounting hole
- Wind-up reel
- Crank axle
- Crank arm
- Rubber washer
- Boom pivot pin
- Crank handle
- Side wall
- ½ x ³⁄₃₂ rabbet
- Floor panel
- Boom

SIDE VIEW — Side wall

- ¹³⁄₁₆
- 17°
- ⁷⁄₁₆
- 1
- ¹⁵⁄₁₆
- ⁷⁄₈

Trailer

SIDE VIEW

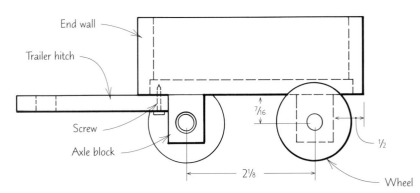

- End wall
- Trailer hitch
- Screw
- Axle block
- ⁷⁄₁₆
- ½
- Wheel
- 2¹⁄₈

TOP VIEW

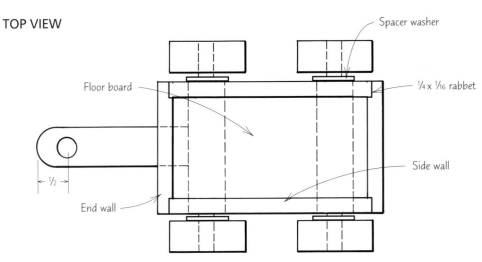

- Spacer washer
- Floor board
- ¼ x ¹⁄₁₆ rabbet
- Side wall
- End wall
- ½

Assembly

8. Once the friction fit is right, remove the right side wall and the wind-up reel and insert the crane pivot pin into the floor panel.

9. Re-assemble all parts, carefully applying glue in the boom pivot pin hole in the right side wall and along the edge of the floor panel.

10. Thread the string through the screw eye on the end of the boom and epoxy it into the

pick-up head. Epoxy the ½-in.-dia. magnet to the pick-up head.

11. Glue the crank arm and handle onto the crank axle (see the photo at bottom).

12. Check to make sure that the crane housing fits and rotates on the chassis. Attach the crane housing by applying glue in the chassis disc hole and then carefully inserting the crane

pivot pin. Don't slop glue onto the disc or use too much because the excess glue could bond the crane housing to the pivot disc.

13. Dry-assemble all wheels with ¼-in. spacer washers between the axle blocks and the wheels and mark the axles for correct length. Disassemble and trim the axles to length. Then crimp the axle ends, apply glue and slip the wheels onto the axles.

TRAILER

1. Glue all the walls onto the floor board and the axle blocks to the underside of the floor board.

2. Assemble the wheels and axles as for the truck.

3. Check to make sure that the hitch fits onto the trailer hook-up peg on the truck chassis before gluing the hitch in place. A small brass screw through the hitch into the underside of the trailer strengthens this joint.

4. Epoxy the washers to the top of the cargo drums.

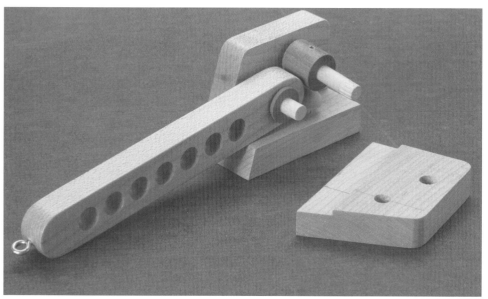

The boom in position, with washers on either side at the pivot pin.

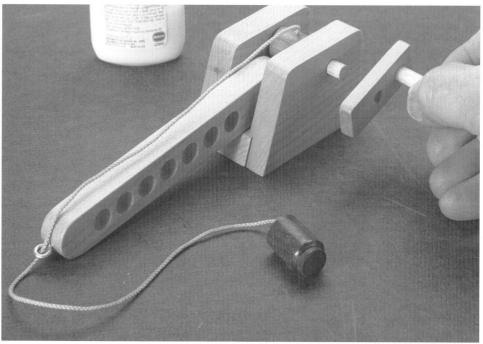

Once the crane housing is assembled, glue the crank arm and handle onto the crank axle.

Jeep with Canopy

Solid-block construction, steel axles and commercial wheels held on with push nuts make this model of a military-style jeep as durable as the real thing, even under the most demanding of play conditions. And the removable top gives you two toys in one. The steering wheel and spare tire add a touch of realism, but for greater authenticity you could paint the jeep in camouflage and add some decals. Or, better yet, let the kids paint it for a vehicle that will be truly their own.

Parts Preparation

BODY

1. Cut the plywood floor panel to size, and then cut dadoes for the axles on the bottom. From the centerlines of the dadoes, measure out ¾-in. on either side and score lines to prevent the finish from flowing into the area where the axle housing will be glued (see p. 18).

2. Cut the front bumper to size and drill holes for the bumper pegs.

3. Cut the hood to size. Cut a rabbet (¹⁄₁₆ in. deep by ¾ in. wide) along each side on top of the hood, and then round the edges of the hood over with a ⅝-in. roundover bit (see the drawing on p. 40). Drill headlight holes ¹⁄₁₆ in. deep before cutting the 10° angle at the back of the hood.

4. Cut the windshield to size with a 10° bevel on the top and bottom edge, and then drill an angled hole for the steering column (see the photo below and p. 10).

5. The side walls are mirror images of each other and can be spot-glued together for cutting and shaping. Cut the blanks oversized (10¼ in. long by 2¾ in. wide). The extra length provides a 1-in. waste area on each end for gluing. Be sure not to glue beyond this waste section. The extra width allows you to drill the back wheelwells without having to worry about tearout on the bottom edge. (If you decide to cut the wheelwells with a bandsaw, the extra width is not necessary.)

Parts List

Quantity	Description	Finished Dimensions	Material
BODY			
1	Floor panel	½ x 3½ x 8	Plywood
1	Hood	1¹³⁄₁₆ x 3½ x 3⅛	Poplar
1	Windshield	⅜ x 2¾ x 3½	Poplar
1	Front bumper	⅜ x ¾ x 4⅜	Poplar
2	Bumper pegs	¼-in.-dia. peg, ¾ in. long with ⅜-in.-dia. head	Birch
1	Back wall	¹³⁄₁₆ x 1¾ x 3½	Poplar
2	Side walls	⅝ x 1¾ x 8¼	Poplar
2	Headlights	⁹⁄₁₆-in.-dia. by ⅛-in.-thick buttons	Plastic
INTERIOR			
2	Front-seat bottoms	¾ x 1½ x 1	Poplar
2	Front-seat backs	⅜ x 1½ x 1⅝	Poplar
2	Back seats	¾ x ¹³⁄₁₆ x 2	Poplar
1	Steering wheel	1 in. dia. by ¼ in. thick	Birch
1	Steering column	¼-in.-dia. dowel by 1 in. long	Plastic
1	Steering wheel screw	¾-in. pan-head screw	Steel
2	Figures	⅞ in. dia. by 2⅜ in. high	Birch
CANOPY			
1	Canopy top	½ x 3½ x 5⅜	Poplar
1	Canopy back	¹³⁄₁₆ x 1⅜ x 3½	Poplar
2	Canopy posts	¼-in.-dia. dowel by 1⅝ in. long	Plastic
WHEELS AND AXLES			
2	Axle housings	⅝ x 1½ x 3⅝	Poplar
2	Axles	¼ in. dia. by 5 in. long	Steel
4	Spacer washers	¼ in.	Steel
5	Wheels	2 in. dia. by ½ in. thick	Birch
5	Push nuts (hub caps)	¼ in.	Steel
1	Spare tire post	¼ in. dia. by ¾ in. long	Steel

Drill an angled hole in the windshield for the steering column, using a jig to hold the workpiece at the correct angle.

Cut the wheelwells with a hole saw, as explained on p. 13, and then make the perimeter cuts. Trim off the glued-together waste at each end to separate the pieces.

6. Cut the back wall to size and rabbet the inside bottom edge. Drill two ¼-in.-dia. holes on the top edge for the canopy posts, and one hole in the back for the spare-tire post.

INTERIOR

1. Cut the front-seat bottoms and backs and the back seats to size.

2. Clamp the front-seat bottoms to the drill-press fence and drill ¾-in.-dia. holes for the two figures. If you use the ⅞-in.-dia. by 2⅜-in.-high commercial figures that I recommend (available from Casey's Wood Products; see Sources of Supply on p. 151), cut a ¹⁄₁₆-in. deep by ⁹⁄₁₆-in. high shoulder at the base of the figures to fit the front seats; alternatively, drill the seat holes to fit the figures (if you do this, you'll need to make the seats a little wider).

3. Adjust the length of the ¼-in.-dia. plastic-dowel steering column as necessary.

CANOPY

1. Cut the canopy top to size, and then cut the back rabbet.

2. Cut the canopy back to size, and then drill it to receive the canopy posts.

3. Dry-assemble the canopy and check the alignment with the windshield before cutting the dado. Adjust the width and depth of the dado to fit.

WHEELS AND AXLES

1. Dimension the axle-housing stock to thickness and width and at least 1 ft. long (depending on how many jeeps you're making). Cut the dado for the axle and the 45° shoulders before cutting the housings to length.

Jeep

TOP VIEW (canopy off)

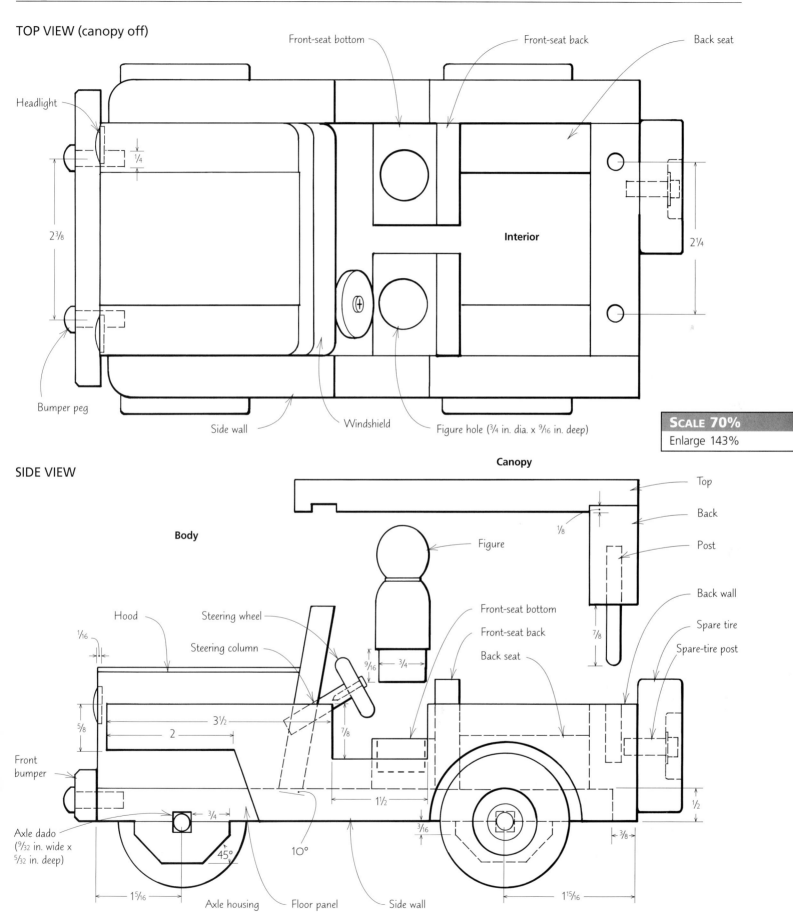

Headlight

Front-seat bottom

Front-seat back

Back seat

1/4

2 3/8

Interior

2 1/4

Bumper peg

Side wall

Windshield

Figure hole (3/4 in. dia. x 9/16 in. deep)

SCALE 70%
Enlarge 143%

Canopy

SIDE VIEW

Body

Top

Back

Post

1/8

Back wall

Figure

Spare tire

Hood

Steering wheel

Front-seat bottom

Spare-tire post

Steering column

Front-seat back

Back seat

7/8

1/16

9/16

3/4

5/8

3 1/2

7/8

2

Front bumper

1 1/2

1/2

Axle dado
(9/32 in. wide x
5/32 in. deep)

3/4

3/16

3/8

45°

10°

1 5/16

Axle housing

Floor panel

Side wall

1 15/16

Jeep with Canopy   39

Assembly

Finish all parts as described on pp. 16-18.

BODY AND INTERIOR

1. Glue all the body parts to the floor panel in the order that they appear in the parts list.

2. Add the interior parts in the following order: steering column, steering wheel, steering-wheel screw, back seats.

3. Glue the front-seat bottoms to their backs, and then butt the front-seat units against the back seats. Leave the figures loose in the seats.

CANOPY

1. Glue the canopy top to the back, and the posts into the bottom edge of the canopy back.

WHEELS AND AXLES

1. Glue the axle housings to the bottom of the floor panel.

2. Insert the steel axles through the axle housings, install the spacer washers and wheels and tap on the push nuts. (Note that commercial wheels are available in smooth and treaded styles. If you use the treaded wheels, you'll have to plug the ⅜-in.-dia. axle holes and re-drill for the ¼-in.-dia. axles.)

3. Install the spare-tire post (either a ¼-in. steel rod or ¼-in. dowel) and spare tire on the back wall.

Jeep

FRONT VIEW

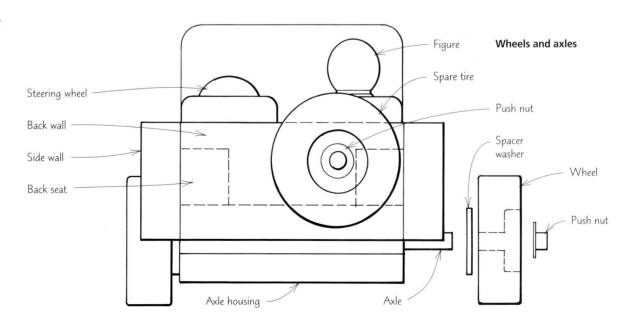

SCALE 70%
Enlarge 143%

REAR VIEW

A Gallery of Heirloom Toys

The photos on the following pages represent all the toy projects in this book. Some toys are shown in more than one version to illustrate material, finishing and design options. Page numbers in parentheses after each toy name indicate the starting page of each project, where you will find parts lists, drawings and detailed construction and assembly information.

U-Fly-It Plane
(p. 140)

Sports Car
(p. 57)

Life Star Helicopter
(p. 63)

Fire Truck
(p. 114)

Police Helicopter
(p. 69)

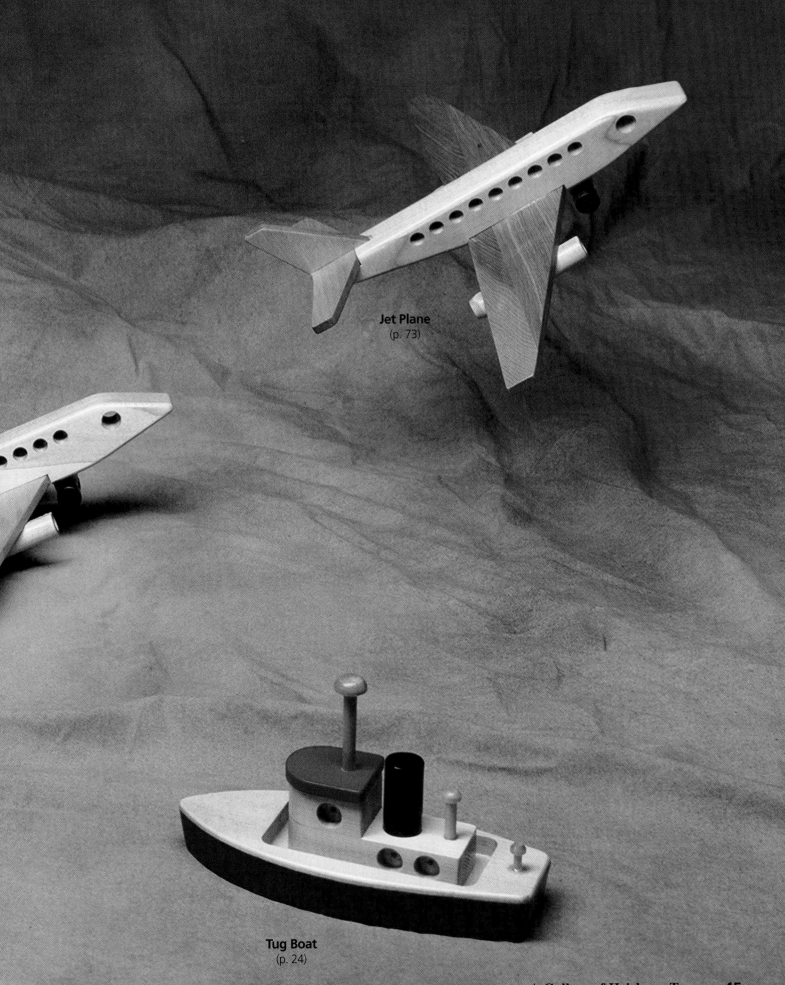

Jet Plane
(p. 73)

Tug Boat
(p. 24)

Jeep with Canopy
(p. 37)

Vintage Truck
(p. 121)

Vintage Truck
(low-side version)

Jeep

Cable Car
(p. 96)

Passenger Train
(p. 89)

Trolley Car
(p. 102)

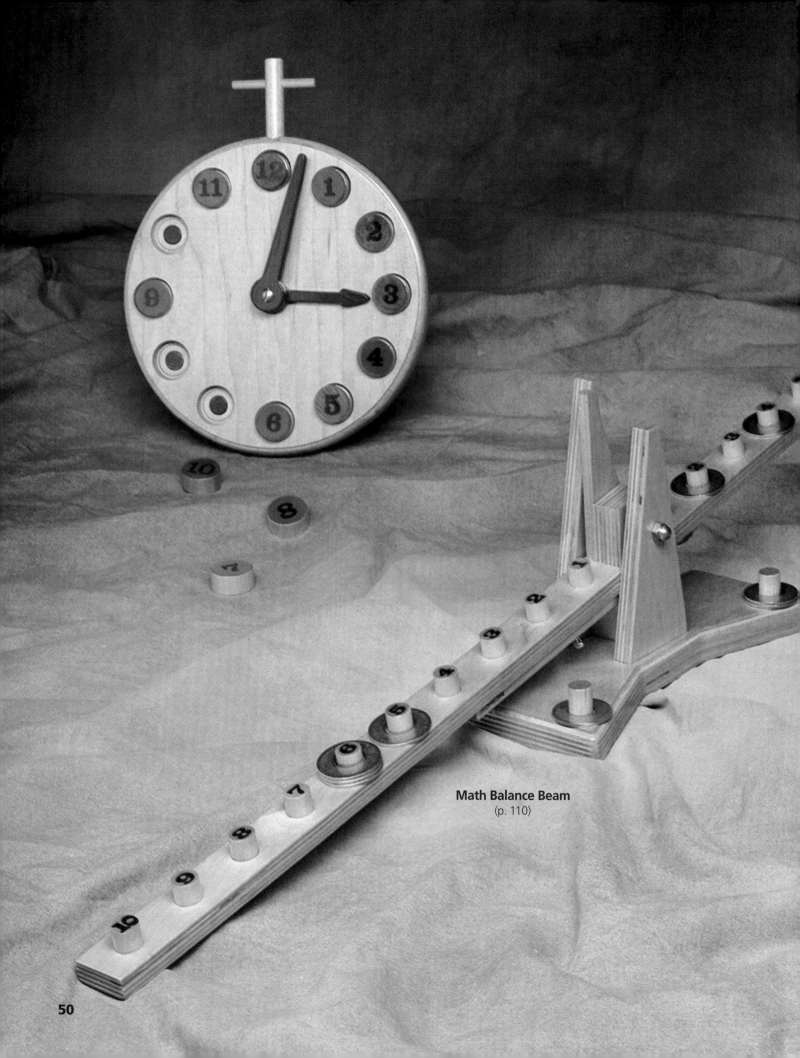

Math Balance Beam
(p. 110)

Walk the Ball
(p. 60)

Woodchuck Clock
(p. 106)

Mary's Ferry Boat with Four Vehicles
(p. 126)

Woodie Wagon
(vehicles, p. 132)

Biplane
(p. 77)

Sedan

Pick-up Truck

Coupe

Dump Truck
(p. 27)

Crane Truck and Trailer
(p. 31)

Freight Train
(p. 82)

Grasshopper
(p. 19)

Sports Car

This toy is sleek, fast and simple in design. With just two body parts, steel axles and commercial wheels, it's solid as a Sherman tank and perfect for active play at any age. The basic design can be embellished with a racing stripe by gluing up the body stock with a contrasting wood (as shown in the gallery photo on p. 43). Headlights, taillights, tailpipes and other accessories could also be added, but for rugged play, the simpler the better.

Parts Preparation

BODY

1. Cut the body blank slightly oversized
(1⁵⁄₁₆ in. x 3³⁄₈ in. x 10³⁄₄ in.) with both ends
square. (The extra width allows you to trim
¹⁄₁₆ in. off each side to remove any chips or
tearout from the cross-grain shaping cuts.)
2. Lay out a full profile drawing on each side of
the blank.
3. Drill 1³⁄₄-in.-dia. by ⁹⁄₁₆-in.-deep wheelwells
(to leave ¹⁄₂-in.-deep wheelwells after the sides
are trimmed). Clamp a block to the bottom of
the stock to prevent tearout, as explained on
p. 12 and shown in the top photo at right.
4. Drill ¹⁄₄-in. holes through the body for the
axles, and then redrill with a ⁹⁄₃₂-in. bit for axle
clearance.
5. Make the four angle cuts to shape the body,
using the angle-cutting technique described on
p. 9. Cut the 20° angle at the back end first,
the 15° angle at the bottom front end second,
the 10° angle on the hood third, and the 20°
angle on the front end last. I make the second
and third cuts in two passes for cleaner and
more accurate cuts.
6. Trim ¹⁄₁₆ in. off each side.
7. Round over the edges with a ³⁄₁₆-in. roundover bit on an overhead or table-mounted
router. Clamp a block to the body for extra
stability on the overhead router. Do not round
over the wheelwells.

ROOF

1. As with the body blank, cut the roof blank
¹⁄₈ in. oversized in width to allow trimming off
tearout after shaping the roof.
2. Cut the windshield slope to a 17° angle and
the back window to 20°.
3. Cut the back-window louvers with a
¹⁄₄-in.-dia. straight router bit chucked in a drill
press running at its highest speed (see the
bottom photo at right). Secure a backing block
to the workpiece with double-sided tape to help
keep the workpiece square to the fence. For
accurate and controlled cuts, use a ¹⁄₁₆-in.-thick
wood shim between the depth-adjustment
screw and the quill to set the depth stop on
the drill press. Position the router bit on the
line of cut with the shim in place, and then
remove the shim to drop the bit down to final
depth (see the drawing detail on the facing
page). Repeat for each louver.
4. Mask the roof off as necessary and paint the
window pattern (I like to use a T-roof design,
as shown in the drawing on the facing page).
The commercially made wheels that I use (see
Sources of Supply on p. 151) are unfinished,
but I paint them black so they are more lifelike.

Parts List

Quantity	Description	Dimensions	Material
BODY AND ROOF			
1	Body	1⁵⁄₁₆ x 3¹⁄₄ x 10¹¹⁄₁₆	Maple
1	Roof	¹³⁄₁₆ x 2¹³⁄₁₆ x 7¹⁵⁄₁₆	Maple
4	Wheels	1¹⁄₂ in. dia. by ¹⁄₂ in. thick	Birch
2	Axles	¹⁄₄-in.-dia. by 3⁵⁄₈ in. long	Steel
4	Spacer washers	¹⁄₄ in.	Steel
4	Push nuts (hub caps)	¹⁄₄ in.	Steel

Assembly

Finish all parts as described on pp. 16-18.
1. Glue the roof to the body.
2. Insert the steel axles through the body holes, install the spacer washers and the wheels and tap on four push nuts to serve as hub caps.

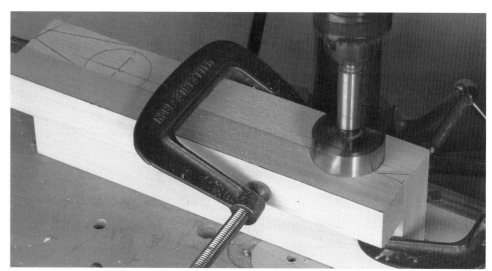

To prevent tearout when drilling the wheelwells, clamp an auxiliary block to the bottom of the body blank.

Cut the back-window louvers with a straight router bit on the drill press.

Sports Car

FRONT VIEW

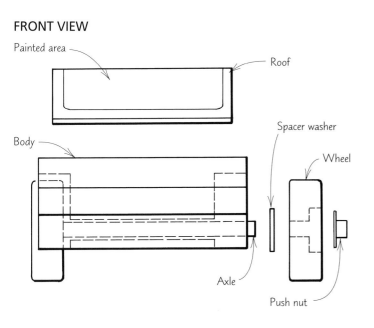

Painted area

Roof

Body

Spacer washer

Wheel

Axle

Push nut

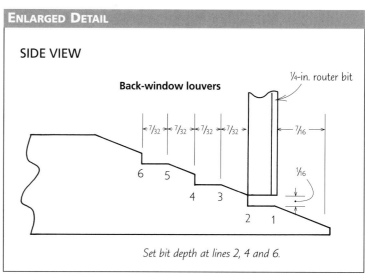

SIDE VIEW

Back-window louvers

¼-in. router bit

⁷⁄₃₂ ⁷⁄₃₂ ⁷⁄₃₂ ⁷⁄₃₂   ⁷⁄₁₆

6 5   4 3   2 1

¹⁄₁₆

Set bit depth at lines 2, 4 and 6.

SCALE 70%
Enlarge 143%

SIDE VIEW

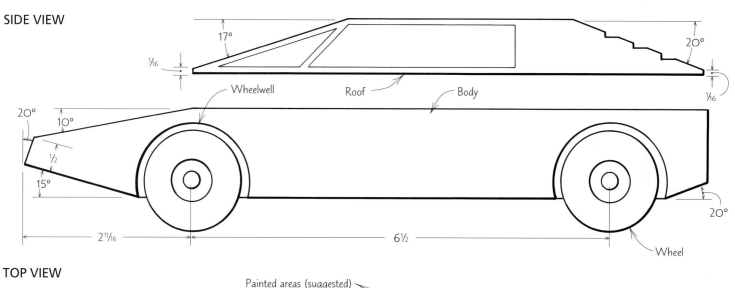

17°

20°

¹⁄₁₆

¹⁄₁₆

Wheelwell

Roof

Body

20°

10°

¹⁄₂

15°

2¹¹⁄₁₆

6½

20°

20°

Wheel

TOP VIEW

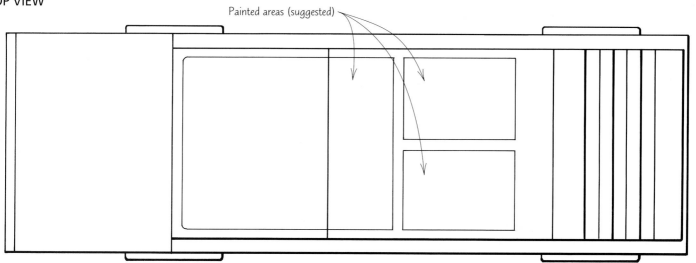

Painted areas (suggested)

Walk the Ball

The object of this game is to walk the Ping-Pong ball across the cradle and back without the ball falling off. It sounds simple, but you'll find it takes patience, coordination and lots of practice to master the game. You move the ball by raising or lowering one or more of the sixteen ½-in.-dia. dowels, coaxing the ball carefully from one dowel to the next. Many people have commented that the game looks like a Viking ship, particularly with the light birch dowels (the "oars") contrasted against the rich, dark walnut cradle. So when you're done playing, this toy makes a great coffee-table or desktop conversation piece.

Parts Preparation

CRADLE

There are two options for making the cradle ends. I chose to shape a single thick piece of walnut, and then resaw it into two pieces on the table saw. You could also use double-sided tape to fasten together two pieces of the proper thickness and then shape them as a single unit.

1. Use the full-size pattern on p. 62 to lay out the profile on the cradle end. Drill two holes to create the radiused shoulder on either side (see the top photo at right).

2. Make the 6° and 35° angle cuts on the cradle ends (a commercial tenoning jig is ideal for these cuts). For safety, stop the second cut short of the drilled hole and finish the cut on the bandsaw.

3. Sand the edges smooth, and then drill the hole for the rod.

4. Resaw the block into two ½-in.-thick pieces.

5. Make the U-shaped cutout on the cradle before beveling the sides to match the ends. To get a smooth radius, I first drilled the corners of the cutout with a ½-in.-dia. drill bit and then cut to the holes on the bandsaw. You could also make this cut on a router table.

WALKING STICKS

1. Apply finish to four full-length (36-in.) dowels with one coat of sanding sealer and two coats of high-gloss urethane. Cut the dowels into 6-in. lengths and apply finish to the ends.

2. Drill the centered holes in the dowels using the guide block shown in the bottom photo at right (see also pp. 10-11).

Assembly

Finish the cradle and cradle ends as described on pp. 16-18, making sure to keep the finish away from the glue areas.

1. Glue the cradle ends to the cradle.

2. Drill the rod holes through the cradle, using the holes in the cradle ends as a guide. Be sure the holes are straight and parallel to the cradle.

3. Glue a dowel plug into one cradle end, and then slide the brass rod into the cradle from the opposite end. Slide the dowels onto the brass rod, alternating from side to side as you feed the rod into the cradle.

4. Glue a dowel plug into the cradle end when the rod is fully inserted.

Parts List

Quantity	Description	Dimensions	Material
CRADLE AND WALKING STICKS			
1	Cradle	⅞ x 1¹³⁄₁₆ x 10	Walnut
2	Cradle ends	½ x 2⅛ x 4⅜	Walnut
16	Walking sticks	½-in.-dia. dowels by 6 in. long	Birch
1	Rod	³⁄₁₆ in. dia. by 9⅛ in. long	Brass
2	Dowel plugs	³⁄₁₆ in. dia. by ⅞ in. long	Birch
1	Ping-Pong ball	1½ in. dia. (standard size)	Plastic

To cut the cradle ends, first drill two holes to create the curved shoulder and finish the cut on the table saw. Use a tenoning jig to hold the workpiece.

Drill the centered holes in the dowels using a guide block and the auxiliary fence on the drill press.

Walk the Ball

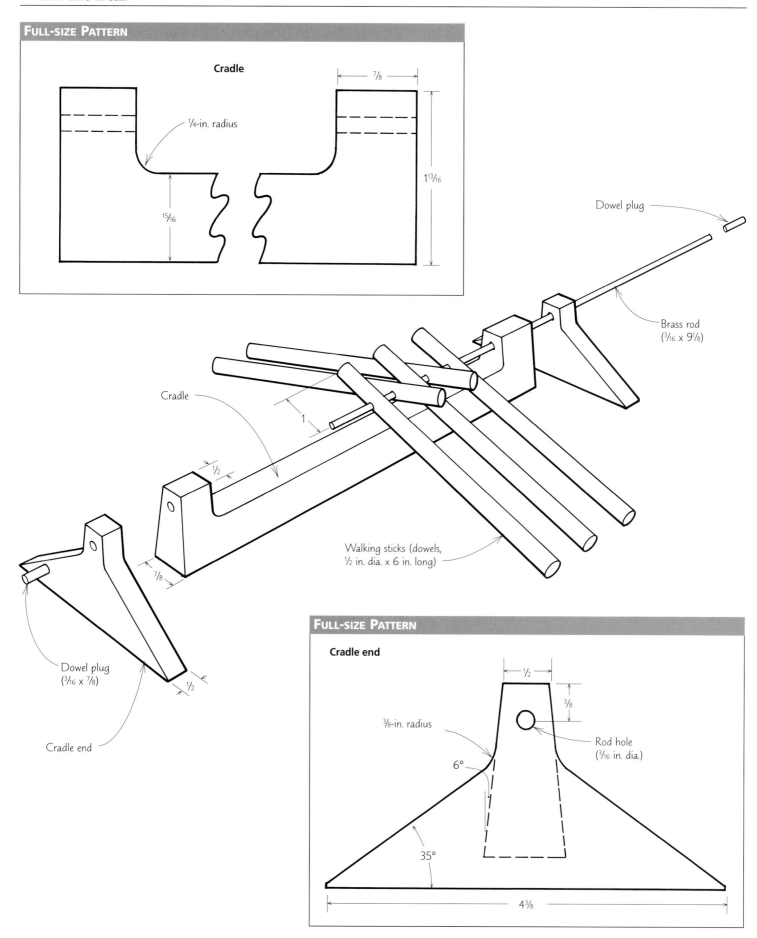

FULL-SIZE PATTERN

Cradle

7/8

1/4-in. radius

1 13/16

15/16

Dowel plug

Brass rod
(3/16 x 9 1/8)

Cradle

1

1/2

Walking sticks (dowels,
1/2 in. dia. x 6 in. long)

7/8

Dowel plug
(3/16 x 7/8)

1/2

Cradle end

FULL-SIZE PATTERN

Cradle end

1/2

3/8

3/8-in. radius

Rod hole
(3/16 in. dia.)

6°

35°

4 3/8

Life Star Helicopter

You don't see too many wooden helicopter toys, yet they offer all kinds of creative possibilities. The Life Star helicopter and the Police helicopter that follows are composite designs inspired by a helicopter calendar given to me by a friend. I'm particularly pleased with the way the propellers capture the feel of whirling motion. The full-size plans for the rotor and stabilizer props in this project could also be used for the Police helicopter.

Parts Preparation

FUSELAGE

The key to building the Life Star helicopter is being able to make accurate cuts at a 30° angle. To do this, I've developed a special jig that holds and positions the piece for cutting on the table saw (see p. 9). With a filler block in the same jig, I can cut smaller pieces, such as the pontoon struts. You could cut all these pieces on the bandsaw, but the angle of the cuts is critical for a precisely assembled model.

1. To make the fuselage sides, tape together two oversized blanks of 1/2-in.-thick Baltic birch plywood (1³/₁₆ in. x 7⁵/₈ in.) with double-sided tape. Using the full-size pattern on p. 67, transfer the fuselage-side profile, including all holes and cuts, onto the plywood.

2. Cut both ends at 30° with an angle jig, as shown in the photo at left below. Cut off the back tip of this parallelogram at 90° and separate the pieces.

3. Lay out the profile of the fuselage center piece, including the holes in the tail section, using the full-size pattern on p. 67.

4. I make the critical cuts that define the top edge of the fuselage center and the two angle cuts on the table saw. Make the first cut with the blank against the fence, being careful not to cut into the curved area that blends into the tail section (clamp a block to the fence to stop

the cut before the saw reaches the tail). Make the second and third cuts using the 30° angle jig (see the photos at center and right below). Finish off the tail section on the scrollsaw or bandsaw.

5. Drill the four holes in the tail section using the spacer-block technique (see pp. 6-7). Drill the hole at the end of the tail section to receive the stabilizer-axle screw.

6. Align and glue the fuselage side pieces on either side of the center piece.

7. Cut and sand the radius on the nose.

8. With the bottom edge of the fuselage against the drill-press fence, locate and drill the three holes through the fuselage.

9. Drill the rotor-shaft hole on the top edge of the fuselage.

10. Cut 1/8-in. saw kerfs into the bottom edge of the fuselage for the pontoon struts. Using a 1½-in. spacer block against the miter fence makes it easy to space the kerfs.

(text continues on p. 68)

Parts List

Quantity	Description	Finished Dimensions	Material
FUSELAGE			
1	Fuselage center	1/4 x 2³/4 x 9¹/8	Baltic birch plywood
2	Fuselage sides	1/2 x 1³/₁₆ x 6³/₁₆	Baltic birch plywood
2	Pontoon struts	1/8 x 1¹/4 x 2⁵/8	Baltic birch plywood
2	Pontoons	1/2-in.-dia. dowels by 3⁵/8 in. long	Birch
PROPELLERS			
1	Main rotor	1/4 in. thick by 4³/4 in. dia.	Baltic birch plywood
1	Rotor shaft	1/2-in.-dia. dowel by 1¹/4 in. long	Birch
2	Rotor washers	3/₁₆ in.	Steel
1	Rotor axle	#6 by 1¹/4-in. round-head screw	Steel
1	Stabilizer	1/8 in. thick by 2¹/2 in. dia.	Baltic birch plywood
2	Stabilizer washers	1/8 in.	Steel
1	Stabilizer axle	#4 by 3/8-in. round-head screw	Steel

To cut the 30° angles for the ends of the fuselage sides, use an angle-cutting jig to guide the workpiece.

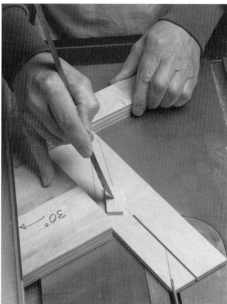

Use the same jig to make the angle cuts on the fuselage center.

Life Star Helicopter

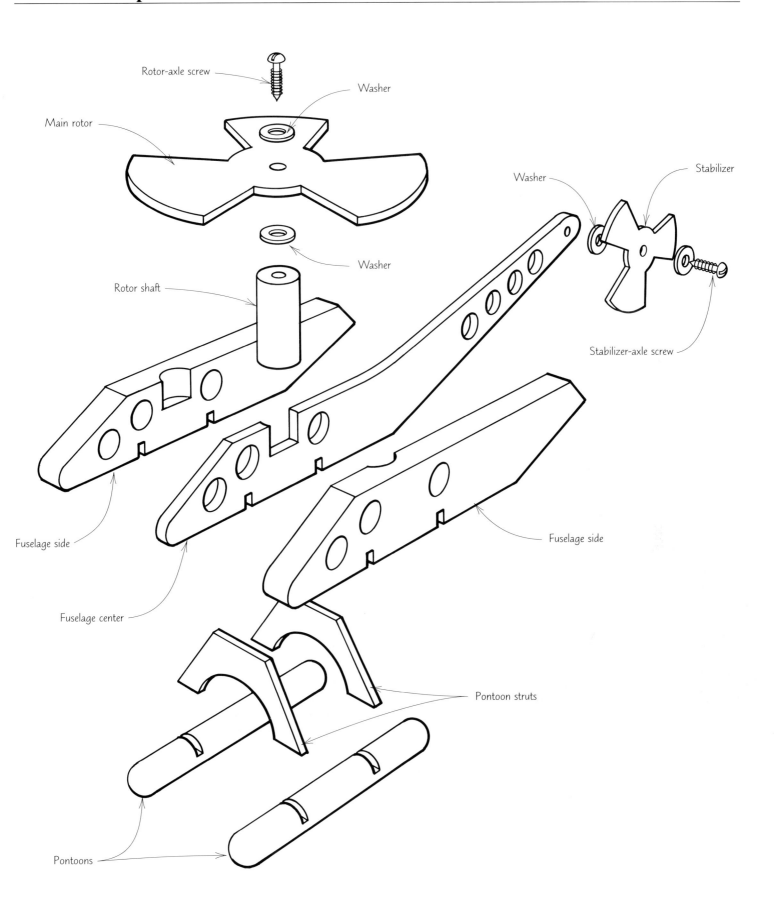

Rotor-axle screw

Washer

Main rotor

Washer

Washer

Stabilizer

Rotor shaft

Stabilizer-axle screw

Fuselage side

Fuselage side

Fuselage center

Pontoon struts

Pontoons

Life Star Helicopter

FRONT VIEW

SCALE 75%
Enlarge 133%

Main rotor

60°

1¼

SIDE VIEW

Stabilizer

Stabilizer-axle screw

Rotor-axle screw

Rotor shaft

¾

13/32

30°

1⁵/₁₆

½

30°

¼

1½

TOP VIEW (main rotor removed)

Pontoon

Fuselage side

Fuselage center

Stabilizer washers

Pontoon strut

Stabilizer-axle screw

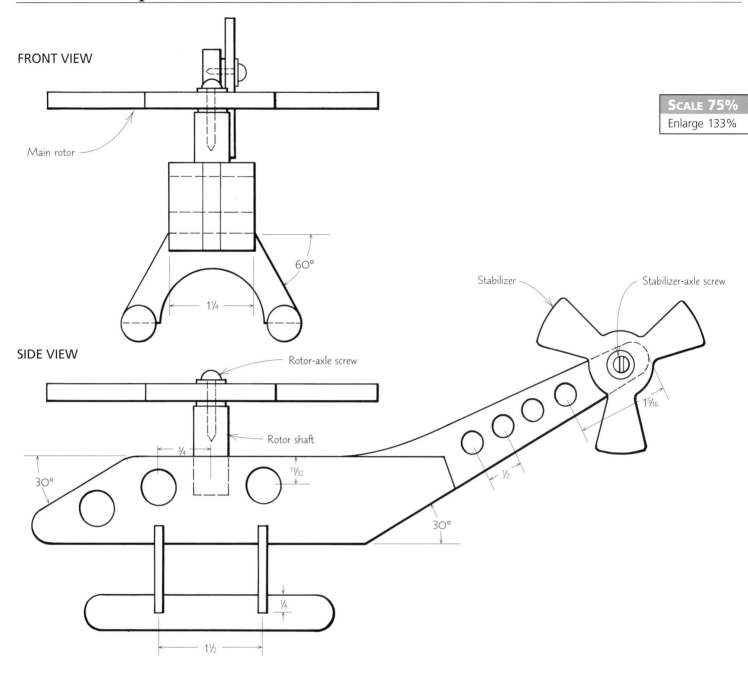
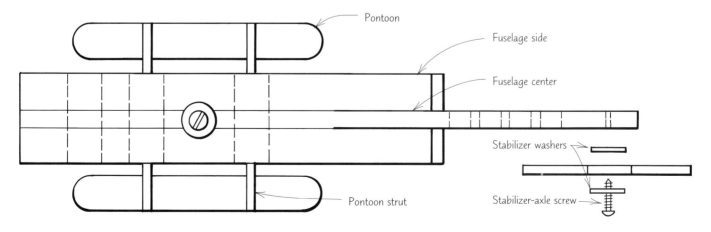

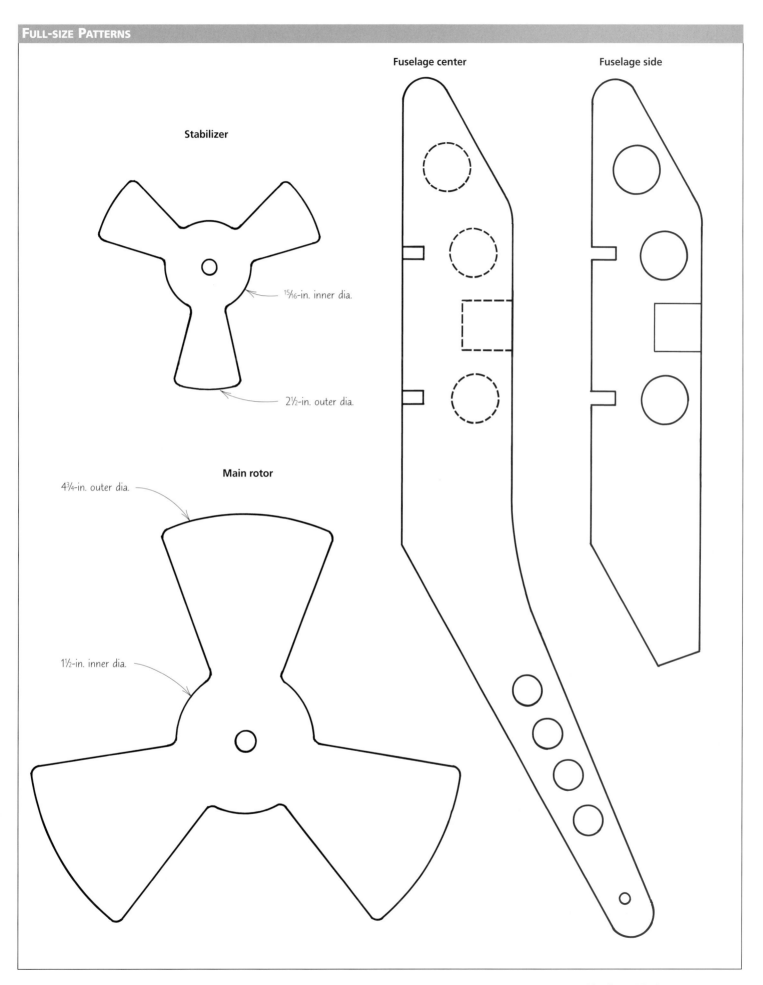

Stabilizer

Fuselage center

Fuselage side

$^{15}/_{16}$-in. inner dia.

2½-in. outer dia.

Main rotor

4¾-in. outer dia.

1½-in. inner dia.

Parts Preparation (continued)

PONTOONS AND STRUTS

1. To make the pontoons, spot-glue two 5-in.-long dowels together with a dab of glue at each end.

2. Using the same technique as in Step 10 on p. 64, kerf the pontoons for a perfect match to the fuselage (see the photo below). Cut the glued ends off the pontoons and round over the ends.

3. Cut perfectly matched struts by fastening the blanks together with double-sided tape.

Cut the 1½-in.-dia. arch on the bandsaw, and then cut the 30° side angles. You can use the same jig used for the fuselage cuts, with a filler block in place, or another 30° jig (see the photo at bottom).

PROPELLERS

1. Cut the main rotor and stabilizer to size using the full-size patterns on p. 67.

2. Drill a hole into the rotor shaft to receive the the rotor-axle screw.

Assembly

Finish all parts as described on pp. 16-18. Refer to the drawing on p. 65 for correct orientation of the parts during assembly.

FUSELAGE

1. Glue the pontoon struts into the fuselage and the pontoons onto the struts. I prefer to use epoxy rather than regular wood glue to add extra strength to these small joints.

PROPELLERS

1. Screw the main rotor and stabilizer in place, with washers on either side of the propellers to reduce friction.

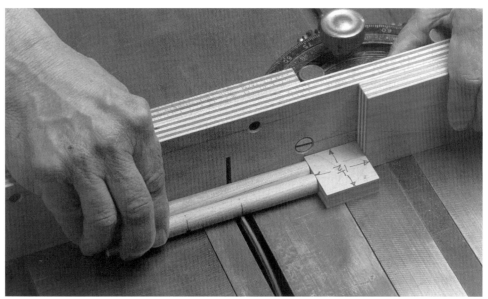

To cut kerfs for the struts in the pontoons, make the first cut with a spacer block in place, and then remove the spacer for the second cut. (This same technique is used to cut the matching kerfs in the fuselage.)

Make the angled cuts for the struts using a 30° angle jig.

Police Helicopter

The Police helicopter builds on some of the skills taught in the Life Star helicopter project (Project 8). The major difference in design is that the fuselage of the Police helicopter is a single piece rather than a three-piece assembly; it requires several challenging cuts. Unlike on the Life Star fuselage, all internal cutting and drilling is performed before any perimeter cutting. Consistent with the lighter appearance of the Police helicopter, the rotor has been slimmed down by using ⅛-in.-thick plywood, but for active play I'd use the same ¼-in.-thick plywood used on the Life Star chopper.

Parts Preparation

FUSELAGE

1. Cut the fuselage blank to size, and then use the full-size pattern on p. 72 to lay out the side and top profiles, including all the internal details (see the photo below).

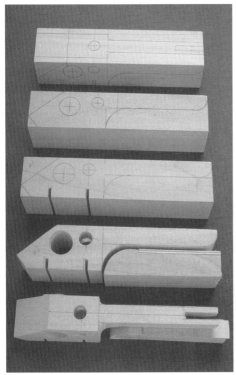

This photo shows the sequence of cuts and drilling operations for shaping the fuselage.

2. Kerf the fuselage for the pontoon struts using the same technique described for the Life Star helicopter on p. 64.

3. Drill the cabin holes through the blank.

4. Drill the ½-in.-dia. rotor-shaft hole in the top of the blank.

5. Form the windshield by cutting off the front of the cabin at 40° using a tenoning jig on the table saw. Finish the front of the helicopter by cutting off the projecting point at 90° to the windshield.

6. Now comes the tricky part—cutting the tail section. If you have a steady hand, you can simply cut the fuselage on the bandsaw using the full-size pattern on p. 72 as a guide. I prefer to use a tenoning jig on the table saw to cut the slot for the rudder and to begin the cuts that define the sides and bottom tail section of the fuselage.

Parts List

Quantity	Description	Dimensions	Material
FUSELAGE			
1	Fuselage	1¹¹⁄₁₆ x 1⁷⁄₁₆ x 7⅝	Poplar
1	Rudder	¼ x 1⁹⁄₁₆ x 2¾	Poplar
2	Pontoon struts	⅛ x 1⅜ x 2⅞	Baltic birch plywood
2	Pontoons	½-in.-dia. dowel by 4 in. long	Birch
PROPELLERS			
1	Main rotor	⅛ in. thick by 4¾ in. dia.	Baltic birch plywood
1	Rotor shaft	½-in.-dia. dowel by 1⅝ in. long	Birch
2	Rotor washers	¼ in.	Steel
1	Rotor axle	¼-in.-dia. peg by ¾ in. long with ⅜-in.-dia. head	Birch
1	Stabilizer	⅛ in. thick by 2¼ in. dia.	Baltic birch plywood
2	Stabilizer washers	⅛ in.	Steel
1	Stabilizer axle	⅛-in.-dia. peg by ⅝ in. long with ⁵⁄₁₆-in.-dia. head	Birch

7. Complete the cut under the tail section on the bandsaw, and then use double-sided tape to fasten the waste piece back in place, with a piece of ⅛-in.-thick plywood filling in the saw kerf. With this scrap supporting the tail section in a true horizontal position, the side cuts can be completed on the bandsaw.

8. To cut the bevels on the sides of the fuselage, set the table-saw blade at 3° and make the first side cut using the top layout line for alignment.

9. To make the second side cut, you'll need a block of wood approximately 1¾ in. wide by 4 in. long and about ¾ in. thick with a 3° angle cut on one side. Fasten the block to the fuselage with double-sided tape, with the tail end facing the blade. Make the cut, as shown in the photo at right. Check to be sure that the top layout line is aligned with the blade. After making both side cuts, you should end up with a 1¼-in.-wide flat area on top of the fuselage.

10. Sand the edges of the fuselage to the desired radius.

PONTOONS AND STRUTS

Make the pontoons and struts using the same technique described for the Life Star helicopter on p. 68.

PROPELLERS AND RUDDER

1. Cut the main rotor, stabilizer and rudder to size using the full-size patterns (the pattern for the main rotor is the same as for the Life Star helicopter; see p. 67).

2. Drill a hole into the rotor shaft for the rotor axle, and a hole in the rudder for the stabilizer.

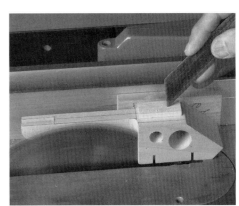

For the second angled side cut on the fuselage, tape a 3° block to the fuselage to support the workpiece.

Assembly

Finish all parts as described on pp. 16-18.

Assembly is essentially the same as for the Life Star helicopter (see p. 68), except that the stabilizer mounts to a rudder, not directly to the tail section. Glue the rudder into the slot in the fuselage tail and then smooth the back curve.

I chose to use wooden pegs instead of screws to mount the propellers for this helicopter. If you use pegs, make sure they're not too tight and don't get any glue on the props or they won't spin freely.

Police Helicopter

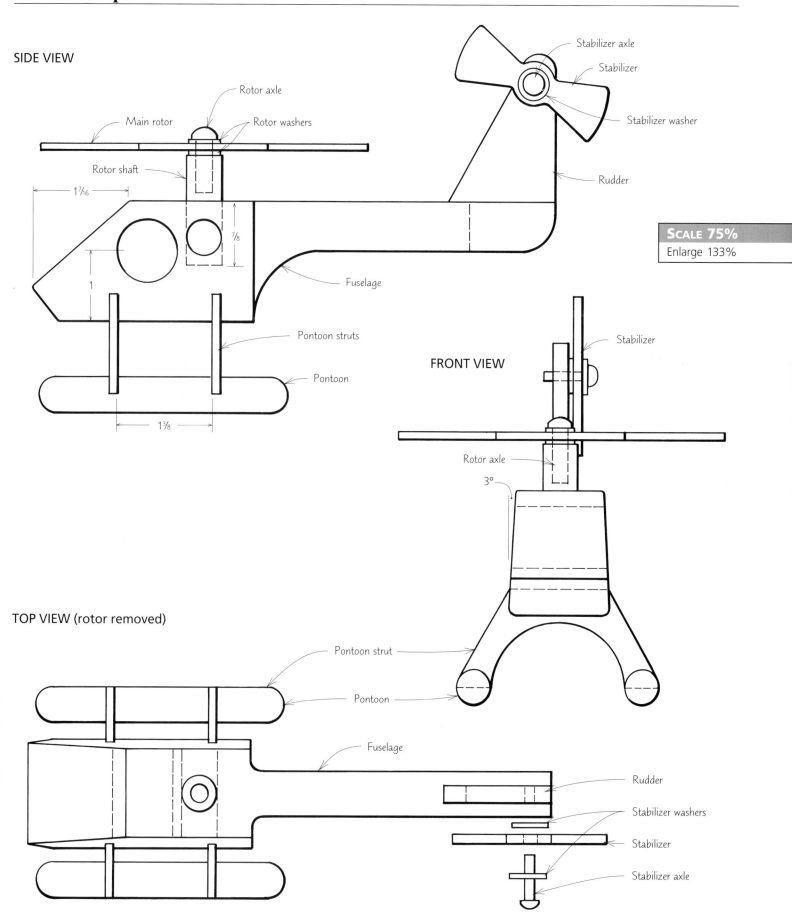

SIDE VIEW

Rotor axle

Main rotor

Rotor washers

Rotor shaft

$1\frac{7}{16}$

$\frac{7}{8}$

1

Fuselage

Pontoon struts

Pontoon

$1\frac{3}{8}$

Stabilizer axle

Stabilizer

Stabilizer washer

Rudder

SCALE 75%
Enlarge 133%

FRONT VIEW

Stabilizer

Rotor axle

3°

TOP VIEW (rotor removed)

Pontoon strut

Pontoon

Fuselage

Rudder

Stabilizer washers

Stabilizer

Stabilizer axle

(See the Life Star helicopter, p. 67, for a full-size pattern of the main rotor.)

Fuselage (side)

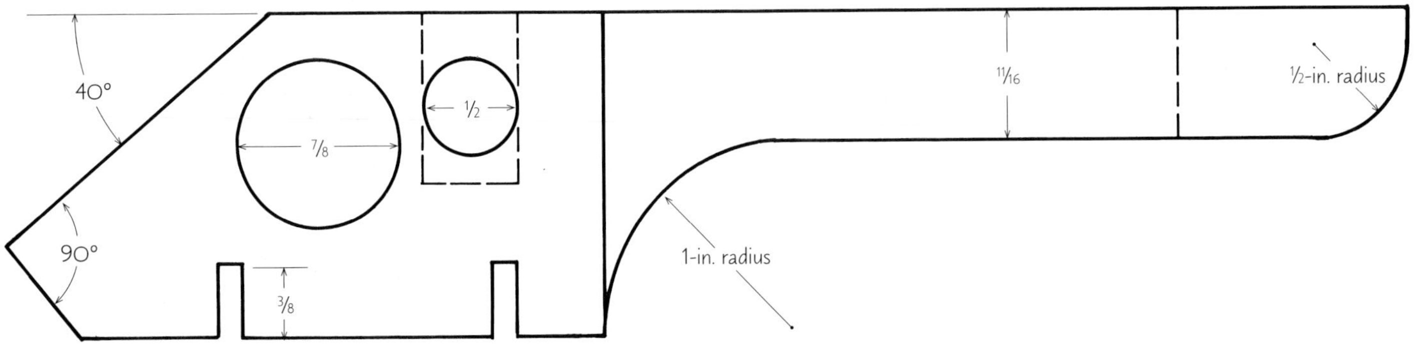

40°

90°

⁷⁄₈

¹⁄₂

³⁄₈

1-in. radius

1¹⁄₁₆

¹⁄₂-in. radius

Fuselage (top)

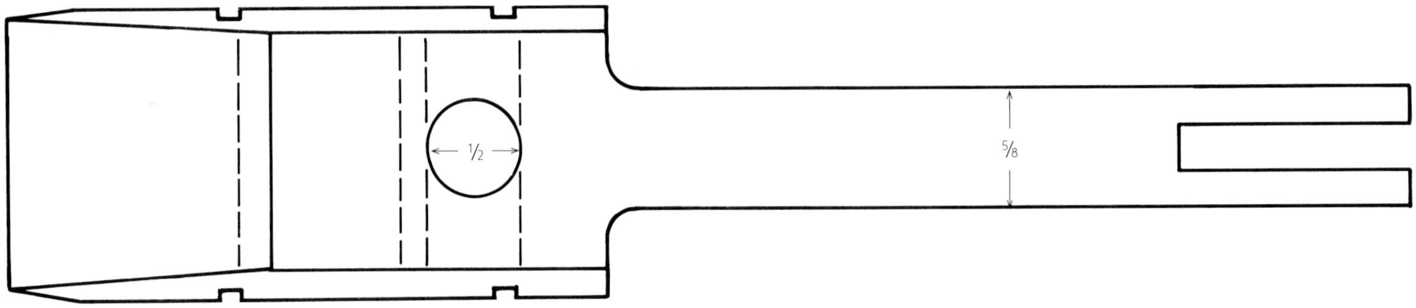

¹⁄₂

⁵⁄₈

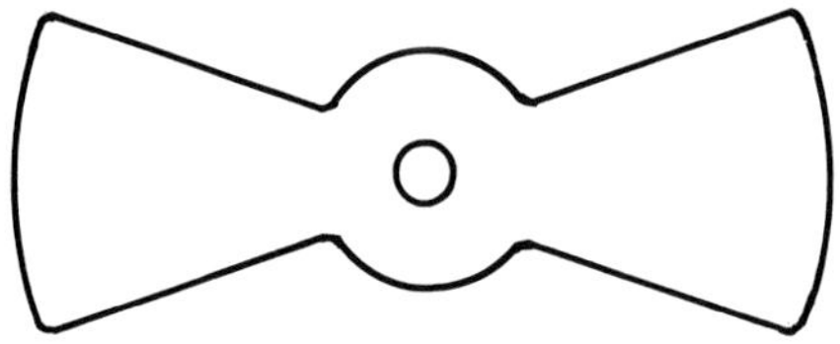

Pontoon strut

Stabilizer

Rudder

30°

1³⁄₈

¹⁵⁄₁₆-in. radius

¹⁄₂

30°

1¹⁄₁₆

1³⁄₁₆

1⁹⁄₁₆

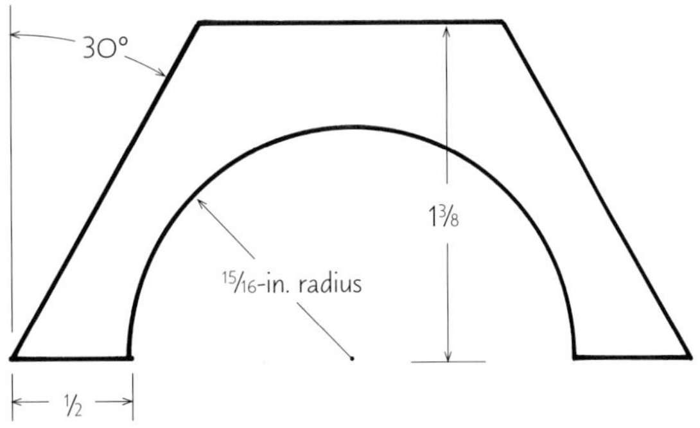

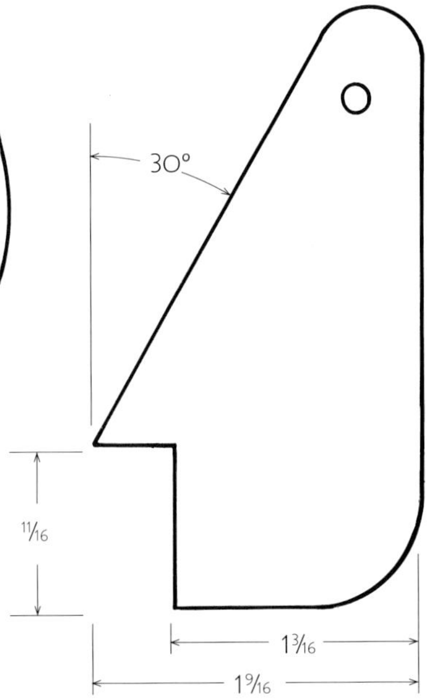

Jet Plane

With just six main parts, plus the landing gear, this plane exemplifies design simplicity. Yet it's form following function, since the plane's long, sweeping wings, rudder and elongated nose create a feeling of forward movement. The landing gear is designed so that the plane can be displayed in a landing position or tilted upward for takeoff (see the photo in the gallery on pp. 44-45).

Parts Preparation

FUSELAGE

1. Cut the fuselage blank slightly oversized to make it easier to lay out the plane profile and to allow for trimming off any tearout that may occur while drilling or shaping the piece.

2. Drill the window holes using the spacer-block technique discussed on pp. 6-7.

3. Trim off the excess length from the tail end of the fuselage, and cut a ¼-in.-deep rabbet for the stabilizer wing with a tenoning jig (see p. 9).

4. Cut a 13° angle on the tail end of the fuselage, leaving a flat area at least ³⁄₁₆ in. long behind the main-wing area so you can cut the dado for the wing. Then cut the two angles on the nose. Use an angle-cutting jig (see the photo on p. 9), a tenoning jig or a bandsaw for the three angled cuts.

5. Cut a ¼-in.-deep dado for the main wing, trim the fuselage to final dimensions with the help of a tenoning jig and then round over the edges with a ⅛-in. roundover bit.

MAIN WING

The main wing can be cut on the bandsaw or on the table saw with an angle-cutting jig (as described below).

1. Cut the blank to size, and then draw the layout on the top side. Using the angle jig shown in the top photo at right, cut the 22° angles on the front edge of the wing, leaving a 1-in.-wide straight area in the center. (I suggest that you first make a test cut about ¼ in. outside the layout line to check the angle of cut, and then make any necessary adjustments.)

2. Cut the back edge of the wing using the same technique (but a different jig). These are stopped cuts—make sure you don't cut into the 1-in. straight area in the center. Finish off the back edge of the wing with a scrollsaw or bandsaw.

STABILIZER WING

1. Cut the blank to size, and then make the angled cuts on the front and back edges as described for the main wing. Again, be sure to leave a 1-in. straight area in the middle of the wing to blend in with the fuselage.

Use an angle jig to cut the front edge of the wing. (Flip the workpiece over to make the second cut.)

Use a second angle jig to cut the back edge of the wing, stopping the cut just before the blade reaches the straight section in the center.

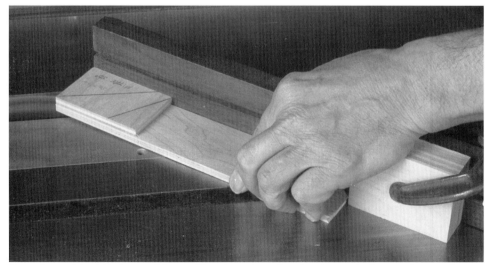

Tape the rudder blank to a thin auxiliary board, and make the angled cuts using a miter gauge and stop block on the table saw.

RUDDER

1. Tape the rudder blank to a thin auxiliary board (approximately 2 in. wide by 10 in. to 12 in. long).

2. Cut both angles on the table saw using a miter gauge and stop block to guide the workpiece, as shown in the bottom photo on the facing page.

LANDING GEAR

1. Cut the wheel struts to size, using the pattern on p. 76. Drill the holes for the axles. The holes should be slightly larger than the diameter of the axles (³⁄₁₆ in.) so the wheels will turn freely.

2. Cut the six wheels from a length of ⁵⁄₈-in.-dia. dowel rod, and then drill the holes to receive the ³⁄₁₆-in.-dia. axles.

ENGINES

1. Cut the engine dowels about 1½ in. longer than specified so you can spot-glue the ends to a flat board and cut the ⁵⁄₁₆-in. flat area for gluing the engine to the wing (see the top photo on p. 83). Cut the dowels loose from the board, and then trim to length.

2. Drill the intake and exhaust holes in each end on a lathe, making sure that the jaw chuck is not resting on the flat area. Taper the back end of the engines to approximately 15°.

Parts List

Quantity	Description	Finished Dimensions	Material
FUSELAGE AND WINGS			
1	Fuselage	1 x 1½ x 10½	Poplar
1	Main wing	¼ x 3³⁄₁₆ x 12¹³⁄₁₆	Birch
1	Stabilizer wing	¼ x 1⁵⁄₈ x 4½	Birch
1	Rudder	¼ x 2⁷⁄₈ x 2	Birch
ENGINES AND LANDING GEAR			
2	Jet engines	⁵⁄₈-in.-dia. dowel by 3⅛ in. long	Birch
3	Wheel struts	¼ x ¹³⁄₁₆ x ¹³⁄₁₆	Baltic birch plywood
6	Wheels	⁵⁄₈-in.-dia. dowel by ³⁄₈ in. long	Birch
3	Axles	³⁄₁₆-in.-dia. dowel by ⁷⁄₈ in. long	Birch

Assembly

Before finishing, sand the sharp corners off all the parts to leave a generous radius, especially on the rudder. Finish all parts as described on pp. 16-18. For this toy, I like to use a high-gloss finish to enhance the feeling of flight.

1. Glue the main wing and stabilizer wing to the fuselage.

2. Clamp the fuselage to a block, and then rout a ¼-in.-wide by ¹⁄₁₆-in.-deep groove for the rudder centered in the top of the stabilizer wing and into the fuselage. You can pre-rout the groove in the stabilizer wing, if you prefer.

(Another alternative is to notch out the rudder—that way you don't have to rout the fuselage at all.) Epoxy the rudder into the groove.

3. Epoxy the wheel struts and engines to the underside of the fuselage and wing, as shown in the drawing on p. 76.

4. Slide the axles through the wheel struts, and then epoxy the wheels onto the axles.

Jet Plane

SIDE VIEW

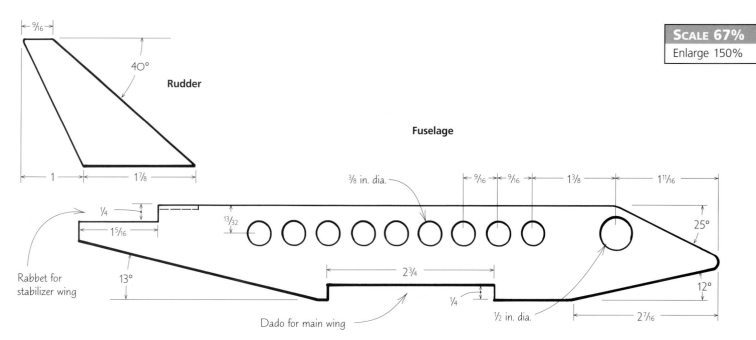

Jet Plane

BOTTOM VIEW

SCALE 54%
Enlarge 185%

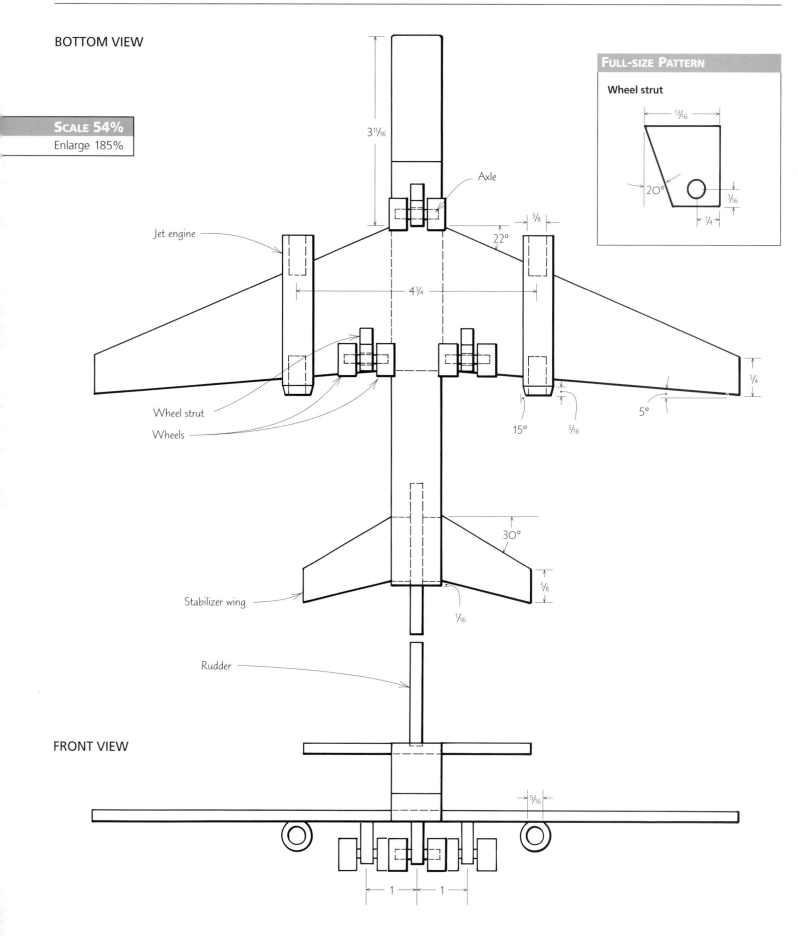

FULL-SIZE PATTERN

Wheel strut

$^{13}/_{16}$

$20°$

$^{3}/_{16}$

$^{1}/_{4}$

$3^{11}/_{16}$

Axle

Jet engine

$^{3}/_{8}$

$22°$

$4^{3}/_{4}$

$^{3}/_{4}$

Wheel strut

Wheels

$15°$

$^{3}/_{16}$

$5°$

$30°$

Stabilizer wing

$^{5}/_{8}$

$^{1}/_{16}$

Rudder

FRONT VIEW

$^{5}/_{16}$

1 1

Biplane

The biplane is one of my favorite toys, on nostalgia value alone—I have such fond memories of these planes as a young boy. Although developed as a toy to be played with, my biplane has found great favor with pilots, who enjoy the plane as a display piece. The landing-gear assembly presented the greatest design challenge during development, while the fuselage involves some interesting cutting techniques. As with most of my projects, this one has gone through several revisions over the years.

PROJECT 11

Parts Preparation

FUSELAGE

Cut the fuselage blank to size, leaving it about ¼ in. thicker than specified for later shaping. To shape the fuselage, follow the instructions below and the drawing on the facing page.

1. Drill holes for the cockpit and tail strut.

2. Make shoulder cuts for the bottom wing and stabilizer wing.

3. Complete the dado cut for the bottom wing by making multiple passes on the table saw, guiding the workpiece with the miter gauge. Complete the rabbet cut for the stabilizer wing using a tenoning jig on the table saw. Bandsaw the cockpit. Taper-cut the rear section with a tenoning jig on the table saw.

4. Tape the wedged offcut from Step 3 back to the underside of the fuselage to support the fuselage for trimming the sides.

5. Bevel each side at 5° on the table saw, to leave a 1⅛-in.-wide flat surface on the top of the fuselage. Round over the edges on a table-mounted router.

6. Taper the tail section on the bandsaw with the table tilted to 5° to maintain the beveled sides (these are compound cuts). Leave the layout lines and clean up any imperfections with a sandpaper block. Round over the edges with a ¼-in. router bit, except the back bottom section, which should be sanded to a minimal radius.

ENGINE COWL AND COCKPIT WINDSHIELD

1. Cut the cowl to size. I roughed out the cowl blank with a 2-in.-dia. hole saw, and then trued it up on a wood lathe. Make sure the hole for the propeller axle (which is drilled by the hole saw) is the correct diameter for the axle peg.

2. Cut the cockpit windshield to size, and then taper the sides (5°) and the front (40°).

WINGS, RUDDER AND PROPELLER

1. Cut out the bottom wing, and then radius each end, using the jig shown in the photo on p. 14.

2. Cut the top wing to shape, including the opening above the cockpit, and radius the ends. Lay out the four holes for the wing struts.

3. Turn ¼-in. by ¼-in. tenons on the ends of the wing struts. If you don't have a lathe, you could forego the tenons and drill holes in the wings to match the dowels.

4. Use double-sided tape to secure the bottom wing to the top wing—centered left to right with both back edges aligned. Drill the four strut holes and separate the wings.

5. Make the angled cuts on the stabilizer wing and the rudder. I use an angle jig on the table saw (see p. 9), and then finish off the radiuses on a scrollsaw.

6. Dado a ¼-in.-wide by ¹⁄₁₆-in.-deep slot on the stabilizer wing to receive the rudder.

7. Use the full-size pattern on p. 81 to lay out and cut the propeller.

LANDING GEAR

1. Tape the side-support blanks together (good sides facing in) with the grain direction running vertically. Cut rabbets for the top plate.

2. Lay out the triangular profile, and drill the holes for the axle and the side-support brace. (The location of this brace is not critical.)

3. Make the exterior cuts on a table saw using an angle jig, and the interior cuts on a scrollsaw.

4. Taper the back edge of the top plate to match the side-support back profile.

Parts List

Quantity	Description	Finished Dimensions	Material
FUSELAGE AND WINGS			
1	Fuselage	1⁵⁄₁₆ x 1⁹⁄₁₆ x 8¼	Birch
1	Top wing	¼ x 2¼ x 11⅛	Baltic birch plywood
1	Bottom wing	¼ x 2 x 10	Baltic birch plywood
1	Stabilizer wing	¼ x 2¼ x 4¼	Baltic birch plywood
1	Rudder	¼ x 2¼ x 2	Baltic birch plywood
1	Engine cowl	1¾ in. dia. by ¹¹⁄₁₆ in.	Walnut
1	Cockpit windshield	⁹⁄₁₆ x ¹¹⁄₁₆ x 1⅜	Birch
1	Propeller	⅛ x ¾ x 4⅜	Baltic birch plywood
1	Propeller axle	¼-in.-dia. peg, ¾ in. long with ½-in.-dia. head	Birch
1	Spacer washer	¼ in.	Steel
1	Pilot	¾-in.-dia. dowel by 1½ in. long	Birch
4	Wing struts	⅜ in. dia. by 2⁷⁄₁₆ in. long	Birch
1	Tail strut	¼-in.-dia. peg, 1 in. long with ⅜-in.-dia. head	Birch
LANDING GEAR			
2	Side supports	¼ x 1¹³⁄₁₆ x 1¾	Baltic birch plywood
1	Top plate	¼ x 1⅜ x 1¹³⁄₁₆	Baltic birch plywood
1	Side-support brace	⅛-in.-dia. dowel by 1¾ in. long	Birch
1	Wheel axle	³⁄₁₆-in.-dia. dowel by 2½ in. long	Birch
2	Wheels	1¼ in. dia. by ⅜ in. thick	Birch

Shaping the Fuselage

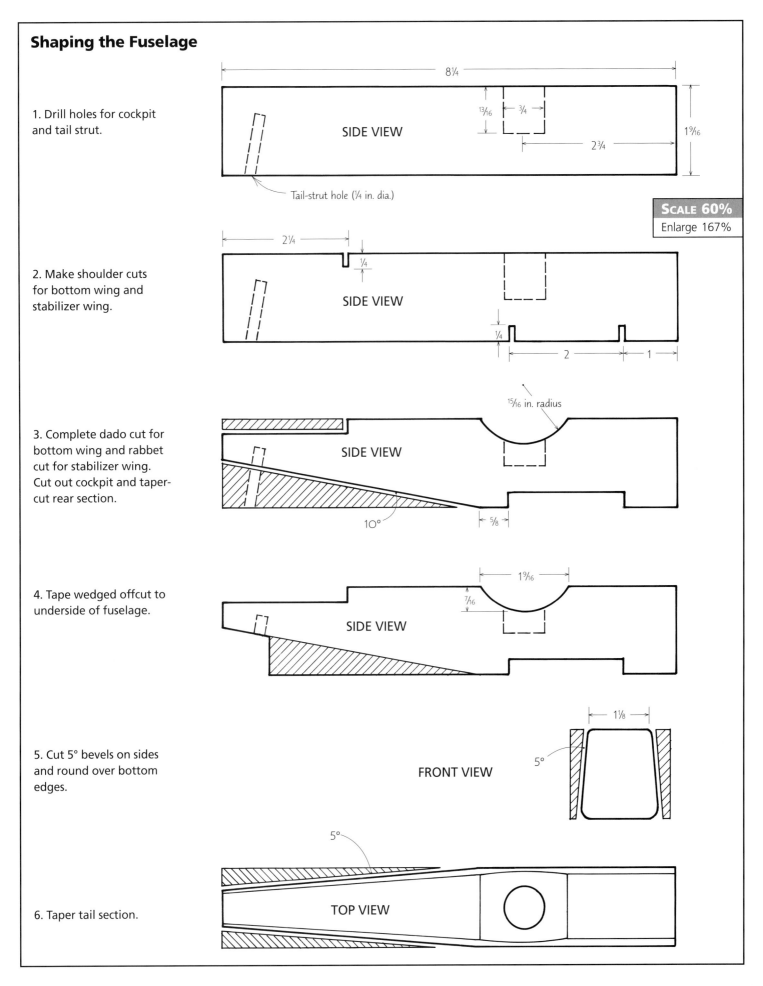

1. Drill holes for cockpit and tail strut.

SIDE VIEW

8¼

13⁄16   ¾

1⁹⁄16

2¾

Tail-strut hole (¼ in. dia.)

SCALE 60%
Enlarge 167%

2. Make shoulder cuts for bottom wing and stabilizer wing.

2¼

¼

SIDE VIEW

¼

2   1

3. Complete dado cut for bottom wing and rabbet cut for stabilizer wing. Cut out cockpit and taper-cut rear section.

15⁄16 in. radius

SIDE VIEW

10°   ⅝

4. Tape wedged offcut to underside of fuselage.

1⁹⁄16

7⁄16

SIDE VIEW

5. Cut 5° bevels on sides and round over bottom edges.

1⅛

5°

FRONT VIEW

6. Taper tail section.

5°

TOP VIEW

Biplane

SIDE VIEW

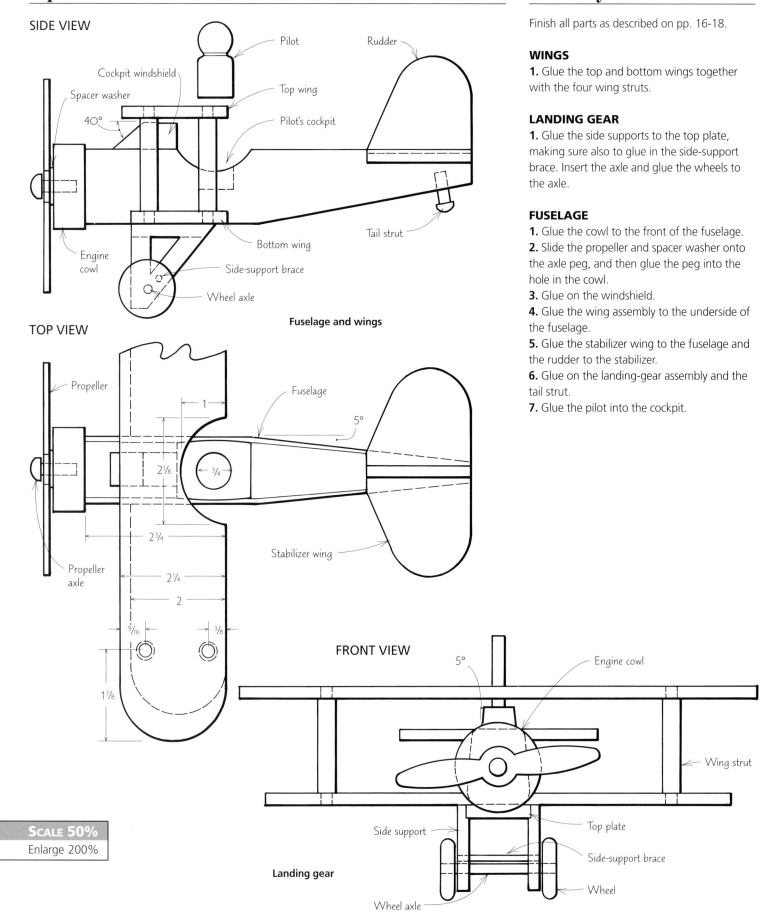

Pilot

Rudder

Cockpit windshield

Top wing

Spacer washer

Pilot's cockpit

40°

Engine cowl

Bottom wing

Side-support brace

Wheel axle

Tail strut

Fuselage and wings

TOP VIEW

Propeller

Fuselage

1

5°

2⅛

¾

2¾

Stabilizer wing

Propeller axle

2¼

2

⁹⁄₁₆

⅜

1⅞

FRONT VIEW

5°

Engine cowl

Wing strut

Side support

Top plate

Side-support brace

Wheel

Wheel axle

Landing gear

Assembly

Finish all parts as described on pp. 16-18.

WINGS
1. Glue the top and bottom wings together with the four wing struts.

LANDING GEAR
1. Glue the side supports to the top plate, making sure also to glue in the side-support brace. Insert the axle and glue the wheels to the axle.

FUSELAGE
1. Glue the cowl to the front of the fuselage.
2. Slide the propeller and spacer washer onto the axle peg, and then glue the peg into the hole in the cowl.
3. Glue on the windshield.
4. Glue the wing assembly to the underside of the fuselage.
5. Glue the stabilizer wing to the fuselage and the rudder to the stabilizer.
6. Glue on the landing-gear assembly and the tail strut.
7. Glue the pilot into the cockpit.

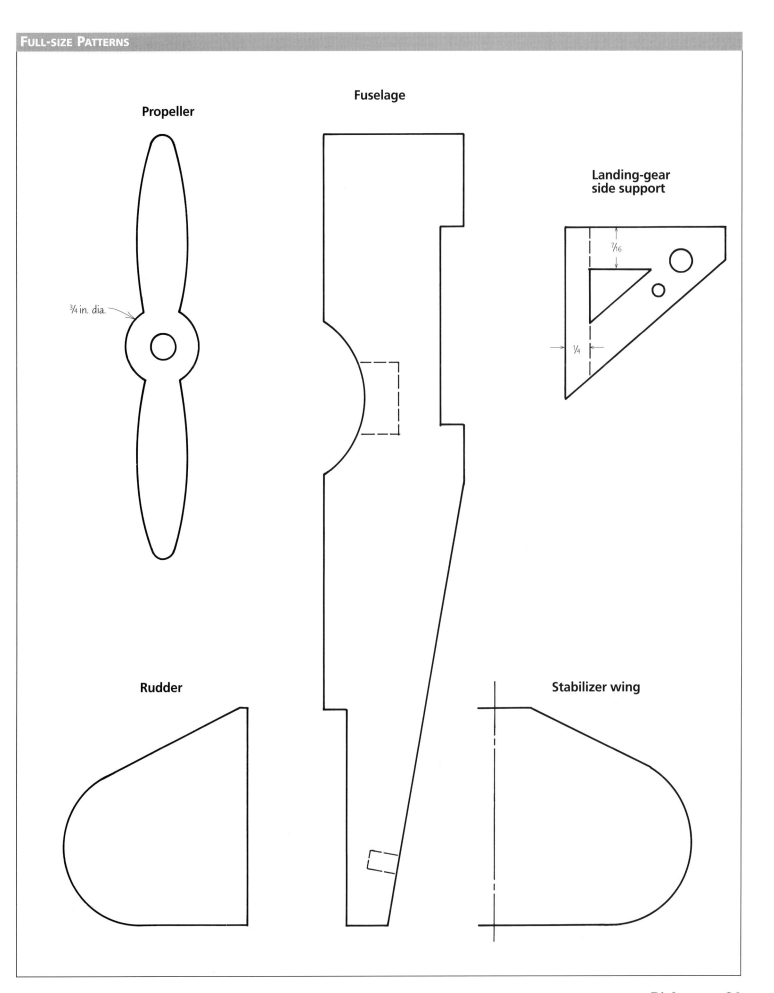

Propeller

Fuselage

Landing-gear side support

³⁄₄ in. dia.

$^{7}/_{16}$

$^{1}/_{4}$

Rudder

Stabilizer wing

Freight Train

This freight train consists of an old-fashioned steam engine with coal tender, box car, oil-tanker car and caboose. Although there are a lot of pieces, the simple shapes and common carriages make it a fairly easy toy to build. In fact, the design lends itself quite readily to mass-production techniques. The car connectors are designed so that a car can be hooked up anywhere in the train, with the exception of the caboose, which has only a front connector, thereby guaranteeing its proper location at the end of the train.

Parts Preparation

ENGINE

The trickiest procedures on the whole train are cutting the flat on the bottom of the boiler (and tanker car) to mate with the carriage and routing the wheel-clearance grooves in the boiler.

1. To cut the flat bottom of the boiler, glue the ends of an over-long dowel to a simple carrier jig and run it along the table-saw fence, as shown in the top photo below. The carrier is made of ³⁄₄-in.-thick plywood glued into an L-shape about 4 in. wide and 8 in. long that registers against the fence. Once the bottom is flattened, cut off the ends of the dowel (and carrier) to release the boiler.

2. Tape the boiler to a large auxiliary block and rout the wheel-clearance rabbet (¹⁄₄ x ¹⁄₄ x 1¹⁄₄), as shown in the bottom photo.

Glue the ends of the boiler to a carrier jig to cut the flat bottom.

With the boiler taped to an auxiliary block, rout the rabbet for the wheel clearance on either side.

Parts List

Quantity	Description	Finished Dimensions	Material
ENGINE			
1	Boiler	1¹⁄₂-in.-dia. dowel by 3¹⁄₈ in. long	Birch
1	Smokestack	¹⁄₂-in.-dia. dowel by 2⁷⁄₈ in. long	Birch
1	Smokestack cap	1-in.-dia. dowel by 1⁷⁄₃₂ in. long	Birch
1	Sand dome	³⁄₈ in. dia. by 1³⁄₈ in. long	Birch
1	Headlight	³⁄₈-in.-dia. peg, 1 in. long with ⁵⁄₈-in.-dia. head	Birch
1	Cab housing	1⁵⁄₈ in. x 2 x 2³⁄₈	Birch
1	Cab roof	⁹⁄₁₆ x 1⁷⁄₈ x 2³⁄₄	Cherry
1	Carriage	¹³⁄₁₆ x 1³⁄₄ x 7¹⁄₈	Birch
3	Axles	³⁄₁₆-in.-dia. dowel by 1⁵⁄₈ in. long	Birch
4	Back wheels	1¹⁄₄-in.-dia. by ³⁄₈ in. thick	Birch
2	Front wheels	1 in. dia. by ⁵⁄₁₆ in. thick	Birch
COAL TENDER			
2	Side walls	⁵⁄₁₆ x 1¹⁄₄ x 3¹⁄₂	Birch
1	Front wall	⁵⁄₁₆ x ⁷⁄₈ x 1	Birch
1	Back wall	⁵⁄₁₆ x 1¹⁄₄ x 1	Birch
1	Carriage	¹³⁄₁₆ x 1 x 5¹⁄₈	Birch
4	Wheels	1 in. dia. by ⁵⁄₁₆ in. thick	Birch
2	Axles	³⁄₁₆-in.-dia. dowel by 1⁵⁄₈ in. long	Birch
1	Coupling pin	³⁄₁₆-in.-dia. dowel by ⁷⁄₈ in. long	Birch
BOX CAR			
1	Box body	1¹⁄₁₆ x 1¹⁄₂ x 4	Birch
1	Roof	¹⁄₂ x 1⁵⁄₈ x 4¹⁄₄	Birch
1	Carriage	¹³⁄₁₆ x 1 x 5⁷⁄₈	Birch
4	Wheels	1 in. dia. by ⁵⁄₁₆ in. thick	Birch
2	Axles	³⁄₁₆-in.-dia. dowel by 1⁵⁄₈ in. long	Birch
1	Coupling pin	³⁄₁₆-in.-dia. dowel by ⁷⁄₈ in. long	Birch
OIL-TANKER CAR			
1	Tanker body	1¹⁄₂-in.-dia. dowel by 4¹⁄₄ in. long	Birch
1	Tanker cap	1 in. dia. by ⁷⁄₈ in. long	Birch
1	Carriage	¹³⁄₁₆ x 1 x 5⁷⁄₈	Birch
4	Wheels	1 in. dia. by ⁵⁄₁₆ in. thick	Birch
2	Axles	³⁄₁₆-in.-dia. dowel by 1⁵⁄₈ in. long	Birch
1	Coupling pin	³⁄₁₆-in.-dia. dowel by ⁷⁄₈ in. long	Birch
CABOOSE			
1	Main-cab body	1¹⁄₁₆ x 1¹⁄₂ x 3⁵⁄₈	Birch
1	Top-cab section	⁵⁄₈ x 1¹⁄₂ x 1¹⁄₂	Birch
2	Main-cab roof caps	³⁄₈ x 1⁵⁄₈ x 1¹⁄₄	Birch
1	Top-cab roof cap	³⁄₈ x 1⁵⁄₈ x 1³⁄₄	Birch
1	Carriage	¹³⁄₁₆ x 1 x 4³⁄₄	Birch
4	Wheels	1 in. dia. by ⁵⁄₁₆ in. thick	Birch
2	Axles	³⁄₁₆-in.-dia. dowel by 1⁵⁄₈ in. long	Birch
1	Coupling pin	³⁄₁₆-in.-dia. dowel by ⁷⁄₈ in. long	Birch

3. Using a lathe or a drill press, drill a hole centered in the front end of the boiler for the headlight peg.

4. Drill the holes for the smokestack and the sand dome in the top of the boiler.

5. The smokestack is a two-piece assembly. Drill through a 1-in.-dia. dowel lengthwise for the cap, and then glue it onto a ½-in.-dia. dowel (the stack). When the glue dries, turn the cap to the proper profile (see the drawing on p. 86). I suggest you make extra smokestack assemblies, since the 1-in. dowel has a tendency to split—it took me three tries to turn one that didn't split.

6. Round over the top of the sand dome on the lathe and cut to length.

7. Cut the cab-housing blank to size and drill the ¾-in.-dia. window holes. Use a 1-in.-dia. bit to create the curve at the top back of the cab, and then finish the profile on the bandsaw.

8. Cut the wheel-clearance rabbets along the bottom of the cab-housing sides.

9. With the cab-roof blank taped to a vertical jig, cut and then sand the curved top (see the photos at left and center below).

10. Cut the engine carriage to size, and then drill the three ⁷⁄₃₂-in.-dia. axle holes.

11. Lay out a full plan view of the carriage on the workpiece (see the drawing on p. 86). Cut a rabbet to form the back-connector tongue, and then drill a ⁷⁄₃₂-in.-dia. hole to receive the coupling pin from the coal tender.

12. Make the angle cuts on the sides of the back-connector tongue.

13. Cut the side and top angles on the cowcatcher with a tenoning jig on the table saw. I used a ⅜-in.-dia. drill bit to create the inside corner radiuses behind the cowcatcher, and then bandsawed to the holes.

CARRIAGES

Use the following procedure (and the drawing on p. 88) to make carriages for all the cars, with minor adjustments for the caboose (no connector tongue on the back) and the coal tender (cut slightly shorter).

1. Cut the carriage blank to size, and then make the shoulder cuts for the front- and back-connector tongues.

2. Drill the holes to receive the coupling pins. The hole for the glued-in pin is ¹⁄₃₂ in. smaller than the hole for the loose pin; for reference, mark the end in which the pin will be glued. Drill the axle holes.

3. Finish the rabbet cut on either end.

4. Make the shoulder cuts for the sides of the front- and back-connector tongues.

5. Finish the rabbet cuts and make the 45° angle cuts on the ends of the connector tongues.

COAL TENDER

1. Cut the side walls to size, and then fasten them together with double-sided tape.

2. Cut the rabbets on each end, and then cut the profile with a bandsaw or scrollsaw.

3. Cut the front and back walls to size.

To save time, you could simply bandsaw the coal tender to shape from a solid block.

BOX CAR

1. Working with an auxiliary wood fence on a miter gauge, use a fine-kerf blade to make three scoring cuts ¹⁄₁₆ in. deep in the box-car blank. These cuts simulate the box car's double doors (see the drawing on p. 87).

2. Shape the roof cap by first making ¹⁄₁₆-in.-deep cuts that define the center ridge. Then, with the workpiece taped to an auxiliary block, bevel-cut from the edges to meet the first cuts, as shown in the photo at right below.

OIL-TANKER CAR

1. Cut the flat bottom of the tanker body using the same technique described for the engine boiler (see p. 83).

2. Drill a centered hole on top of the tanker body for the 1-in.-dia. cap.

CABOOSE

1. Cut the main cab body and the top cab section to size. Drill window holes in the top cab.

2. Round over the edges of a 6-in.-long strip of roof stock, and then cut the blank to the required lengths for the three roof caps.

Assembly

Finish all parts as described on pp. 16-18.

There is no special order required for assembly. I usually glue up the upper sections of the cars, assemble them to the carriage and then add the axles and commercial wheels last.

Tape the cab-roof blank to a vertical jig, and then cut and sand the curved top.

With the box-car roof taped to an auxiliary block and kerfs cut in the roof top, make bevel cuts on either side.

Freight Train

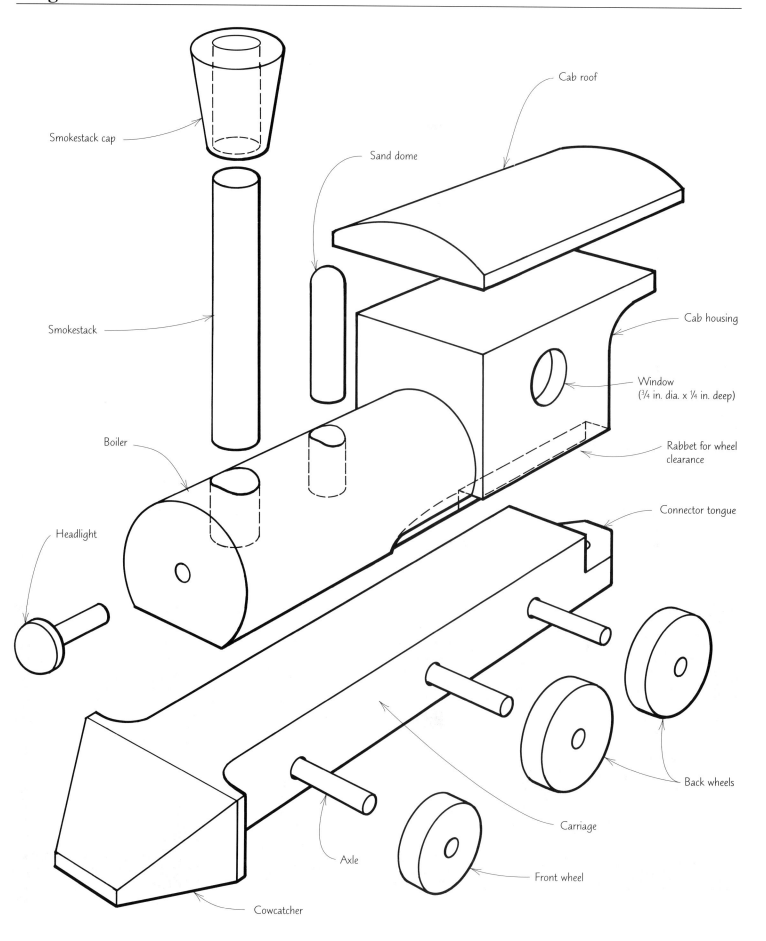

Smokestack cap

Smokestack

Boiler

Headlight

Cowcatcher

Sand dome

Cab roof

Cab housing

Window
(¾ in. dia. x ¼ in. deep)

Rabbet for wheel
clearance

Connector tongue

Axle

Carriage

Back wheels

Front wheel

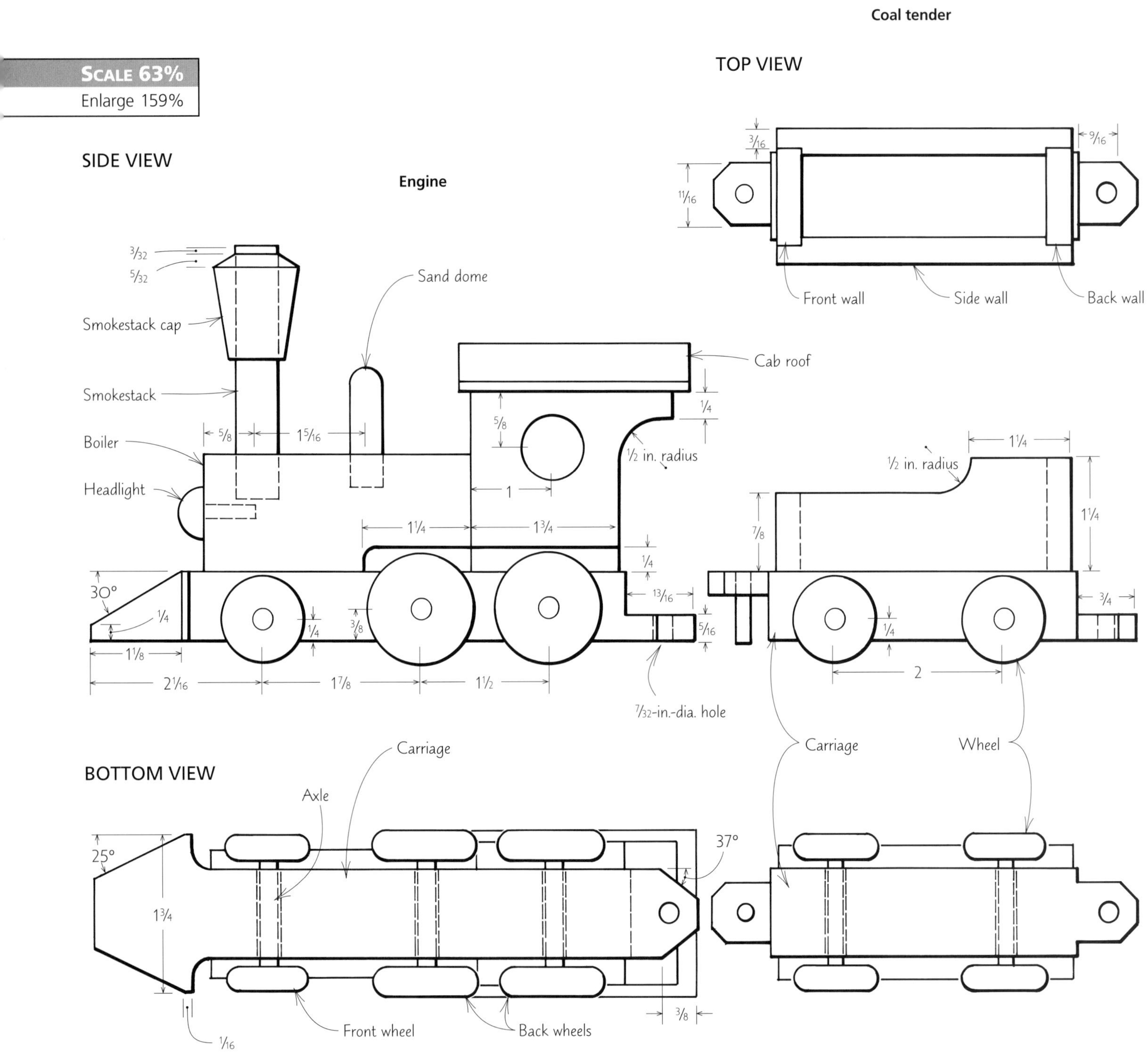

Freight Train

Coal tender

TOP VIEW

3/16

9/16

11/16

Front wall   Side wall   Back wall

SIDE VIEW

Engine

3/32

5/32

Smokestack cap

Smokestack

Boiler

Headlight

5/8   1 5/16

5/8

1/2 in. radius

1

1 1/4   1 3/4

1/4

30°

1/4

1/4

3/8

13/16

5/16

1 1/8

2 1/16   1 7/8   1 1/2

7/32-in.-dia. hole

Sand dome

Cab roof

1/4

Cab roof

1/2 in. radius   1 1/4

7/8

1 1/4

1/4

3/4

2

Carriage   Wheel

BOTTOM VIEW

Carriage

Axle

25°

1 3/4

1/16

Front wheel   Back wheels

37°

3/8

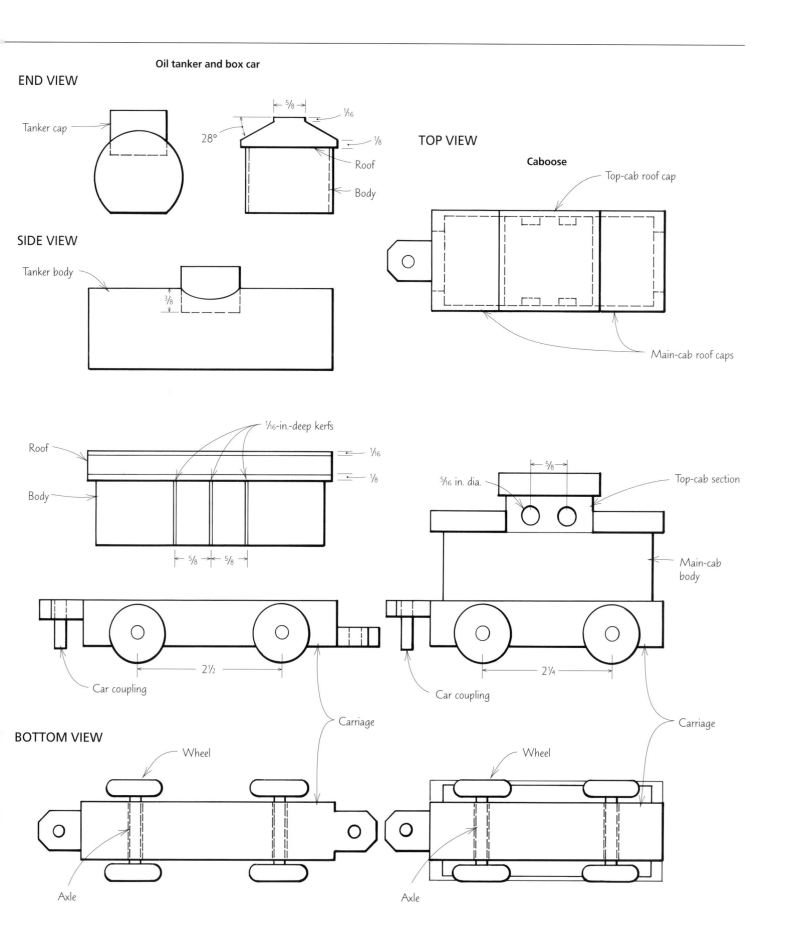

Oil tanker and box car

END VIEW

Tanker cap

5/8

1/16

28°

1/8

Roof

Body

TOP VIEW

Caboose

Top-cab roof cap

SIDE VIEW

Tanker body

3/8

Main-cab roof caps

1/16-in.-deep kerfs

Roof

1/16

Body

1/8

5/16 in. dia.

5/8

Top-cab section

5/8   5/8

Main-cab body

2 1/2

2 1/4

Car coupling

Carriage

Car coupling

Carriage

BOTTOM VIEW

Wheel

Wheel

Axle

Axle

Making a Carriage

Note: The length of the carriage varies for the coal tender, the caboose (which has no back tongue) and the regular cars; the couplings are identical for all cars.

SIDE VIEW

1. Make shoulder cuts for connector tongues.

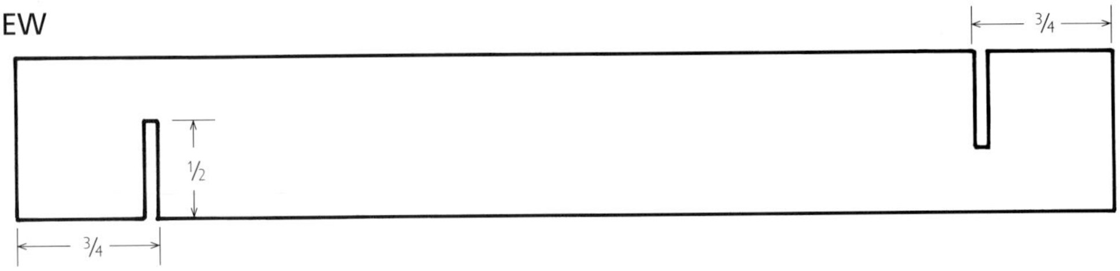

$^3/_4$

$^1/_2$

$^3/_4$

2. Drill coupling holes and axle holes.

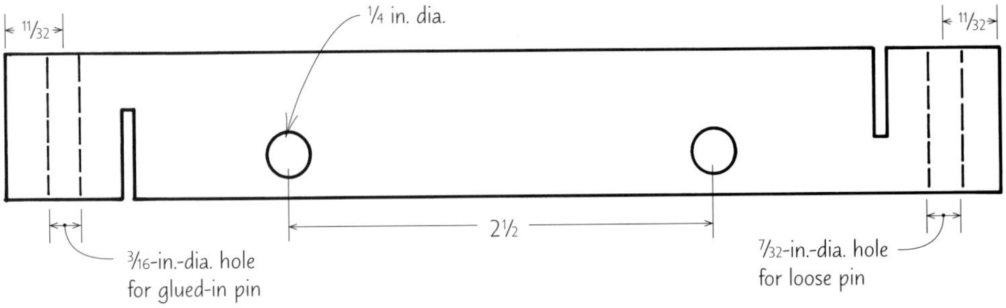

$^{11}/_{32}$

$^1/_4$ in. dia.

$^{11}/_{32}$

$2^1/_2$

$^3/_{16}$-in.-dia. hole for glued-in pin

$^7/_{32}$-in.-dia. hole for loose pin

3. Finish rabbet cuts.

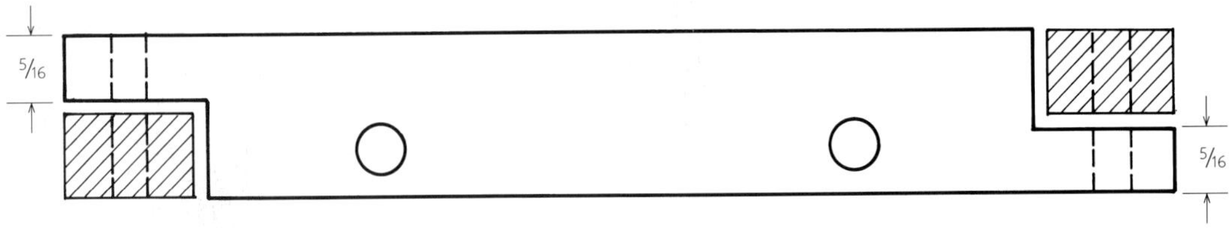

$^5/_{16}$

$^5/_{16}$

TOP VIEW

4. Begin shaping tongues.

$^3/_4$

$^5/_{32}$

5. Finish shaping tongues.

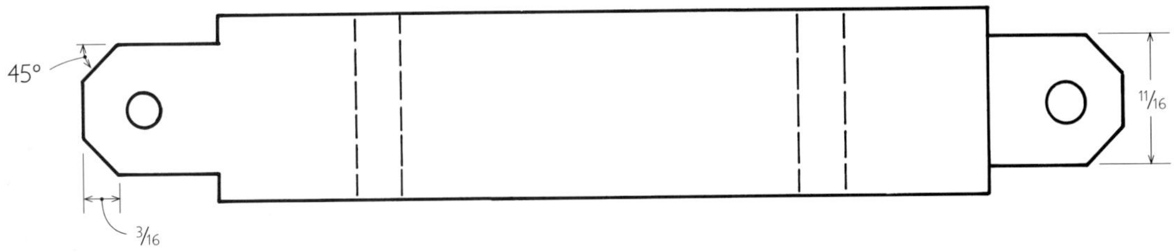

45°

$^{11}/_{16}$

$^3/_{16}$

Passenger Train

There's nothing quite so nostalgic as an old steam passenger train. This one's a re-creation of a Boston & Maine RR train, complete with Pullman passenger cars, that I rode on a few times in the 1940s. The undercarriages and roofs are made of solid birch (you could also use maple), but the passenger and cargo compartments are cut from Baltic birch plywood, with up to 14 openings in each to hone your scrollsaw skills. As with the freight train (Project 12), all cars feature the same car-coupling design to allow for any hook-up order desired. However, in the old Wild West, the combo car (passenger/mail car) was usually located right behind the coal tender so the engineer could spot train robbers.

Parts Preparation

The engine assembly comprises three sections: the carriage, boiler and cab.

ENGINE CARRIAGE

1. Cut the carriage blank to size, and then lay out the side and top view.

2. Mark and drill all holes in the blank, including the three axle holes ($^{11}/_{32}$ in. dia.), the coupling-pin hole ($^5/_{16}$ in. dia.) and the four holes in the face of the cowcatcher ($^5/_{16}$ in. dia.). I also drilled $^5/_{16}$-in.-dia. holes to create the inside radius behind the cowcatcher.

3. Glue a $^1/_4$-in.-thick piece of solid birch to the bottom front of the carriage to add thickness to the cowcatcher (this piece is the "lower cowcatcher" in the parts list). Using double-sided tape, temporarily fasten an additional $^1/_4$-in.-thick piece to the underside of the carriage behind the lower cowcatcher. (This $^1/_4$-in. shim creates a level bottom surface to help support the workpiece during subsequent operations.)

4. Make the compound cuts on the face of the cowcatcher by setting the miter gauge and the table-saw blade to 25°. Tilt the blade to 15° to make the side cuts.

5. Trim off each side of the carriage from the back to the cowcatcher to create the $1^5/_8$-in. body width. I cut just short of the cowcatcher on the table saw (using a tenoning jig), and then finished the cut on the bandsaw.

6. Cut the rabbet for the car coupling, and then radius the back end of the carriage.

7. Sand the carriage to eliminate sharp edges and glue in the coupling pin.

ENGINE BOILER

1. Cut the boiler blank a little long, and then chuck it in a lathe to shape the front end. (I used a $1^5/_8$-in.-dia. dowel for the boiler, but if you have trouble finding the right size dowel, you can turn your own or simply make some minor modifications to accommodate the size you are using.) Trim off the nub in the center where the tailstock was.

2. Trim the boiler to correct length, and then cut a flat surface on the bottom, using the same technique as for the freight train (see p. 83).

3. Drill holes in the boiler for the smokestack and sand domes.

4. Drill the hole in the $1^1/_2$-in.-dia. dowel for the smokestack cap, and then glue the cap onto the smokestack. Turn the cap to shape on the lathe.

5. Cut the sand domes to size and radius the tops on the lathe.

ENGINE CAB

1. Cut the front and two side panels of the cab to size.

2. Rabbet both inside edges and the bottom edge of the front panel. Tape the side panels together (with outside surfaces facing in) and cut the rabbet on the bottom edge.

3. Lay out the windows in the three panels. I used a $^3/_4$-in.-dia. bit to drill the radiused tops of the windows in the side panels (and a $^7/_8$-in.-dia. bit for the radiused corners on the front panel), and then finished the cutouts on a scrollsaw.

4. Cut the floor panel and cab block to size.

5. Rabbet the underside of the roof to fit between the cab walls.

6. Cut and sand the radiused roof with the same vertical support jig used on the freight train (see p. 84).

COAL TENDER

1. Make the carriage for the coal tender as described for the freight train (see p. 84 and the drawing on p. 88), except for the addition of two axle blocks. The larger axles on this train require holes close to the edge of the carriage, so I've reinforced this area by gluing blocks right under the axle locations.

2. Drill the $^{11}/_{32}$-in.-dia. axle holes.

3. Cut the side panels to size and temporarily fasten them together with double-sided tape. On both pieces, cut rabbets on each end and on the bottom. Scrollsaw the profile and separate the pieces.

4. Cut the front and back panels to size and rabbet the bottom edges.

5. Cut the floor panel to size.

PULLMAN CARS

1. Cut out and shape the carriages as explained for the freight train (see p. 84 and the drawing on p. 88). All the carriage cuts are made on the table saw, using a tenoning jig for the vertical cuts on the coupling tongues. Note that the tongue with the coupling pin is the full width of the carriage.

2. Glue on the axle blocks, and then drill the axle holes ($^{11}/_{32}$ in. dia.) and the hole for the coupling pin ($^5/_{16}$ in. dia.). Glue the pin in place. Drill the hole for the loose coupling pin in the front-coupling tongue slightly oversize ($^{11}/_{32}$ in. dia.).

3. Cut all passenger-compartment panels to size.

4. Fasten the side panels together with double-sided tape and rabbet the bottom edge.

5. Working with a drill press with an auxiliary fence, drill the regularly spaced window holes in the side walls as described on pp. 6-7. Finish the window cutouts on the scrollsaw. Use a flat stick and a dowel covered with sandpaper to clean the sides and the arches.

6. Drill and cut the door opening in the end panels.

7. Cut the roof blank to size.

8. Rabbet the sides and ends of the roof to fit inside the walls of the car.

9. To shape the outside of the roof, make two parallel cuts lengthwise and spaced to create the crown in the center. For extra support when bevel-cutting the edge of the roof, I tape the workpiece to a straight piece of scrap wood, as shown in the photo at right on p. 84. Cut the ends at 45°, and then sand to blend the ends into the crown of the roof.

COMBO CAR

1. Make the combo car in the same way as the Pullman car, but note that the side panel has a different cutout pattern (three windows and a doorway) and the mail-car section has no door cutout on the end panel (see the photo on p. 89).

2. Cut the three pieces for the internal sliding-door unit. Assemble the unit as shown in the drawing on p. 94 (but don't glue in the pegs for the door handles just yet).

WHEELS

All the wheels on this train are cut slightly oversized with a hole saw and finished to correct diameter on a wood lathe (see p. 13). Use spacer washers to keep the wheels from rubbing against the carriage.

Parts List

Quantity	Description	Finished Dimensions	Material
STEAM ENGINE: CARRIAGE			
1	Carriage	$^{13}/_{16}$ x 3 x 9$^7/_{16}$	Birch
1	Lower cowcatcher	$^1/_4$ x 3 x 3	Birch
3	Axles	$^5/_{16}$-in.-dia. dowel by 2$^3/_4$ in. long	Birch
6	Spacer washers	$^5/_{16}$ in.	Steel
2	Front wheels	1$^5/_{16}$ in. dia. by $^1/_2$ in. thick	Birch
4	Back wheels	1$^5/_8$ in. dia. by $^1/_2$ in. thick	Birch
1	Coupling pin	$^5/_{16}$-in.-dia. dowel by $^{13}/_{16}$ in. long	Birch
STEAM ENGINE: BOILER			
1	Boiler	1$^5/_8$-in.-dia. dowel by 4$^3/_8$ in. long	Birch
1	Smokestack	$^5/_8$-in.-dia. dowel by 3 in. long	Birch
1	Smokestack cap	1$^1/_2$-in.-dia. dowel by 1$^3/_8$ in. long	Birch
2	Sand domes	$^5/_8$-in.-dia. dowel by 1$^5/_8$ in. long	Birch
STEAM ENGINE: CAB			
1	Cab block	$^5/_8$ x 1$^5/_8$ x 2$^3/_4$	Birch
1	Floor panel	$^1/_4$ x 1$^7/_8$ x 2$^{11}/_{16}$	Baltic birch plywood
1	Front panel	$^1/_4$ x 2$^1/_4$ x 2$^5/_8$	Baltic birch plywood
2	Side panels	$^1/_4$ x 3$^3/_8$ x 2$^5/_8$	Baltic birch plywood
1	Roof	$^{11}/_{16}$ x 2$^3/_4$ x 3$^3/_4$	Birch
COAL TENDER			
1	Floor panel	$^1/_4$ x 1$^3/_4$ x 4	Baltic birch plywood
2	Side panels	$^1/_4$ x 4$^1/_4$ x 2$^1/_4$	Baltic birch plywood
1	Front panel	$^1/_4$ x 1$^3/_4$ x 1$^3/_8$	Baltic birch plywood
1	Back panel	$^1/_4$ x 1$^3/_4$ x 2$^1/_4$	Baltic birch plywood
1	Carriage	$^{13}/_{16}$ x 1$^5/_8$ x 6	Birch
2	Axle blocks	$^1/_4$ x $^3/_4$ x 1$^5/_8$	Birch
2	Axles	$^5/_{16}$-in.-dia. dowels by 2$^3/_4$ in. long	Birch
4	Spacer washers	$^5/_{16}$ in.	Steel
4	Wheels	1$^1/_4$ in. dia. by $^1/_2$ in. thick	Birch
1	Coupling pin	$^5/_{16}$ in. dia. by $^{13}/_{16}$ in. long	Birch
PULLMAN CARS			
1	Floor panel	$^1/_4$ x 1$^3/_4$ x 7	Baltic birch plywood
2	End panels	$^1/_4$ x 2 x 2$^1/_4$	Baltic birch plywood
2	Side panels	$^1/_4$ x 7 x 2$^1/_4$	Baltic birch plywood
1	Roof	$^{13}/_{16}$ x 2$^1/_4$ x 8	Birch
1	Carriage	$^{13}/_{16}$ x 1$^5/_8$ x 9$^3/_4$	Birch
2	Axle blocks	$^1/_4$ x $^3/_4$ x 1$^5/_8$	Birch
2	Axles	$^5/_{16}$ in. dia. by 2$^3/_4$ in. long	Birch
4	Spacer washers	$^5/_{16}$ in.	Steel
4	Wheels	1$^1/_4$ in. dia. by $^1/_2$ in. thick	Birch
1	Coupling pin	$^5/_{16}$-in.-dia. dowel by $^{13}/_{16}$ in. long	Birch
COMBO PASSENGER/MAIL CAR			

(The only differences between the combo car and the Pullman car are the side-panel cutouts and the addition of the following parts to create a sliding door.)

2	Doors	$^1/_4$ x 1$^3/_4$ x 1$^{13}/_{16}$	Baltic birch plywood
1	Door floor board	$^1/_4$ x 1$^3/_{16}$ x 1$^3/_4$	Baltic birch plywood
2	Door handles	$^1/_8$-in.-dia. dowels by $^5/_8$ in. long	Birch

Assembly

Finish all parts as described on pp. 16-18.

There is no special order required for assembly of the engine. For the Pullman cars, glue the side and end panels first, and then add the floor panels and roofs. For the combo car, insert the three-piece sliding-door assembly before attaching the roof. Slide the door over to the larger opening and glue in the door handles (making sure that the pegs are on the side closest to the end panel).

Glue the assembled compartments to the carriages and add the wheels and axles last to keep the cars from rolling around.

Passenger Train

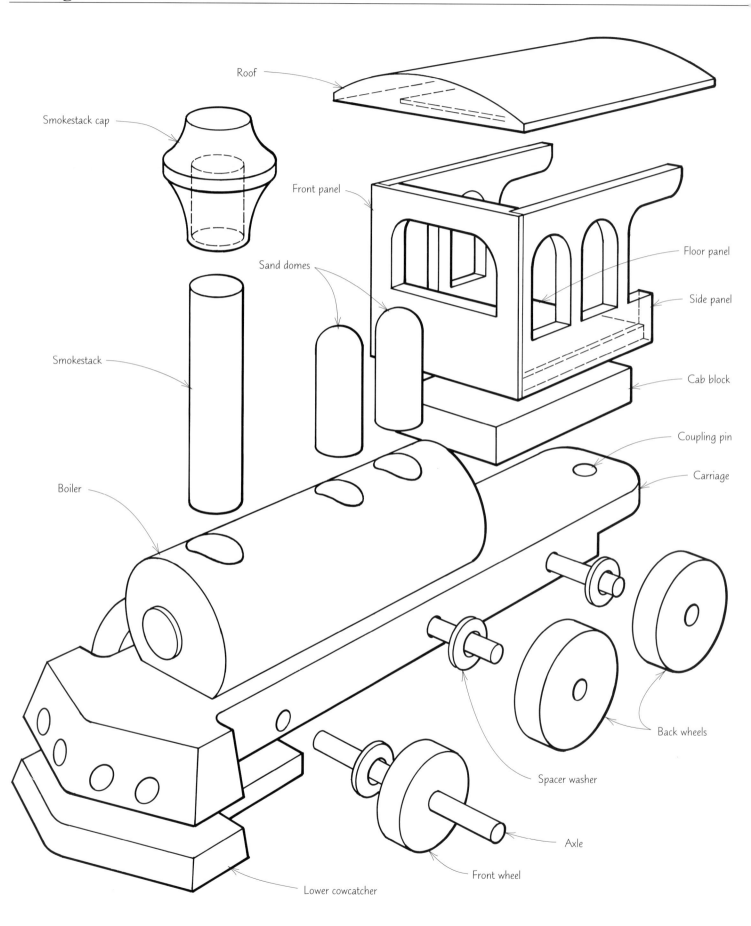

Roof

Smokestack cap

Front panel

Floor panel

Sand domes

Side panel

Smokestack

Cab block

Coupling pin

Carriage

Boiler

Back wheels

Spacer washer

Axle

Front wheel

Lower cowcatcher

SIDE VIEW

Steam engine

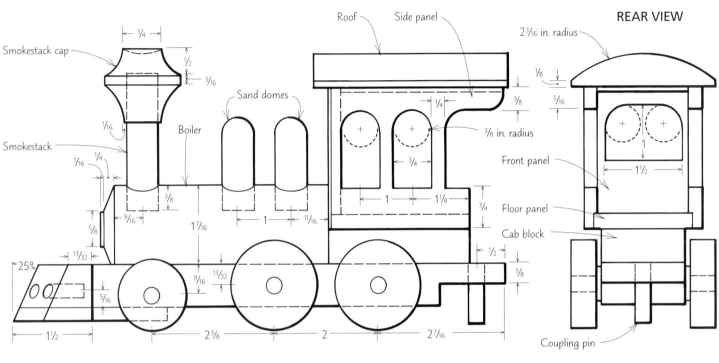

Smokestack cap

Smokestack

Boiler

3/4

1/2

3/16

1/16

1/16   1/4

3/8

9/16

5/8

13/32

25°

1 7/16

9/16   13/32

1 1/2

2 3/8

2

2 7/16

Sand domes

Roof   Side panel

1/4

3/4

1

11/16

1

1 1/8

3/8

3/8 in. radius

3/4

1/2

3/8

REAR VIEW

2 3/16 in. radius

1/8

5/16

1

1 1/2

Front panel

Floor panel

Cab block

Coupling pin

Lower cowcatcher

TOP VIEW

Carriage

Axle

13/32

5/32 in. radius

2 1/2

25°

13/16

Front wheel

Spacer washer

Back wheels

1 1/4

1 5/8

5/16-in.-dia. hole

1/2

FRONT VIEW

Front panel

15°

5/16-in.-dia. hole

1/2   11/16   1/2

Passenger Train

Pullman car

SIDE VIEW

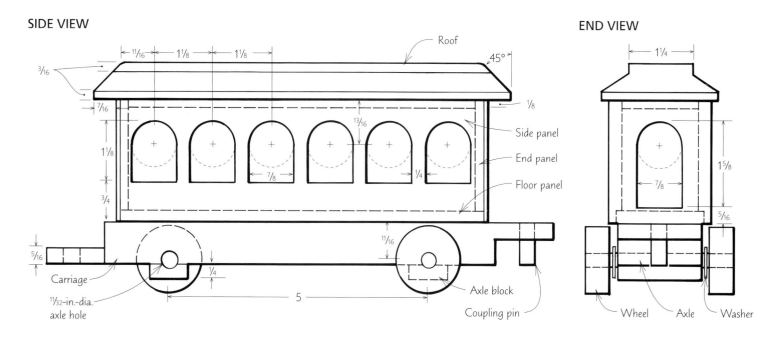

END VIEW

Roof

45°

³/₁₆

¹¹/₁₆ 1¹/₈ 1¹/₈

⁷/₁₆

1¹/₈

³/₄

1¼

Side panel

End panel

Floor panel

¹/₈

¹³/₁₆

⁷/₈

¹/₄

1⁵/₈

⁵/₁₆

⁷/₈

⁵/₁₆

¹¹/₁₆

Carriage

⁵/₁₆

¹¹/₃₂-in.-dia. axle hole

¹/₄

5

Axle block

Coupling pin

Wheel   Axle   Washer

BOTTOM VIEW

Carriage

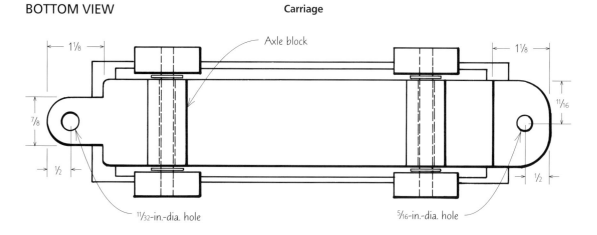

Axle block

1¹/₈

⁷/₈

¹/₂

¹¹/₃₂-in.-dia. hole

1¹/₈

¹¹/₁₆

¹/₂

⁵/₁₆-in.-dia. hole

SIDE VIEW

Combo passenger/mail car (side panel)

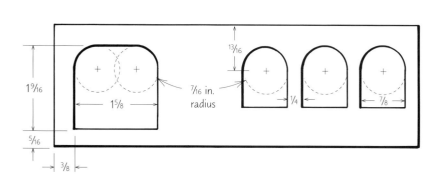

1⁹/₁₆

1⁵/₈

⁵/₁₆

³/₈

¹³/₁₆

⁷/₁₆ in. radius

¹/₄

⁷/₈

SIDE VIEW   END VIEW

Sliding doors (mail-car section)

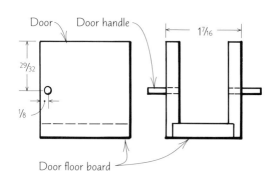

Door   Door handle

29/32

¹/₈

1⁷/₁₆

Door floor board

SIDE VIEW

FRONT VIEW

Coal tender

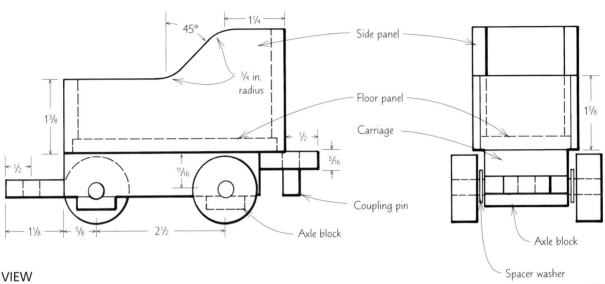

TOP VIEW

Cable Car

This cable car is a modified version of a life-size cable car (my biggest toy ever!) that I made with the kids in my neighborhood for a 1979 parade float. Modeled after the cars that daily climb San Francisco's fabled hills, this car features a high-domed roof in solid walnut that contrasts nicely with the light birch plywood that makes up the paneled sides and ends.

Parts Preparation

SIDE WALLS

Use ¼-in.-thick Baltic birch plywood for the side walls if the cable car is to be a play toy; for a display model, I'd select solid cherry instead.

1. Cut the blanks 1 in. longer than finished size.

2. To ensure that the pieces will be shaped identically, spot-glue the panels together at the corners. (I also use a couple of strips of double-sided tape at the top and bottom edges so I can sand all interior and exterior edges as one piece after the ends are cut off.) Glue the panels with the best faces together to prevent tearout on what will be the exposed faces.

3. Use the full-size pattern on p. 99 to lay out the side-wall profile.

4. Drill out the bottom corners of each of the three windows, and then finish cutting the windows with a scrollsaw. I use the spacer-block technique to drill the holes (see pp. 6-7), only this time the blocks alternate between ½ in. wide (the distance between centerlines of the holes within the windows) and ¾ in. wide (the distance between centerlines of the holes from one window to the next; see the pattern on p. 99).

5. Cut the end profiles on the side walls, drilling three ½-in.-dia. holes and finishing the cut with a scrollsaw.

6. Using a ¼-in. router bit in an overhead router or a drill press, dado the side walls for the floor boards (see the photo on p. 98). Rabbet the top edge for the roof.

Parts List

Quantity	Description	Finished Dimensions	Material
BODY			
2	Side walls	¼ x 7½ x 4⅜	Baltic birch plywood
1	Center floor board	¼ x 2½ x 4	Baltic birch plywood
2	End floor boards	¼ x 2½ x 1⁹⁄₁₆	Baltic birch plywood
1	Wheel chassis	1¹⁄₁₆ x 1¼ x 4⅞	Poplar
2	Axles	¼ in. dia. by 2¼ in. long	Birch
4	Spacer washers	¼ in.	Steel
4	Wheels	1¼ in. dia. by ⅜ in. thick	Birch
2	Headlight panels	¹³⁄₁₆ x 3 x 1¼	Walnut
2	Headlight-panel caps	¼ x ²⁹⁄₃₂ x 3	Baltic birch plywood
2	Headlights	¹¹⁄₁₆-in.-dia. pearl buttons	Plastic
4	End walls	¼ x ¾ x 3¼	Baltic birch plywood
ROOF			
1	Roof	¹⁵⁄₁₆ x 3 x 7¾	Walnut
1	Roof cap	⅝ x 1⅝ x 4	Walnut

7. Sand all edges, and then separate the two side-wall pieces. If you're using cherry, be careful separating the pieces from the double-sided tape because the outer ends will be weak because of the short-grain orientation.

ROOF

1. Cut the roof blank to size, and then cut the rabbets on the underside along each side and each end. For appearance, I like to bevel the vertical face of the end rabbets at 30°, but a straight cut is fine.

2. The roof is a modified version of a raised panel. Create a centered rectangle by cutting a ¹⁄₁₆-in.-deep shoulder across both ends and along both sides. Make the bevel cut, setting the blade depth to meet the shoulder cut. Cut the ends first, then readjust the depth of cut and cut the sides (see the photos at left and center below). Use a tenoning jig for the end cuts and an auxiliary block (and double-sided tape) to support the roof for the side cuts.

While you've got the table saw set up, bevel an extra length of stock for the front and back headlight panels, which have the same cross section as the roof.

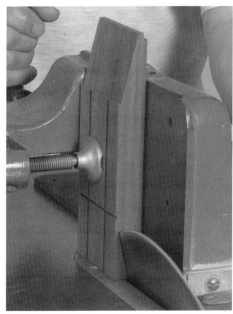

Use a tenoning jig to make the end cuts on the car roof.

For the angled side cuts, fasten the roof to an auxiliary board with double-sided tape.

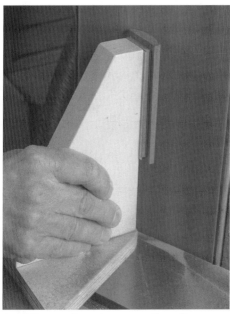

Sand the roof cap to a smooth radius, using a vertical jig for support.

Parts Preparation (continued)

3. Cut the roof cap to size, and then rabbet all four edges of the underside to create a rectangle that matches the rectangle on the top of the roof.

4. Cut the top profile of the cap, and then sand to a smooth radius with a vertical shaping jig (see the photo at right on p. 97).

5. Glue the roof cap to the roof.

FLOOR

1. Cut the three floor pieces to size. Rabbet the center board on each end to receive the end-wall panels. Round over the inward-facing end of the end boards (see the photo below).

2. Glue the end boards to the center board, making sure that the floor assembly will fit into the dado cuts in the side walls. (But don't glue the floor assembly to the side walls yet.)

WHEEL CHASSIS

1. Cut the wheel chassis to size, and then cut a ¼-in.-deep rabbet on each end so that the chassis fits between the end floor boards.

2. Drill the two ¹¹/₃₂-in.-dia. axle holes through the chassis.

3. Bevel the ends of the chassis at 45°.

HEADLIGHT PANELS

1. The headlight panels were beveled as a single unit while shaping the roof (see p. 97). Now cut the front and back panels to finished length.

2. Rabbet the ends of each panel for the side walls and cut a ¼-in. dado for the floor panel.

3. Use the pattern on the facing page to lay out and cut the headlight-panel caps.

4. Use a spade bit to drill the headlight recess to match the button chosen for the headlight (I use ¹¹/₁₆-in.-dia. pearl buttons; see Sources of Supply on p. 151). The sides of a spade bit are easily ground to match the size of the button, and the point creates a recess for the stud in the back of the button.

END WALLS

1. Cut these partial panels slightly long, and then use the full-size pattern on the facing page to shape the profile.

2. Trim the panels to length to fit between the ceiling and the rabbet on the end of the center floor board.

Assembly

Finish all parts as described on pp. 16-18.

1. Glue the side walls to the floor boards and to the roof.

2. Glue the headlight panels to the side walls, and then glue the headlight-panel caps in place. Epoxy the headlights into the headlight panels.

3. Insert the axles into the wheel chassis, add the spacer washers and then glue the wheels to the axles. Glue the wheel chassis to the underside of the floor boards.

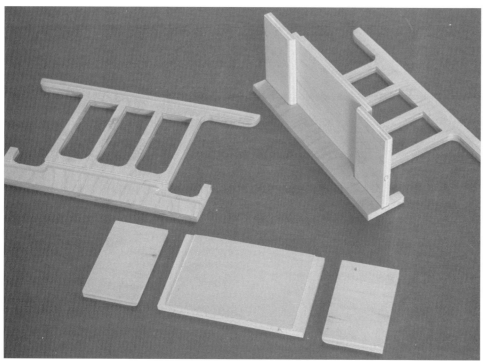

Test-fit the floor assembly into the side walls.

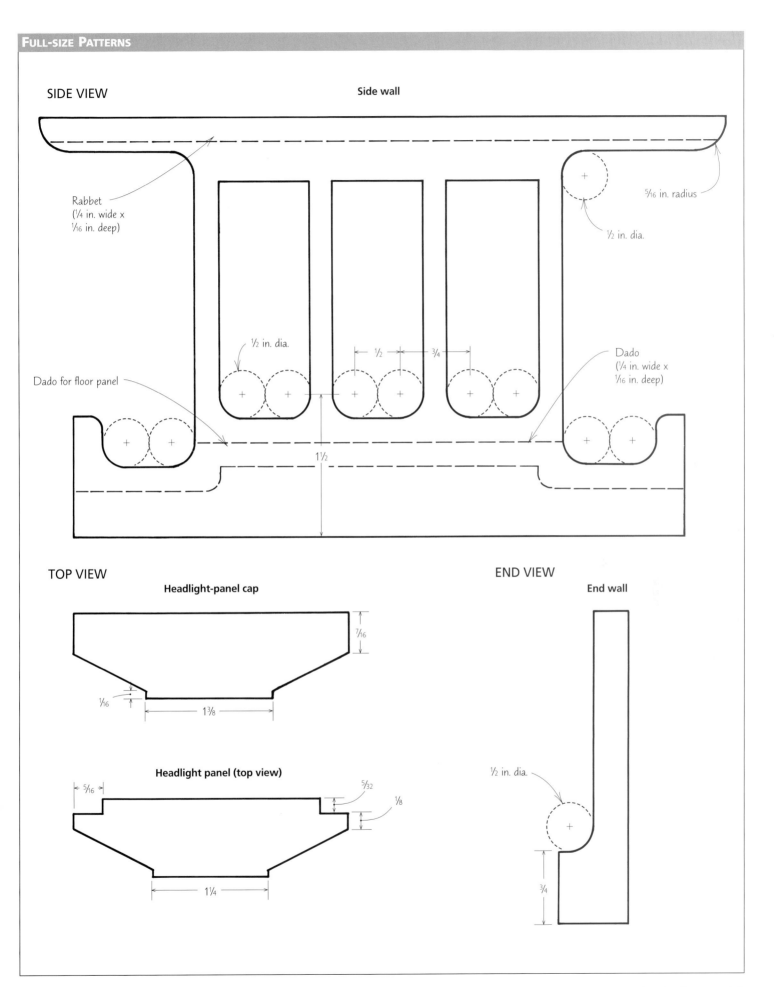

SIDE VIEW

Side wall

Rabbet
(¼ in. wide x
1⁄16 in. deep)

5⁄16 in. radius

½ in. dia.

½ in. dia.

½

¾

Dado for floor panel

Dado
(¼ in. wide x
1⁄16 in. deep)

1½

TOP VIEW

Headlight-panel cap

7⁄16

1⁄16

1⅜

Headlight panel (top view)

5⁄16

5⁄32

⅛

1¼

END VIEW

End wall

½ in. dia.

¾

Cable Car

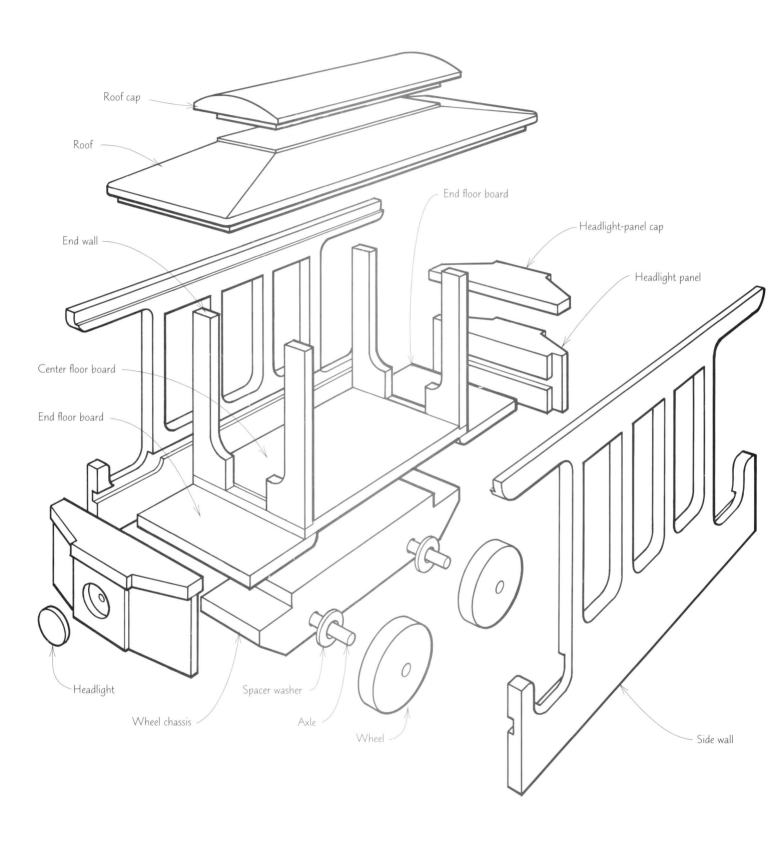

Roof cap

Roof

End wall

Center floor board

End floor board

Headlight

Wheel chassis

Spacer washer

Axle

Wheel

End floor board

Headlight-panel cap

Headlight panel

Side wall

SIDE VIEW

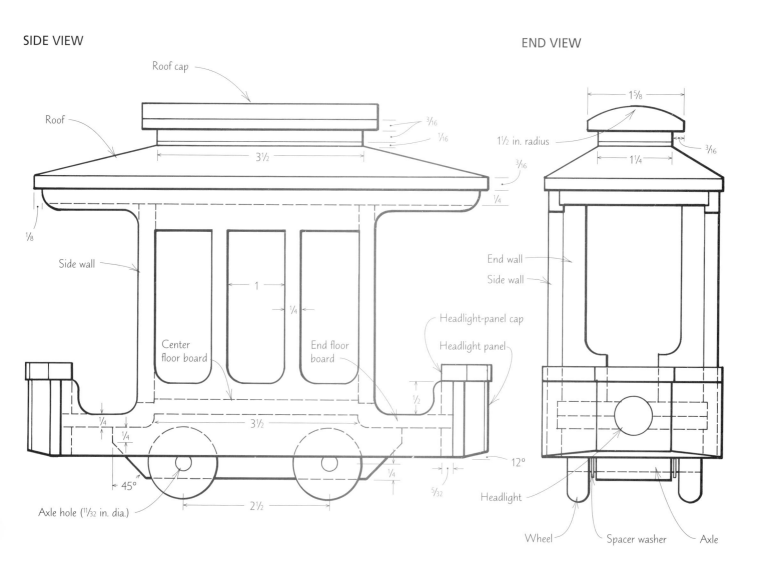

Roof cap

Roof

3/16
1/16

3½

3/16

1/4

1/8

Side wall

1

1/4

Center
floor board

End floor
board

Headlight-panel cap

Headlight panel

1/2

3½

1/4

1/4

1/4

1/4

45°

2½

12°

5/32

Axle hole (11/32 in. dia.)

END VIEW

1⁵/₈

1½ in. radius

3/16

1¼

3/16

End wall

Side wall

Headlight

Wheel

Spacer washer

Axle

BOTTOM VIEW

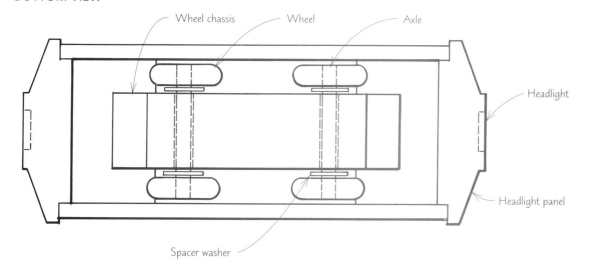

Wheel chassis

Wheel

Axle

Headlight

Headlight panel

Spacer washer

SCALE 65%
Enlarge 155%

Trolley Car

This toy evolved from my research into vehicles of the 1930s.
I developed the design without giving too much thought to
how I would build it—coming up with the techniques to turn
design into reality is always the fun part of woodworking for
me. The neatly aligned rows of holes and posts give the trolley
car a light, open and airy appearance. Yet the combined
strength of the posts creates a piece that's amazingly sturdy.

Parts Preparation

SEATING PLATFORM

1. Cut the seating platform to length and thickness, but leave it about ½ in. wider than specified in the parts list. The extra width will be cut away to remove tearout and splinters after all interior cutting and drilling are completed.

2. With the workpiece on edge against the drill-press auxiliary fence, drill six evenly spaced holes for the seats using the spacer-block technique described on pp. 6-7. The holes through the platform are almost 3 in. deep, so a sharp drill bit with a long shaft is a must.

Using 1⅛-in. spacer blocks, drill holes for the seats in the seating-platform blank.

3. To complete the seats, attach a wooden auxiliary fence to the miter gauge and cut a ⅜-in.-wide channel into each hole on the table saw. The technique is basically the same as for drilling the holes (and the same spacer blocks are used); the only difference is that two cuts are required to cut the channel.

Make the first series of cuts so the kerfs are offset 3/16 in. from the centerline of the drilled hole (see the top photo at right). To complete the channels, flip the platform end for end and make a second series of cuts (see the bottom photo at right). The width of the channel will be twice the distance of the offset.

4. Trim the seating platform to width.

ROOF

1. Cut the roof blank to size, and then apply finish to the underside, or ceiling. (Finishing the ceiling before drilling the post holes gets around the problem of the holes filling with urethane.)

Parts List

Quantity	Description	Finished Dimensions	Material
BODY			
1	Seating platform	1 1/16 x 2⅜ x 7⅜	Pine
1	Floor panel	½ x 2¾ x 10⅝	Pine
2	Headlight panels	⅞ x 1⅛ x 2¾	Pine
2	Headlights	11/16-in.-dia. pearl buttons	Plastic
1	Wheel chassis	13/16 x 1 x 5 31/32	Maple
2	Axles	¼ in. dia. by 2 1/16 in. long	Birch
4	Spacer washers	¼ in.	Steel
4	Wheels	1 5/16 in. dia. by ½ in. thick	Maple
ROOF			
1	Roof cap	7/16 x 1½ x 8⅛	Pine
1	Roof	½ x 2¾ x 10⅝	Pine
14	Posts	3/16-in.-dia. dowels by 3 5/16 in. long	Birch

To cut the channels for the seats, make the first series of cuts with the blade slightly offset from the center of the holes (using the same spacer blocks as for drilling the holes).

Flip the platform end for end and make the second series of cuts.

Parts Preparation (continued)

2. Use the spacer-block technique (and the same spacer blocks again) to drill the evenly spaced post holes in the seating platform and the mating holes in the underside of the roof.

To ensure alignment, drill both sets of holes with just one setup. Secure the seating platform (channels facing down) to the underside of the roof with double-sided tape. The platform should be centered on the ceiling in both directions (see the photo below).

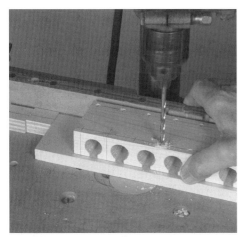

With the seating platform taped to the roof blank, drill the holes for the posts. The holes extend through the platform into the underside of the roof.

Set the drill-bit depth to penetrate through the seating platform and $3/16$ in. into the ceiling. Because of the depth of the holes in the seating platform, I used a No. 11 drill (0.191-in.) to avoid a tight fit of the $3/16$-in.-dia. posts.
3. Separate the roof and seating platform, and then shape the top side of the roof. Create a centered rectangle by cutting a $1/16$-in.-deep kerf across both ends and along both sides (see the photos on p. 97). Making angled cuts from the edges to meet this kerf will create the beveled edges around the centered panel. Cut the ends first using a tenoning jig. Then secure the roof to some straight scrap stock with double-sided tape and run it through the saw to bevel the edges.
4. Radius the ends of the roof, using the technique described on p. 14.

ROOF CAP
1. Cut the roof cap to size, and then cut $3/16$-in. rabbets around the edges to create a raised rectangle in the roof cap to match the raised panel on the roof.

2. To sand the radiused top, tape the roof cap to a vertical shaping jig (as shown in the photo at right on p. 97).
3. Glue the cap to the roof.

FLOOR PANEL AND HEADLIGHT PANELS
1. Cut the floor panel to the same size and perimeter shape as the roof. Round over the bottom edge on the curved ends, to leave a $1/16$-in. lip.
2. Cut the centered opening in the floor panel.
3. Drill a centered hole for the $11/16$-in.-dia. headlight buttons in each headlight panel, and then cut the radius. (For a slightly different headlight-panel design, see the photo in the gallery on p. 49.)
4. Glue the headlight panels to the ends of the floor panel, and then sand the curved surfaces.

WHEEL CHASSIS
1. Cut and fit the wheel chassis to the opening in the floor panel, making sure there's room on either side for the wheels.
2. Cut the wheels with a hole saw, and then true them up on the lathe, as described on p. 13.

Assembly

Finish all parts as described on pp. 16-18.
1. Glue the posts into the seating platform with white or yellow glue, and the roof to the posts with epoxy. (I use epoxy for the roof-to-post joints because it's such a small gluing area.)
2. Glue the seating platform centered onto the floor panel.
3. Assemble the wheels to the chassis, and then glue the assembly to the bottom of the seating platform, centered in the floor-panel cutout.

Trolley Car

FRONT VIEW

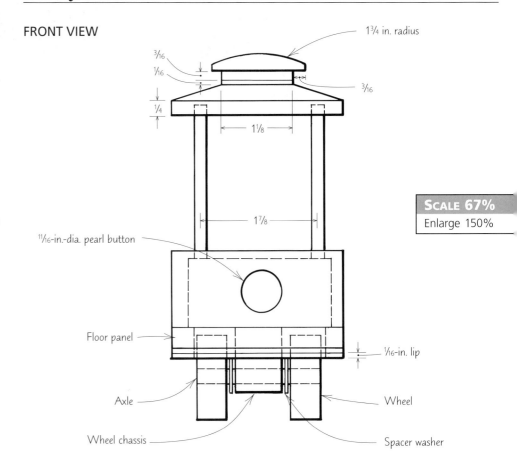

SCALE 67%
Enlarge 150%

Trolley Car

TOP VIEW

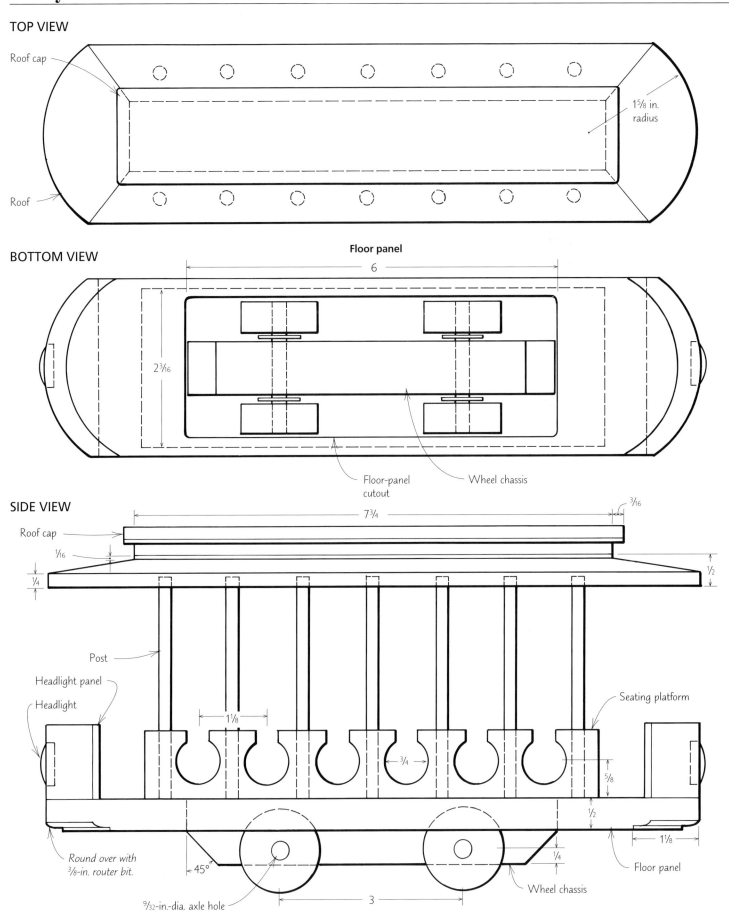

Roof cap

1⁵⁄₈ in. radius

Roof

BOTTOM VIEW

Floor panel

6

2³⁄₁₆

Floor-panel cutout

Wheel chassis

SIDE VIEW

3⁄₁₆

Roof cap

7³⁄₄

1⁄₁₆

1⁄₄

1⁄₂

Post

Headlight panel

Headlight

Seating platform

1¹⁄₈

3⁄₄

5⁄₈

1⁄₂

Round over with 3⁄₈-in. router bit.

45°

1⁄₄

1¹⁄₈

Floor panel

9⁄₃₂-in.-dia. axle hole

3

Wheel chassis

Woodchuck Clock

This clock was the first in a series of educational toys that I've developed over the years. The simple design and painted hands create a playful image, while helping to teach a child to tell time. The addition of a T-handle encourages the child to pick up the clock, further contributing to the playful image of an oversized pocket watch. The stand holds the clock for play or display. If you want, you can convert it to a working clock by installing a quartz movement in the back. (By the way, I am the "Woodchuck"—it's the name I've been known by for as long as I've been teaching toymaking classes.)

Parts Preparation

FACE

1. Cut the clock face slightly oversized, and then turn it to the correct diameter on a wood lathe. If you don't have a lathe, you could use a circle-cutting attachment for the bandsaw or a router jig.

2. Smooth the perimeter with a sanding block and round over the edge with a ¼-in.-radius bit, leaving a 1/16-in. lip.

3. From the center point, draw a reference circle for the number and magnet holes, which are drilled on the same centerline. Divide this line into 12 equally spaced segments and mark for reference only.

4. Draw a vertical line across the clock's face between the twelve and six o'clock positions and continue the line onto the sides.

5. Drill the 3/16-in.-dia. hand-mounting hole in the center of the clock face.

6. Clamp the clock face to a squared-off block for vertical support, and drill the T-handle-stem hole into the edge of the clock at the 12 o'clock position.

7. Dry-assemble the T-handle. Glue the stem and insert it into the stem hole in the clock, adjusting the stem until the crossbar is parallel to the clock face. Glue in the crossbar.

NUMBER AND MAGNET HOLES

To drill the double set of holes, one for the number discs and one for the recessed magnets, use the auxiliary drill-press table described in the sidebar at right.

1. Cut a cardboard or plastic template (the index wheel) approximately 10 in. in diameter. Divide the perimeter of the wheel into 12 equal segments and punch a hole in the center.

2. Tape the index wheel to the back of the clock face, with the 12 o'clock line on the side of the clock face aligned with any layout line on the index wheel and the center holes aligned.

3. Slide the clock face and the index wheel onto the pivot pin of the auxiliary table.

4. Drill the number holes first, using an adjustable bit set at 1 1/16 in. dia. Center the drill bit over the 12 o'clock mark on the reference circle drawn on the clock face. Clamp the face to the auxiliary drill-press table and drill the first hole.

5. Release the clamp, rotate the clock face/index wheel until the pointer on the auxiliary table aligns with the next mark on the index wheel, clamp and drill the next hole. Repeat until all the number holes are drilled.

Parts List

Quantity	Description	Finished Dimensions	Material
CLOCK			
1	Clock face	¾ in. thick by 8⁵/₁₆ in. dia.	Baltic birch plywood
1	Minute hand	¼ x ¹⁵/₁₆ x 4⁷/₃₂	Birch
1	Hour hand	¼ x ¹⁵/₁₆ x 3³/₃₂	Birch
12	Number discs	1-in.-dia. dowels by ⁷/₁₆ in. long	Birch
12	Ceramic magnets	½ in. dia. by ¼ in. long	Magnet
12	Washers	³/₁₆ in.	Steel
2	Washers	⁷/₈ in. dia.	Rubber
1	Set of transfer numbers	To fit 1-in.-dia. dowel	
1	Oval-head machine screw and nut	#8-32 ³/₁₆ in. dia. by 1 in. long	Chrome
T-HANDLE			
1	Stem	½-in.-dia. dowel by 2¾ in. long	Birch
1	Crossbar	¼-in.-dia. dowel by 2¼ in. long	Birch
STAND			
1	Stand base	¾-in.-dia. dowel by 4¾ in. long	Birch
2	Stand supports	³/₈-in.-dia. dowel by 3⁷/₈ in. long	Birch

Auxiliary Drill-Press Table

Drilling the holes in the clock face accurately is easy with the auxiliary drill-press table shown in the photo below. The table is made of ¾-in.-thick plywood and has a pointer and a pivot pin that fits into the hand-mounting hole drilled into the clock-face blank. The pointer registers with marks on an index wheel that is taped to the back of the clock face. Aligning the marks on the index wheel with the pointer positions the blank for drilling holes for the numbers and the recessed magnets. A toggle clamp mounted on the auxiliary table holds the clock face securely for drilling. You may want to use a second clamp (as shown) for added stability.

An auxiliary drill-press table with a pivot pin and pointer simplifies the task of drilling the evenly spaced holes in the clock face.

Drill one set of holes for the numbers and another set for the recessed magnets.

6. To drill the smaller holes for mounting the recessed magnets, switch to a ½-in.-dia. metal-cutting bit (a wood-cutting bit may break through the back of the hole). Repeat the process used to drill the number holes.

7. Clean and sand all the holes. (If the bottoms of the holes are a little rough, they can be sanded smooth by gluing a sanding disc to a 1-in.-dia. dowel.)

8. Press-fit the magnets, making sure they sit flat. Do not hammer them in—the ceramic magnets will shatter. If the magnets are loose, use a little dab of epoxy glue to hold them in place. Apply one coat of sanding sealer in the cavities.

NUMBER DISCS

1. Sand and finish a length of a 1-in.-dia. dowel (see pp. 16-18).

2. Cut 12 pieces of dowel ⁷⁄₁₆ in. long. Drill a shallow hole in the back side to receive a ³⁄₁₆-in.-dia. washer. I drill the recess on the lathe, using a three-jaw chuck to hold the number disc. Alternatively, you could epoxy a thin washer to the back of the number disc.

3. Sand the face of the number discs smooth and apply one coat of sanding sealer.

4. Sand the face again and rub on the transfer numbers. (I use Letraset numbers, which are available from any art-supply store. The font I chose for my clock is 48-point Franklin Gothic Condensed; many other sizes and styles are available.)

5. Gently apply a thin coat of high-gloss urethane. When the finish is dry, apply two or three coats more to create a lens as well as a protective coating for the transfers.

HANDS

1. Cut the minute and hour hands to shape using the full-size patterns below. If you choose to paint the hands (I painted mine red—see the gallery photo on pp. 50-51), use two coats of a non-toxic paint.

2. Countersink a hole into the back of the clock for a press fit of the nut that receives the hands' center-axle screw.

3. Install the hands on the clock face with one rubber washer made from an inner tube between the hour hand and the clock face and another washer between the hands. The rubber washers create some drag on the hands so that they'll hold a set position. Some minor adjustments may be required. If you have a problem moving the hands, try removing the washer between the clock face and the hour hand.

DISPLAY STAND

1. Drill two holes in the back of the clock to receive the stand supports. Drill a matching set of holes in the stand base.

2. Glue the supports into the base but not into the clock. The stand can then be removed easily for storage or wall hanging.

Now that you've built the clock, here's some advice on using it as a teaching tool. The objective is for the child to understand the correct locations of the numbers and be able to tell the time without them. For example, with the hands of the clock set at 4 o'clock, ask the child to insert the correct number disc. The child quickly learns to associate the position of the hands with the correct time, and consequently is able to tell time from a clock with Roman numerals, dots or even no reference indicators at all.

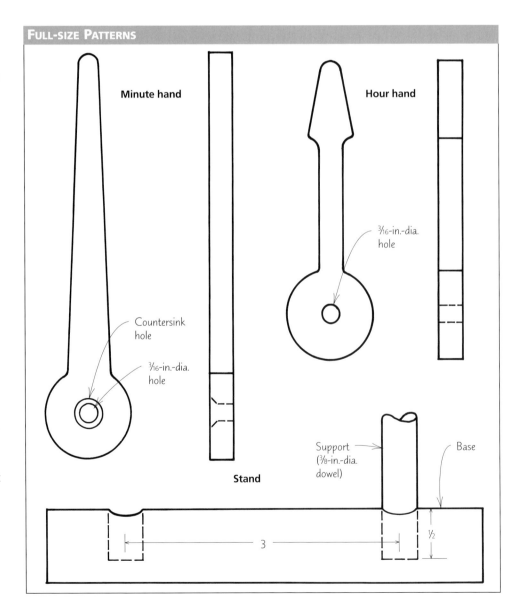

FULL-SIZE PATTERNS

Minute hand

Hour hand

³⁄₁₆-in.-dia. hole

Countersink hole

³⁄₁₆-in.-dia. hole

Stand

Support (³⁄₈-in.-dia. dowel)

Base

½

3

Woodchuck Clock

Number disc

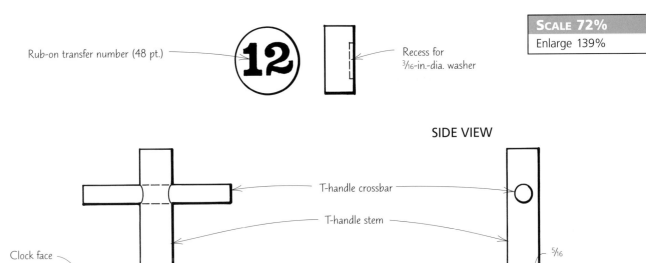

Rub-on transfer number (48 pt.)

Recess for
³⁄₁₆-in.-dia. washer

SCALE 72%
Enlarge 139%

FRONT VIEW

SIDE VIEW

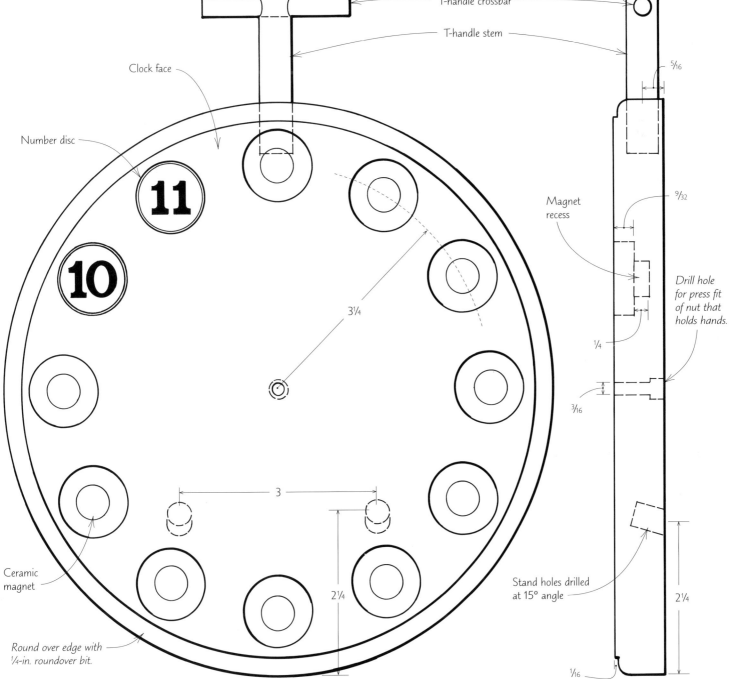

T-handle crossbar

T-handle stem

Clock face

Number disc

Magnet recess

⁵⁄₁₆

⁹⁄₃₂

Drill hole for press fit of nut that holds hands.

¹⁄₄

³⁄₁₆

3¹⁄₄

3

2¹⁄₄

Ceramic magnet

Stand holes drilled at 15° angle

2¹⁄₄

Round over edge with ¹⁄₄-in. roundover bit.

¹⁄₁₆

Math
Balance Beam

This toy makes learning addition, subtraction and multiplication fun. The idea is to set up a problem with weights on one side of the beam and have the child solve the problem with the right combination of weights on the other side. For example, placing a weight on a number on the left side, say "8," will require the correct combination on the right side—say, one weight on "5" and another on "3"—to balance the beam. The weights are washers that slide over numbered posts. There are two storage posts built into the base, and the beam has a built-in sliding adjustment feature for accuracy. Because balance is critical, choose only the best materials and make sure your measurements are accurate. I used Baltic birch plywood throughout and high-quality stainless-steel washers.

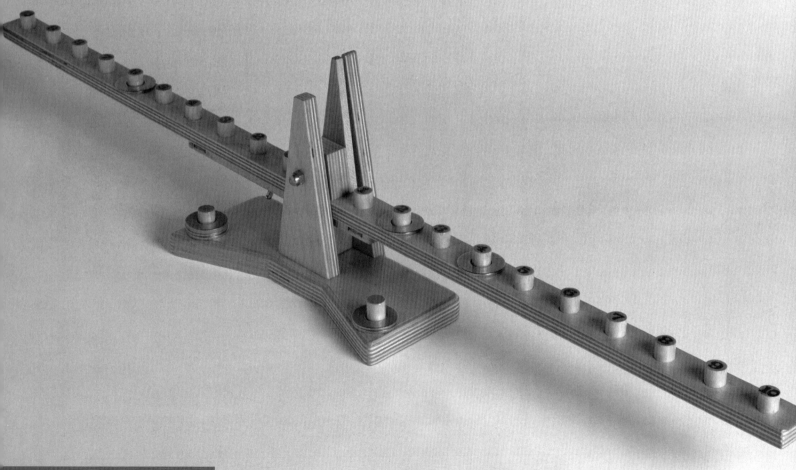

Parts Preparation

MATH BEAM

1. Cut the beam to size and lay out the number-post positions, working from the centerline out in both directions. Check the spacing with a divider.

2. Apply finish to the beam, and then drill the ½-in.-dia. post holes. I used the spacer-block technique (see pp. 6-7) to make sure the holes were equally spaced.

3. To control balance and alignment, and to compensate for any variation in the weight of the materials used to build the scale, you need to be able to adjust the balance point of the beam. This is done by attaching a weighted bar, or "balance adjuster" (see below), to the underside of the beam. For now, drill a ³⁄₁₆-in.-dia. hole to receive a ³⁄₁₆-in. machine screw (with its head cut off) between the "1" and "2" posts on the left side. Epoxy the screw into the bottom of the bar, being careful not to get any glue on the exposed threads (the balance adjuster will slide along this screw with wing-nut adjustment).

4. Because the balance adjuster is offset from the center of the beam, you need to add a weight to the other end of the beam to offset the balance. Drill a recess about ⅛ in. deep to receive a 1-in.-dia. washer on the underside of the beam, between posts "8" and "9" on the right side. Epoxy the washer in place.

NUMBER POSTS

1. Apply finish to a length of birch dowel, and then cut the number posts (and storage posts) to length.

2. Epoxy the posts into the beam.

3. Sand the end of each number post, apply one coat of sanding sealer and sand again with 220-grit production paper.

4. Rub transfer numbers (see p. 108) onto the finished post ends and apply a light coat of urethane, being careful not to disturb the numbers. After the first coat has dried, apply two or three more coats of urethane for protection.

BALANCE ADJUSTER

1. Lay out the balance adjuster, and then rout the center slot (approximately ⁷⁄₃₂ in. wide).

2. Cut the bar to size and drill a ⅛-in.-deep recess into each end to receive the 1-in.-dia. washers.

3. Apply finish to the bar and then epoxy the washers into the recessed areas.

Parts List

Quantity	Description	Finished Dimensions	Material
MATH-BEAM ASSEMBLY			
1	Math beam	½ x 1⅛ x 31½	Baltic birch plywood
20	Number posts	½-in.-dia. dowel by ¾ in. long	Birch
1	Set of transfer numbers	To fit ½-in.-dia. dowel	
3	Weight washers	1 in.	Stainless steel
1	Balance adjuster	¼ x ⅞ x 8	Birch
1	Machine screw (with washer and wing nut)	³⁄₁₆ in. dia. by 1 in. long	Steel
1	Pointer	¼ x 1⅜ x 3⅝	Birch
1	Pointer block	¾ x 1⅜ x 1¼	Baltic birch plywood
10	Game washers	½ in. (1¼ in. dia.)	Stainless steel
1	Swivel tube	¼ in. dia. by 1³⁄₁₆ in. long	Brass
STAND ASSEMBLY			
1	Base	¾ x 3⅝ x 8½	Baltic birch plywood
1	Front taper support	½ x 2⅛ x 4⅞	Baltic birch plywood
1	Back taper support	½ x 2¼ x 6½	Baltic birch plywood
1	Support partition	½ x 1¼ x 1¼	Baltic birch plywood
2	Storage posts	½-in.-dia. dowels by 1 in. long	Birch
1	Axle	³⁄₁₆-in.-dia. rod by 2⅝ in. long (threaded on ends)	Brass
2	Acorn nuts	³⁄₁₆ in. by #10-24 thread	Brass

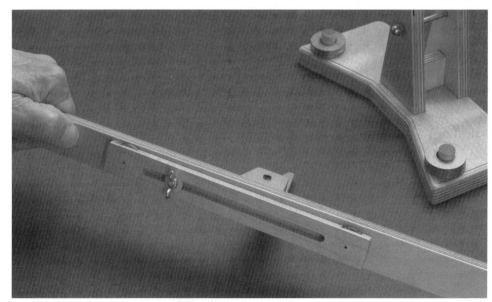

Attach the balance adjuster to the bottom of the beam.

4. Slip the balance adjuster over the screw protruding from the bottom of the beam and secure with a washer and a wing nut (see the photo above).

POINTER

The pointer indicates when the math beam is perfectly balanced (that is, when the correct answer has been given).

1. Cut the 10° sides of the triangular pointer and pointer block with an angle jig (see p. 9), and then glue the two pieces together (see the drawing on p. 113).

2. Drill the hole for the ¼-in.-dia. brass swivel tube. Insert the tube so that it protrudes slightly on either side of the pointer; it should fit tightly without distorting. The end of the tube can be filed to center the balance beam in the stand.

Parts Preparation (continued)

STAND

1. Cut the base to shape and round over the top edge with a ¼-in. roundover bit, leaving a slight lip on the top surface.
2. Cut the front and back taper supports using the same 10° angle jig used to cut the pointer. Drill holes for the ³⁄₁₆-in.-dia. pivot axle.
3. Cut the support partition to size.
4. Cut out the back edge of the base to receive the back taper support.
5. Drill ½-in. dia. holes for the two storage posts.

Assembly

Finish all parts as described on pp. 16-18.
1. Glue the pointer assembly to the beam, making sure it is perfectly centered.
2. Glue the tapered supports and partition to the base, and the storage posts into the base.
3. To install the beam on the stand, insert the axle rod through the swivel tube in the pointer assembly. You may want to lubricate the rod with a little oil.
4. Thread the acorn nuts onto the ends of the axle.

Math Balance Beam

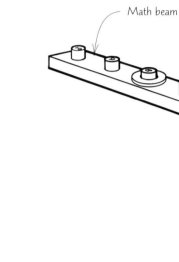

Math beam

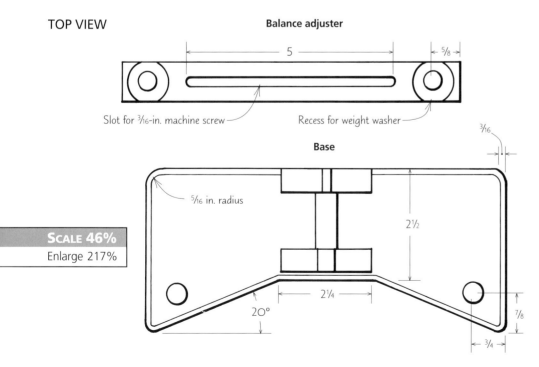

The stand assembly.

TOP VIEW

Balance adjuster

5

⁵⁄₈

Slot for ³⁄₁₆-in. machine screw

Recess for weight washer

Base

³⁄₁₆

⁵⁄₁₆ in. radius

2½

20°

2¼

⁷⁄₈

³⁄₄

SCALE 46%
Enlarge 217%

SIDE VIEW

Base

Back taper support

Front taper support

Axle hole

Support partition

Storage post

2⁵⁄₈

3³⁄₈

¹⁄₁₆

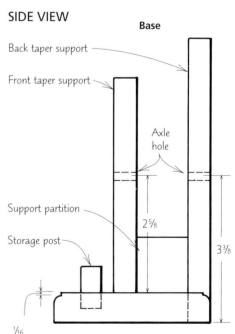

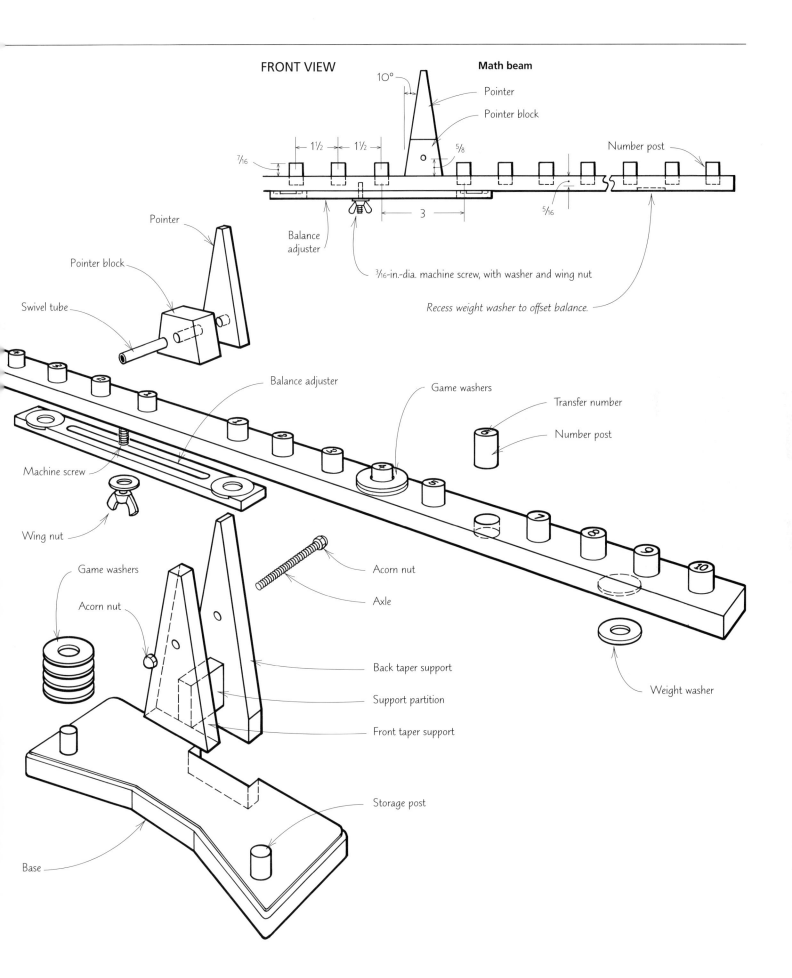

FRONT VIEW

Math beam

10°

Pointer

Pointer block

1½   1½

7/16

5/8

Number post

Balance adjuster

5/16

3

3/16-in.-dia. machine screw, with washer and wing nut

Recess weight washer to offset balance.

Pointer

Pointer block

Swivel tube

Balance adjuster

Game washers

Transfer number

Number post

Machine screw

Wing nut

Game washers

Acorn nut

Acorn nut

Axle

Back taper support

Support partition

Front taper support

Weight washer

Storage post

Base

Fire Truck

This 17-in. long fire truck is a composite study of several fire engines that I developed after visiting a couple of local fire stations. The combination hook-and-ladder and pumper fire engine includes more than 80 pieces and takes about a week's worth of shop time to complete. Instructions for making an optional extension ladder are given on p. 120.

Instructions for making an optional extension ladder are given on p. 120.

PROJECT 18

Parts Preparation

CHASSIS AND COMPONENTS

1. Cut the chassis to size, and then cut out four 2³⁄₁₆-in.-wide by ½-in.-deep wheelwells. Drill two ³⁄₈-in.-dia. holes for the posts for mounting the firemen on the back of the truck.
2. Cut the axle housings to size, rout the axle channel and bevel the edges, as shown in the drawing on p. 117.
3. Cut the bumpers to size and drill ¼-in.-dia. holes for the bumper pegs. Chamfer all front edges and groove the back of the bumper to fit the chassis at the front and rear.

CAB ASSEMBLY

1. Cut the cab body to size, and then drill two ¹¹⁄₁₆-in.-dia. holes for the headlights. (Optionally, drill for four headlights, as shown on the cab in the photo on the facing page.)
2. Temporarily clamp a scrap block to the bottom of the cab, and then drill the wheel-wells (see pp. 12-13).
3. Rout a minimal radius along both top sides, across the top front and down the front corners.
4. Cut the cab top to size, including bevels on the sides (3°) and front (15°). Drill a ⁵⁄₁₆-in.-dia. hole for the emergency-light peg.
5. Glue the cab top to the cab body with the back edges aligned and the top centered left to right.
6. Cut the angled ends of the light bar, and then tape the bar to a scrap block to bevel the sides. Glue the light bar to the top of the cab.

PUMPER ASSEMBLY

1. Cut the pump housing to size and drill holes in both ends for the dials (flat-head rivets) and hose spigots (dowels).
2. Cut the step blank to size, and then rabbet the ends to create steps (as shown in the photo below).

The pump housing (with predrilled holes) and steps.

Parts List

Quantity	Description	Finished Dimensions	Material
CHASSIS AND COMPONENTS			
1	Chassis	½ x 4 x 16½	Poplar
2	Axle housings	½ x 2³⁄₁₆ x 3	Birch
2	Axles	¼-in.-dia. dowels by 4⅛ in. long	Birch
4	Wheels	2 in. dia. by ½ in. thick	Birch
4	Spacer washers	¼ in.	Steel
4	Push nuts	¼ in.	Steel
2	Bumpers	¼ x ¾ x 4⅜	Birch
4	Bumper pegs	¼-in.-dia. peg by ¾ in. long	Birch
2	Mounting posts	³⁄₈-in.-dia. dowel by ¾ in. long	Birch
2	Firemen	⅞ in. dia. by 2⅜ in. high	Birch
CAB ASSEMBLY			
1	Cab body	1¹³⁄₁₆ x 3¹⁵⁄₁₆ x 4⁵⁄₁₆	Birch
1	Cab top	1¹⁄₁₆ x 3⅝ x 4⅛	Birch
1	Emergency light	⁵⁄₁₆-in.-dia. peg with ⅝-in.-dia. head	Birch
1	Light bar	⁵⁄₁₆ x ¼ x 1¹³⁄₁₆	Birch
2	Headlights	¹¹⁄₁₆-in.-dia. flat-head pearl buttons	Plastic
PUMPER ASSEMBLY			
1	Pump housing	1½ x 1¹³⁄₁₆ x 3¼	Birch
1	Pump housing steps	¹³⁄₁₆ x 1¹⁄₁₆ x 3¼	Birch
4	Pump dials	⁵⁄₁₆-in.-dia. flat-head rivets	Steel
2	Hose spigots	⁵⁄₁₆-in.-dia. dowels by 1 in. long	Birch
WATER TANK AND HOSE ASSEMBLY			
1	Water tank	1⅝ x 3⅛ x 6½	Birch
1	Water-hose coil	⅞ x 1¾ x 3⅛	Birch
2	Side walls	½ x 2½ x 7¼	Birch
4	Hose brackets	¼ x ⅝ x 1⁷⁄₁₆	Baltic birch plywood
4	Hoses	⁵⁄₁₆-in.-dia. dowels by 5⅜ in. long	Birch
4	Hose connectors	⁵⁄₁₆ in. dia. by ⅞ in. long	Aluminum
4	Hose keepers	¹⁄₁₆-in.-dia. dowel by ⅜ in. long	Birch
SWIVEL STAND			
1	Base block	1¹⁄₁₆ x 2 x 2	Birch
1	Fender washer	⁵⁄₁₆ in.	Steel
1	Rotation pin	⁵⁄₁₆-in.-dia. peg, 1 in. long with ⅝-in.-dia. head	Birch
1	Rotating disc	2 in. dia. by ½ in. thick	Birch
1	Swivel mount	1 x 1¹¹⁄₁₆ x 2	Birch
2	Pivot pins	¼-in.-dia. pegs by ¾ in. long	Birch
2	Friction washers	⅝ in.	Rubber
LADDER			
2	Rails	⁵⁄₁₆ x ⁹⁄₁₆ x 14½	Birch
20	Rungs	³⁄₁₆-in.-dia. dowels by 1½ in. long	Birch
2	Rail pivot blocks	½ x 1 x 1¼	Maple

Fire Truck

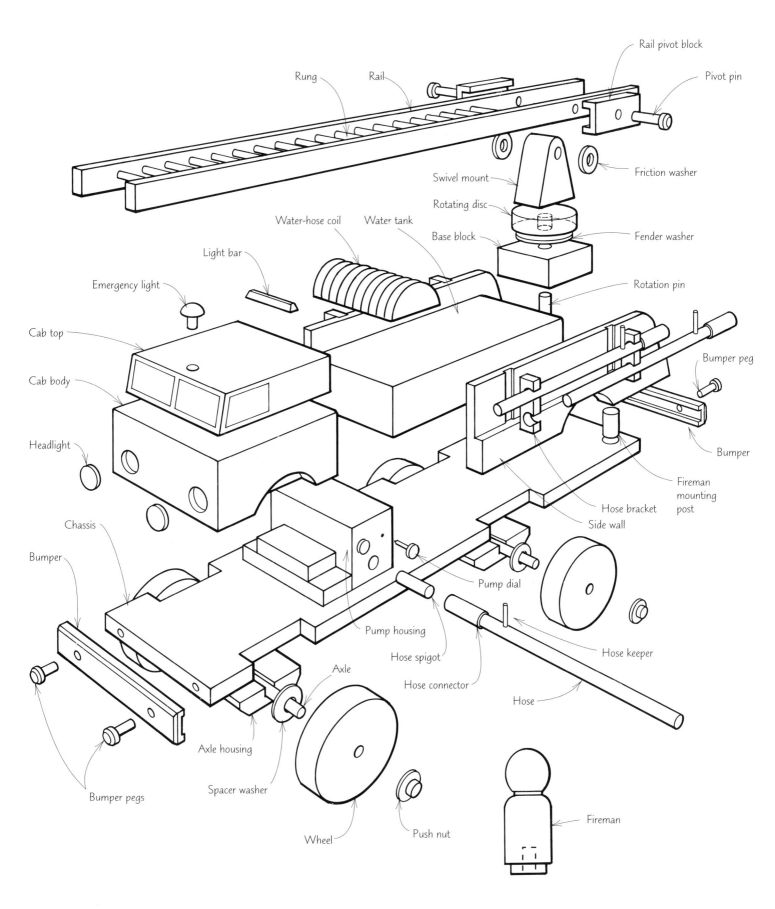

Rail pivot block

Pivot pin

Rung

Rail

Friction washer

Swivel mount

Rotating disc

Water-hose coil

Water tank

Base block

Fender washer

Light bar

Rotation pin

Emergency light

Cab top

Bumper peg

Cab body

Headlight

Bumper

Fireman mounting post

Chassis

Hose bracket

Side wall

Pump dial

Bumper

Pump housing

Hose keeper

Hose spigot

Hose connector

Hose

Axle

Axle housing

Spacer washer

Bumper pegs

Wheel

Push nut

Fireman

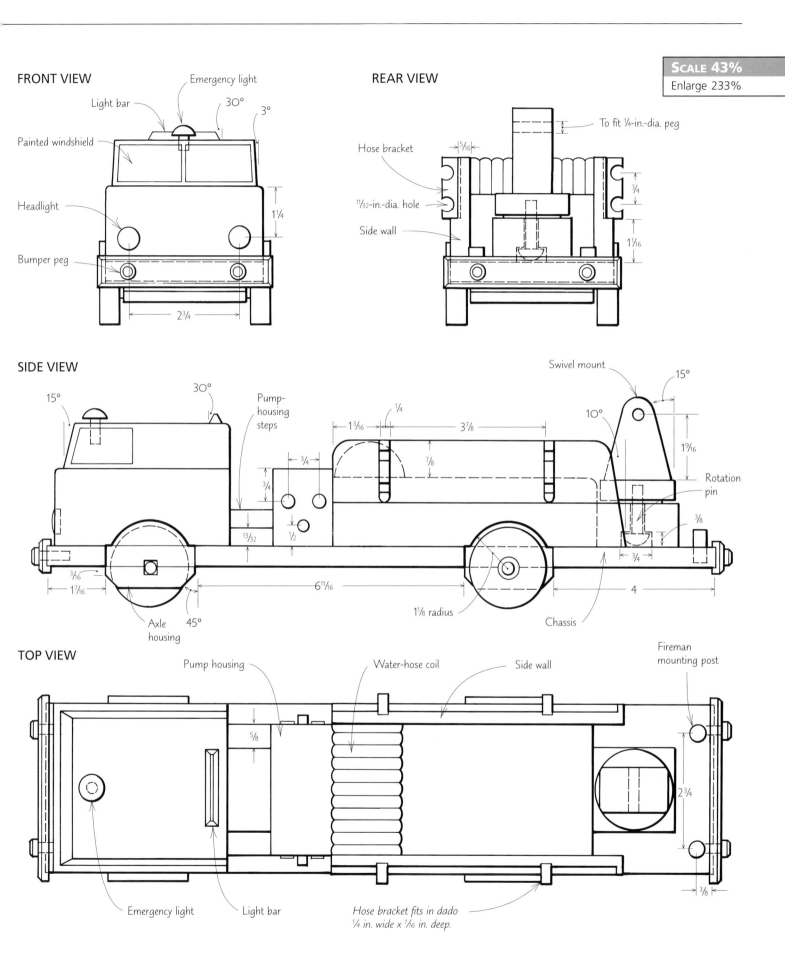

FRONT VIEW

Emergency light
Light bar
30°
3°
Painted windshield
Headlight
Bumper peg
1¼
2¾

REAR VIEW

To fit ¼-in.-dia. peg
Hose bracket
5/16
¾
11/32-in.-dia. hole
Side wall
1 1/16

SIDE VIEW

15°
30°
Pump-housing steps
¼
1 3/16
3 7/8
Swivel mount
15°
10°
1 9/16
¾
7/8
Rotation pin
3/4
⅜
13/32
½
3/16
1 7/16
6 11/16
1⅛ radius
4
Axle housing
45°
Chassis

TOP VIEW

Pump housing
Water-hose coil
Side wall
Fireman mounting post
5/8
2¾
⅜
Emergency light
Light bar
Hose bracket fits in dado
¼ in. wide x 1/16 in. deep.

Parts Preparation (continued)

WATER TANK AND HOSE ASSEMBLY

1. Cut the water tank to size and radius the top back edge.

2. To make the water-hose coil, turn a series of beads on a 1¾-in. dowel and then bandsaw the dowel in half. If you can't find a dowel this size, use glued-up stock; make the blank a couple of inches longer than needed and spot-glue the pieces together at the ends. Turn the coil, and then saw off the glued ends.

3. Cut the side walls to size, and then rabbet the top outside faces to create stepped sides. Rout ¹⁄₁₆-in. stopped dadoes for the hose brackets. Cut the back end of the side walls at a 10° angle, and radius the top corners at the front and the back. Cut out the wheelwells in the side walls using a bandsaw or scrollsaw.

4. Cut and drill the hose brackets, as shown in the top right drawing on p. 117.

5. Epoxy a hose connector (a short piece of aluminum tube) to the end of a painted dowel to make the hoses. The hose connector should extend past the end of the dowel about ⁷⁄₁₆ in. to allow a second hose to slide into the connector. Drill holes in the dowels and glue in the hose keepers.

SWIVEL STAND

1. Cut and drill the base block, rotating disc and swivel mount, as detailed in the parts list and the drawing on p. 117.

LADDER

1. Cut the ladder rails to the correct thickness and width but 1½ in. longer than specified in the parts list. Spot-glue the rails together at each end with the insides facing out for drilling the rung holes. For added insurance, it's a good idea to use double-sided tape in the center section.

2. Make a reference mark for the pivot-pin holes at the bottom of the ladder and use that mark for spacing out the rung holes. The proper alignment of the rails is critical.

3. Use the spacer-block technique (see pp. 6-7) to drill the stopped holes. Position the auxiliary fence and stop block, drill the first hole in the first rail, flip the piece over, and then drill the second rail. Add a spacer block between the stop block and the workpiece, and repeat the process, drilling the length of both rails.

4. Drill a ⁹⁄₃₂-in.-dia. hole for the pivot pins on the original reference line, drilling through

both pieces. Cut off the extra length on each end of the rails.

5. Cut and groove the rail pivot blocks, and then glue them on the outside face of each rail, centered over the pivot hole. Drill holes through the pivot blocks from the inside of the rail, using the pivot hole in the rail as a guide.

6. Apply finish to a 36-in. length of ³⁄₁₆-in.-dia. dowel before cutting the dowel into rungs. Also, apply finish to the ladder rails.

7. Before assembling the ladder, dry-fit three or four rungs to the side rails and check to make sure the ladder fits inside the swivel mount. Trim the rungs as necessary for a snug fit. To assemble the ladder, glue four equally spaced rungs across the length of one side rail (rail #1). For example, glue rungs in the third, eighth, thirteenth and eighteenth holes. Insert the unglued ends of each rung in the matching holes in rail #2 before the glue sets. Adjust both rails for square alignment. Repeat this procedure until all 20 rungs are glued into rail #1. *Do not* glue rail #2 until the ladder is assembled onto the swivel mount (see the bottom photo on the facing page).

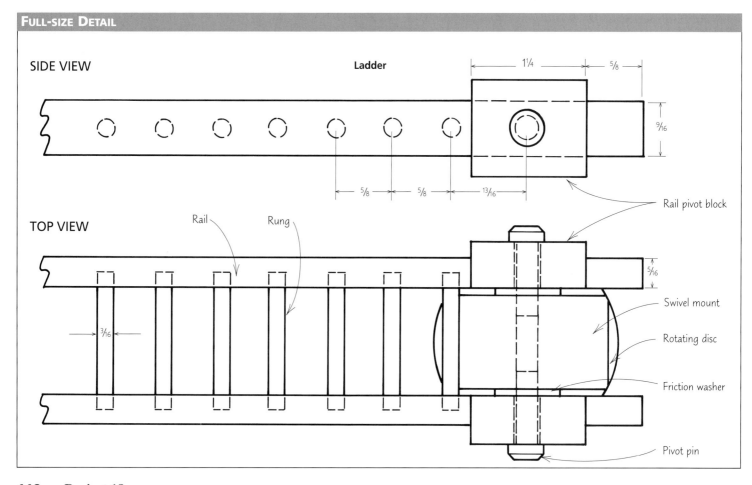

FULL-SIZE DETAIL

SIDE VIEW

Ladder

1¼   ⁵⁄₈

⁹⁄₁₆

⁵⁄₈   ⁵⁄₈   ¹³⁄₁₆

Rail pivot block

TOP VIEW

Rail   Rung

⁵⁄₁₆

³⁄₁₆

Swivel mount

Rotating disc

Friction washer

Pivot pin

Assembly

Finish all parts as described on pp. 16-18.

LADDER AND SWIVEL-STAND ASSEMBLY

1. To assemble the swivel stand, insert the rotation pin through the bottom of the base block. Slip a fender washer over the pin, and then glue on the rotating disc, as shown in the top photos at right. Glue the swivel mount onto the rotating disc. Make sure that the swivel mount rotates freely.

2. To assemble the ladder, insert a pivot pin through ladder rail #1 (the one with the preglued dowels), and then slide a rubber washer (I made mine from an old bicycle inner tube) over the pin between the rail and the swivel mount. Insert the pivot pin into the swivel mount.

3. Insert a pivot pin through rail #2 and push this rail onto rail #1, again with a rubber washer between the swivel mount and rail #2 (see the bottom photo at right). Check for friction movement of the ladder, and add additional rubber washers, if necessary, to make sure the ladder will hold its position at any angle.

4. After achieving the desired friction movement, attach rail #1 by gluing its pivot pin into the swivel mount. Now glue rail #2 onto the rungs (it's not necessary to glue all the rungs—one out of three is sufficient). Clamp the ladder until the glue sets.

FINAL ASSEMBLY

1. Glue the bumper to the chassis, and then redrill the holes to receive the ¼-in.-dia. bumper pegs (see p. 29).

2. Epoxy the headlights in place.

3. Glue the assembled cab centered on the chassis, with wheelwells aligned to the cutouts.

4. Glue the steps and the pumper assembly behind the cab.

5. Glue the water tank centered left to right and butted to the pumper assembly. Glue the hose coil on top of the water tank and butted to the pumper assembly.

6. Glue the side walls to the chassis and water tank, with the front edge butted against the pumper assembly.

7. Glue the hose brackets into the dadoes on the side walls.

8. Glue the axle housing onto the chassis, aligned with the wheelwell cutouts. Slide the axle into the housing, with a ¼-in.-dia. washer on each end, and glue on the wheels.

9. Glue the ladder and swivel-stand assembly behind the water tank.

Assemble the swivel stand with a steel fender washer between the base and the rotating disc.

The swivel stand assembled.

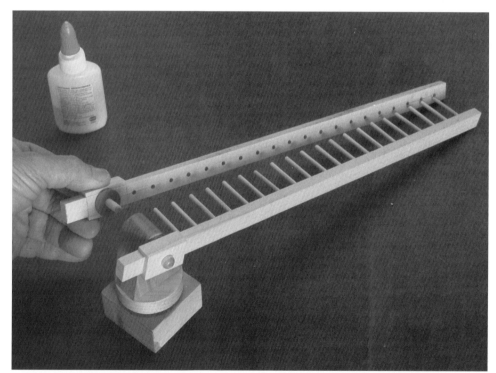

Insert a pivot pin through the rail and pivot block into the swivel mount. The rubber washer between the rail and the swivel mount enables the ladder to stay in raised positions.

Making an Extension Ladder

Adding an extension ladder will allow your little firemen to scale new heights. Fabrication and assembly are basically the same as for the single ladder described in the text, and the extension ladder fits the same swivel-stand assembly. The main construction differences are that I used $1/8$-in.-dia. dowels for the rungs and spaced them $3/4$ in. on center. Also, a rubber friction wheel bears against the extension section of the ladder to hold it in position when extended. The friction wheel is simply a rubber faucet washer, available at any hardware store.

1. Use double-sided tape to fasten the two base rails together back to back. Drill the stopped holes for the rungs using the spacer-block technique (see pp. 6-7).
2. With the rails still taped together, cut the $1/8$-in. by $1/8$-in. grooves in which the extension ladder slides.
3. On the top edge of one rail (between the second and third rungs), drill a hole for the $1/8$-in. axle that receives the friction wheel.
4. Drill the holes for the rungs of the extension section as described in Step 1.
5. Rabbet the sides of the extension rails to create a $1/8$-in. by $1/8$-in. lip.
6. Rabbet the ends of the rails to receive the end stop.

Before assembling the ladders, it's critical that you dry-fit them together and test the fit of the extension section into the base section. Adjust the length of the rungs for a snug but smooth-sliding fit.

SCALE 50%
Enlarge 200%

Quantity	Description	Finished Dimensions	Material
BASE SECTION			
2	Rails	$5/16 \times 3/4 \times 16\frac{1}{2}$	Birch
2	Rail pivot blocks	$7/16 \times 1 \times 1\frac{1}{4}$	Birch
19	Rungs	$1/8$-in.-dia. dowels by $1\frac{5}{8}$ in. long	Birch
1	Friction-wheel axle	$1/8$-in.-dia. dowel by $1/2$ in. long	Birch
1	Friction wheel	$1/2$ in. dia. by $1/8$ in. thick	Rubber
EXTENSION SECTION			
2	Rails	$5/16 \times 9/16 \times 14$	Birch
1	End stop	$1/4 \times 5/16 \times 1\frac{3}{4}$	Birch
18	Rungs	$1/8$-in.-dia. dowels by $1\frac{3}{16}$ in. long	Birch

END VIEW

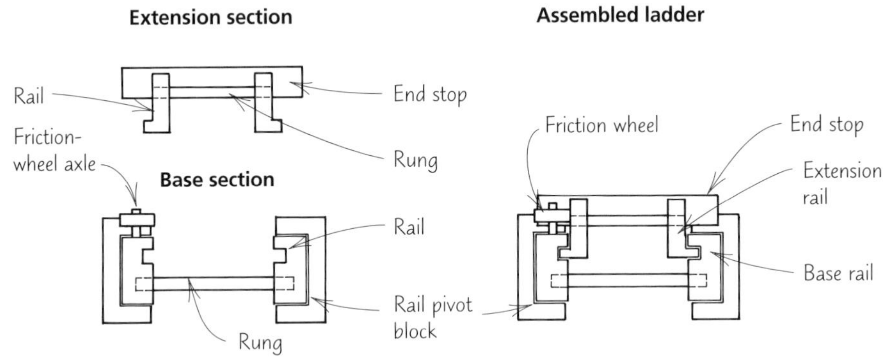
Extension section
Assembled ladder
Rail
End stop
Friction-wheel axle
Rung
Base section
Friction wheel
End stop
Extension rail
Rail
Base rail
Rail pivot block
Rung

SIDE VIEW

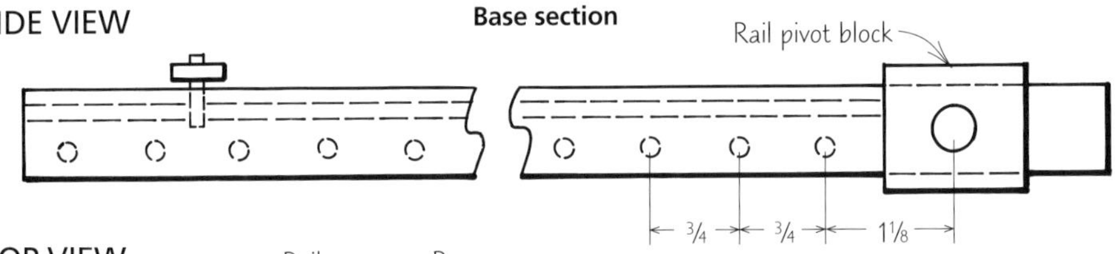
Base section
Rail pivot block
3/4
3/4
1 1/8

TOP VIEW

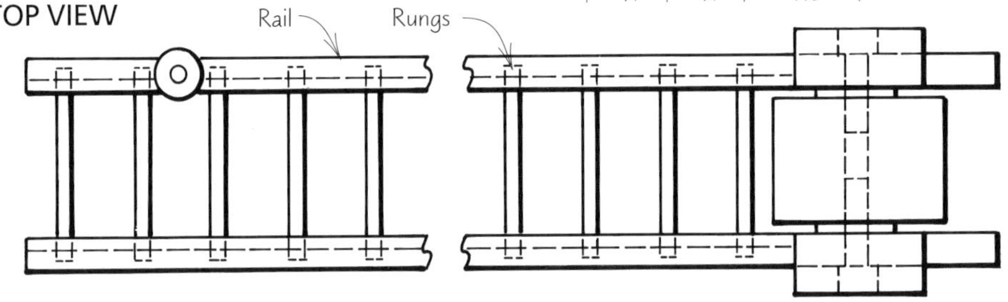
Rail
Rungs

SIDE VIEW

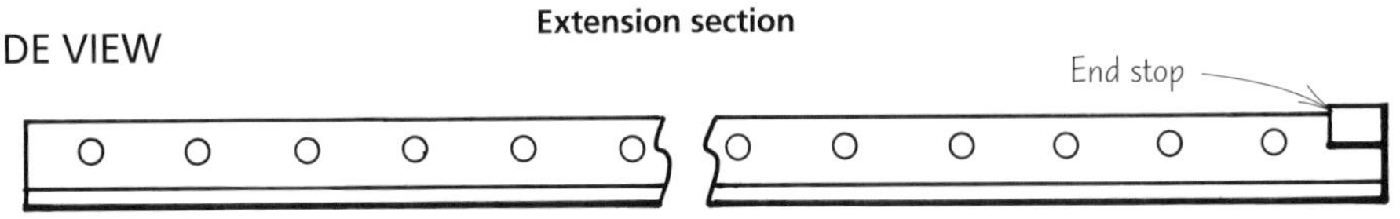
Extension section
End stop

TOP VIEW

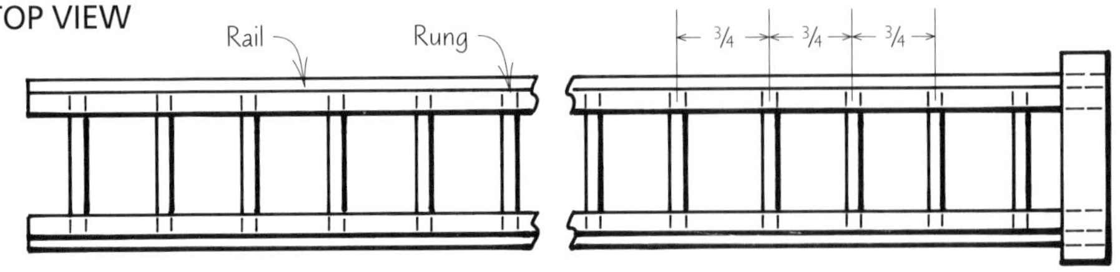
Rail
Rung
3/4
3/4
3/4

Vintage Truck

This 1930s' vintage truck is one of my favorite display pieces. It was made from a piece of cherry that I found on a side road in Maine near an old abandoned sawmill. The walnut wheels enhance the natural warmth and charm of the piece. To make a truck for active play, I'd substitute maple or birch for the cherry (see the gallery photo on p. 47). This toy is one of the most challenging to build in the book, so to make the job easier I've separated the process into four different subassemblies: cab, front end, rolling chassis and bed.

Parts Preparation

CAB

1. Cut the door-panel blanks to size. Fasten the panels together with double-sided tape (with the best sides together). Rabbet both sides and the bottoms, and cut out the window using the full-size pattern on p. 125.

2. Cut the back wall and windshield to size, and then make the window cutout in the windshield.

3. Cut the cab floor to size.

4. Drill an angled hole (10°) for the steering column in the steering-column support while the support is still in block form (see p. 10). Then secure the support to an auxiliary block to make the 45° cut on the bandsaw.

5. Use the full-size pattern on p. 125 to lay out the roof profile, bandsaw the curve in the top surface and then sand smooth (see p. 84).

6. Shape the seat blank using the full-size pattern on p. 125. Make the angle cut last.

7. Cut the steering wheel with a hole saw.

8. Cut the steering column to length.

FRONT END

1. Cut and shape the hood, and then drill a $3/16$-in.-dia. hole in each side for mounting the headlights.

2. To make the headlights, use a brad-point bit to drill a $1/2$-in.-dia. recess about $1/16$ in. deep in the end of two cherry dowels (see the photo below). Turn the back end round.

End-drill a cherry dowel to make the recessed hole for the headlight button.

3. Cut and shape the radiator, and then drill the top for the radiator cap, which is turned from a $1/4$-in.-dia. walnut dowel.

4. Lay out and cut the fenders and fender supports. Because of the short grain just above the running board, the fenders will be fragile; I glue the fender supports to the fenders at this time to add structural strength and minimize the risk of breakage.

Parts List

Quantity	Description	Finished Dimensions	Material
CAB			
2	Door panels	$1/4$ x $2^{5}/16$ x $3^{9}/16$	Cherry
1	Back wall	$1/4$ x $2^{7}/8$ x $3^{9}/16$	Cherry
1	Windshield	$1/4$ x $2^{7}/8$ x $3^{9}/16$	Cherry
1	Cab floor	$1/4$ x $1^{13}/16$ x $2^{7}/8$	Cherry
1	Roof	$1/2$ x $3^{3}/16$ x $2^{1}/2$	Cherry
1	Seat	$13/16$ x $1^{1}/4$ x $2^{9}/16$	Birch
1	Steering-column support	$11/16$ x $11/16$ x $2^{9}/16$	Cherry
1	Steering column	$3/16$-in.-dia. dowel by $2^{1}/4$ in. long	Birch
1	Steering wheel	1 in. dia. by $1/4$ in. thick	Cherry
FRONT END			
1	Hood	$1^{5}/8$ x 2 x $1^{11}/16$	Cherry
1	Radiator	$1/4$ x $2^{1}/8$ x $1^{11}/16$	Cherry
1	Radiator cap	$1/4$-in.-dia. dowel by $5/8$ in. long	Walnut
2	Fenders	$11/16$ x $1^{11}/16$ x $4^{1}/2$	Cherry
2	Fender supports	$5/16$ x $15/16$ x $2^{1}/2$	Cherry
2	Headlights	$5/8$-in.-dia. dowel by $3/4$ in. long	Cherry
2	Headlight brackets	$3/16$-in.-dia. dowel by $5/8$ in. long	Birch
2	Headlight lens	$1/2$-in.-dia. studded pearl buttons	Plastic
ROLLING CHASSIS			
1	Main chassis	$9/16$ x $2^{1}/4$ x $9^{13}/16$	Maple
1	Bed chassis	$9/16$ x $2^{3}/4$ x $5^{3}/4$	Maple
2	Axle housings	$5/8$ x $3/4$ x $2^{3}/4$	Birch
2	Axles	$5/16$ in. dia. by $4^{1}/8$ in. long	Birch
4	Spacer washers	$5/16$ in.	Steel
4	Wheels	$1^{7}/8$ in. dia. by $9/16$ in. thick	Walnut
BED			
1	Floor panel	$1/4$ x 6 x $4^{5}/8$	Cherry
6	Posts	$1/4$ x $5/16$ x $3^{1}/2$	Cherry
2	Side walls	$1/4$ x $1^{1}/4$ x $5^{13}/16$	Cherry
4	Side rails	$3/16$ x $5/16$ x $5^{13}/16$	Cherry
1	Front wall	$1/4$ x $1^{1}/4$ x $4^{5}/8$	Cherry
2	Front rails	$1/4$ x $5/16$ x $4^{5}/8$	Cherry

ROLLING CHASSIS

1. Cut the main chassis to size. Bevel the front (5°) and back (10°) ends and cut a $5/8$-in.-wide by $1/4$-in.-deep dado in the bottom for the axle housings.

2. Cut the bed chassis to size, beveling just the back edge at 10°. Glue the bed chassis to the main chassis, centered left to right and with the rear bevels aligned.

3. Cut and drill the axle housing (see p. 12).

4. Cut the wheels with a hole saw, and true them up on the lathe (see p. 13).

5. Cut the axles to rough length, and trim to final length after dry assembly.

BED

1. Cut the floor panel to size, and then run a $1/4$-in. by $1/16$-in. dado along each side ($1/8$ in. in from the edge) for the side panels. Cut a $1/4$-in. by $1/16$-in. rabbet in the front edge for the front wall.

2. Cut the side walls and front wall to size. Cut a $3/8$-in. by $1/16$-in. rabbet in each end of the front wall.

3. The vertical posts are rabbeted on their lower ends to fit over the side walls and notched in the middle and at the top for the side rails. Make the cuts using the technique described in the sidebar on the facing page.

4. Rip the side and front rails to size. Make a rabbet cut on each end of the front rails.

If this truck is destined for the playground rather than the display shelf, I'd forego the fancy (and fragile) post-and-rail bed, and substitute some lower, solid-panel sides (as shown in the gallery photo on p. 47).

Assembly

Finish all parts as described on pp. 16-18. Note that this toy is pre-assembled in four sections before final assembly.

CAB

1. Glue the cab floor and door panels to the back wall, and then glue the windshield to the door panels. The front corners of the cab may have to be notched to clear the fenders; this should be determined during dry assembly.
2. Glue the steering-column support to the floor and the seat to the back wall. Glue the steering wheel to the steering column, and then glue the lower end of the steering column into the hole in the steering-column support.
3. Glue on the roof.

FRONT END

The fenders and fender supports were glued together before sanding and finishing.

1. Glue the radiator to the front of the hood and the radiator cap into the radiator.
2. Epoxy the pearl buttons and the headlight brackets into the headlights.
3. Epoxy the headlight brackets into the holes in the sides of the hood.

ROLLING CHASSIS

1. Glue the axle housings into the chassis dadoes.
2. Insert the axles into the housings, add washers and glue on the wheels.

BED

1. Because the glue areas on the bed parts are so small, I use epoxy for all glue joints here. Glue the front and side walls to the floor panel, and the posts to the side walls. Glue the front and side rails to the posts.

ASSEMBLING THE COMPONENTS

1. Glue the assembled bed onto the bed chassis, centered left to right and with front edges aligned.
2. Glue the cab onto the main chassis, centered from left to right and flush against the front end of the bed.
3. Glue the hood assembly onto the main chassis, centered and butted against the cab.
4. Glue the fenders and fender supports onto the main chassis, with the back edge of the support aligned with the back edge of the cab. Some minor shaping on the fenders may be necessary to clear the headlights. Once the fenders are fitted, add some epoxy glue between the headlight and fender for additional support.

Making Posts

The bed for the vintage truck includes posts that are rabbeted and notched to receive the side rails and side walls. Machining parts this small is dangerous, so I cut the rabbet and the dadoes in a larger block, as shown in the drawing, and then rip the individual posts from this block. Use the spacer-block technique to cut six identical, 1/4-in.-wide posts, as shown in the photo below.

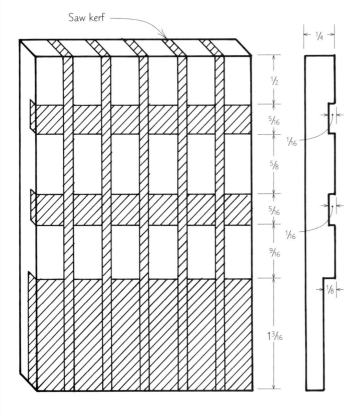

Rip posts for the bed from a precut board. Use spacer blocks to set the rip fence, removing one spacer for each cut.

Vintage Truck

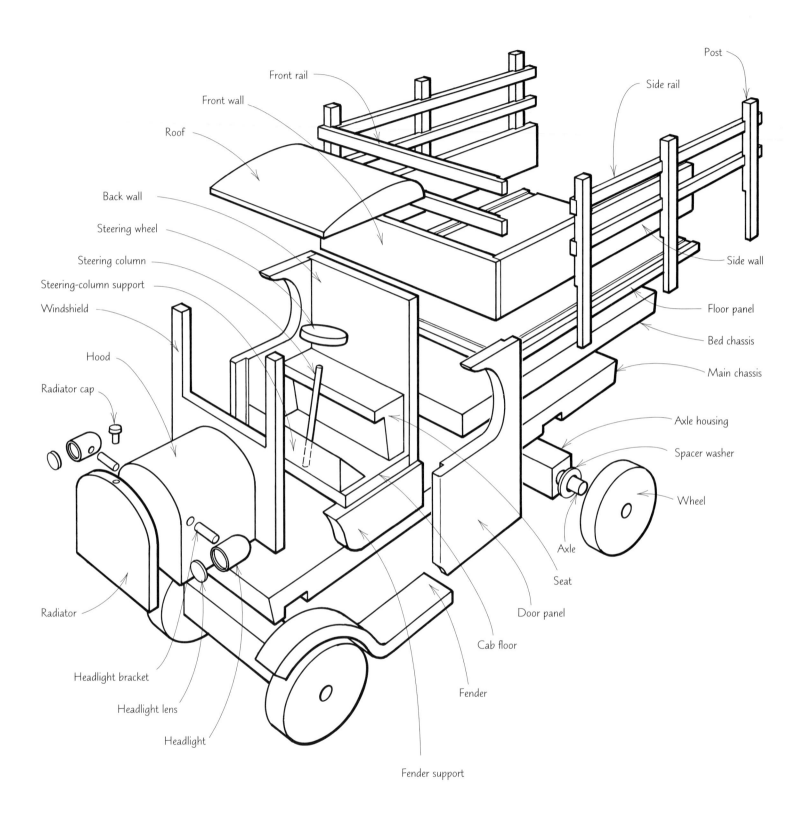

Front rail

Front wall

Roof

Back wall

Steering wheel

Steering column

Steering-column support

Windshield

Hood

Radiator cap

Radiator

Headlight bracket

Headlight lens

Headlight

Post

Side rail

Side wall

Floor panel

Bed chassis

Main chassis

Axle housing

Spacer washer

Wheel

Axle

Seat

Door panel

Cab floor

Fender

Fender support

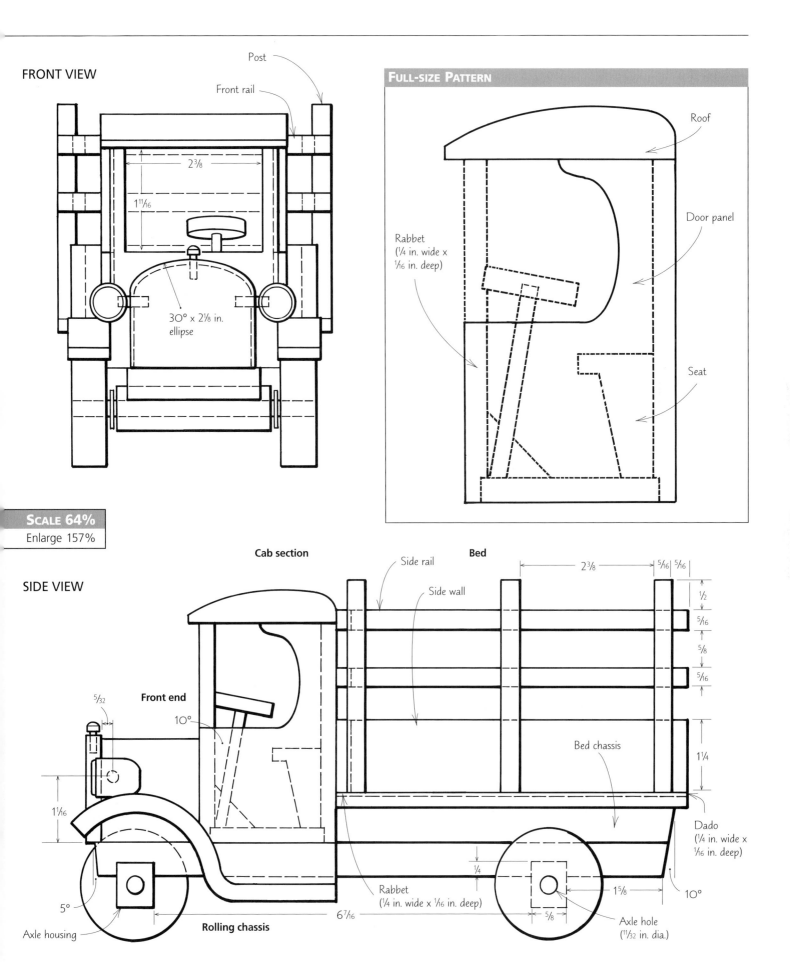

FRONT VIEW

Post

Front rail

2³⁄₈

1¹¹⁄₁₆

30° x 2⅛ in.
ellipse

Roof

Door panel

Rabbet
(¼ in. wide x
¹⁄₁₆ in. deep)

Seat

SCALE 64%
Enlarge 157%

SIDE VIEW

Cab section

Side rail

Bed

Side wall

2³⁄₈   ⁵⁄₁₆ ⁵⁄₁₆

½

⁵⁄₁₆

⅝

⁵⁄₁₆

Front end

5⁄32

10°

Bed chassis

1¼

1¹⁄₁₆

Dado
(¼ in. wide x
¹⁄₁₆ in. deep)

5°

Axle housing

Rolling chassis

Rabbet
(¼ in. wide x ¹⁄₁₆ in. deep)

6⁷⁄₁₆

¼

⅝

Axle hole
(¹¹⁄₃₂ in. dia.)

1⁵⁄₈

10°

Mary's Ferry Boat

Back in the 1950s, the best bargain in the Big Apple was a five-cent ferry-boat ride from lower Manhattan to Staten Island. I made the trip many times to visit my sister, Mary, and promised her that one day I would design a ferry-boat toy for her. This version of the Staten Island ferry is in memory of Mary. Although the ferry is the largest project in this book, it requires only basic woodworking skills and the use of a table saw, drill press and scrollsaw or router.

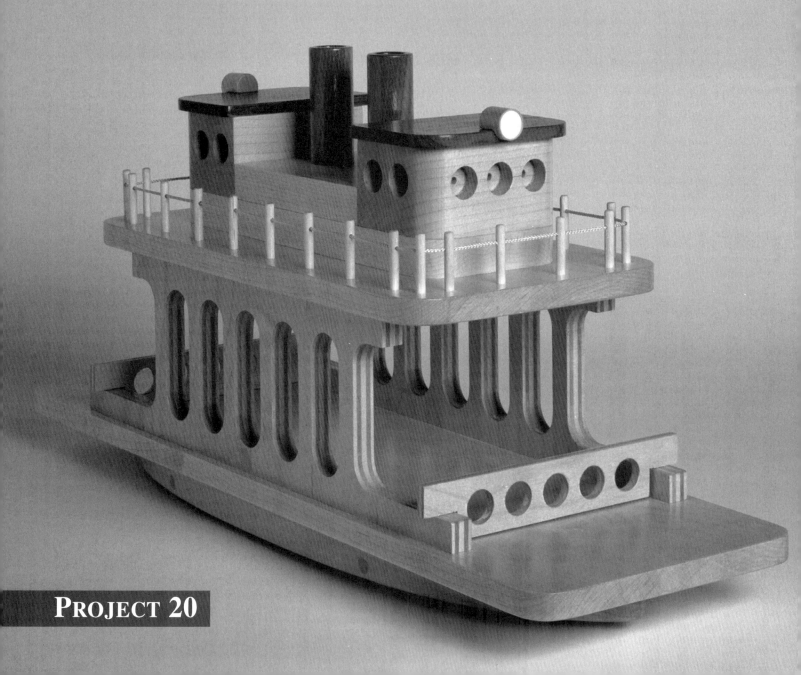

PROJECT 20

Parts Preparation

HULL ASSEMBLY

1. Cut a rectangular blank to the overall dimensions of the hull (see the parts list on p. 130).

2. Lay out the hull perimeter, using the full-size, half-section pattern on p. 131. Cut the perimeter so that it tapers in 5° from top to bottom. Cut out the roller wells and drill the holes for the roller axles.

3. Cut the rollers to length and drill the axle holes, using the technique shown on p. 12.

MAIN DECK AND GATES

1. Cut the main-deck blank to size and radius the four corners. Use the hull to lay out ³⁄₁₆-in.-deep roller wells in the bottom surface of the deck, and then rout the wells.

2. On the top surface of the deck, lay out the area where the side walls will be glued and drill holes for the dowel joints that connect the deck to the side walls (see the bottom drawing on p. 129).

3. Cut the side-wall blanks a little long and draw a full layout, including all the window openings with a vertical centerline on each.

The window openings can be made with a router or with a drill press and scrollsaw. If you choose to rout the window openings, make a template of a single window cutout, as shown in the photo below. Draw a centerline on the template for referencing it to the windows'

centerlines. Drill an entry hole for the router bit in each window, including the half windows at each end. Clamp the template to the workpiece in a bench vise. Rout the first window opening, move the template to the next window and repeat the process until all openings are routed out. Complete the perimeter cuts on a bandsaw or scrollsaw.

If you'd rather drill and cut the window openings, fasten the side-wall blanks together with double-sided tape and shape them as a single unit. Drill 1-in.-dia. holes at the top and bottom of the window openings, and then complete the cutout by scrollsawing from one hole to the next. Sand the edges of the cutouts smooth, using a sanding block for the sides and a dowel for the inside curves.

4. Drill holes at each end of the side walls for the four side-railing posts and oversized holes for the ⅛-in.-dia. gate pins.

5. Make the gates as shown in the drawing on p. 130, but don't install the pins until the ferry boat is assembled.

UPPER-DECK ASSEMBLY

1. Cut the upper-deck blank to size and radius the corners.

2. Locate and lay out the railing-post holes. Note that the posts are aligned between the windows, and the posts at each end of the side walls extend through the deck and into the

side walls. Drill these four holes through the deck and the other 20 holes to a depth of ³⁄₈ in.

3. Cut the railing posts ¼ in. longer than finished length, and then drill holes in the posts for the string railing. Use a simple drilling jig to hold the posts (see pp. 10-11). To reduce the risk of the posts splitting, drill the holes about ½ in. from the end and then trim off the excess at the top end.

4. Cut the cabin-deck blank to size but don't radius the corners yet.

5. Cut the cabin blanks to size, and then drill the ⁵⁄₈-in.-dia. portholes about ³⁄₈ in. deep. Glue the cabins on each end of the cabin deck. Once the glue has set, radius each corner of the cabin/deck unit.

6. Cut the smokestack deck to fit between the cabins. Drill the two 1-in.-dia. stack holes, and then glue the smokestack deck in place.

7. Drill a ⁵⁄₈-in.-dia. hole about ¾ in. deep in one end of the smokestack dowel blanks.

8. Cut the cabin roofs to size, radius the corners and glue them onto the cabins.

9. To make the headlights, drill a centered hole into the end of the dowel blanks with a brad-point drill bit (see the photo on p. 122). Cut the rabbet for fitting the light to the cabin roof (I used an X-Acto razor saw for this tiny cut). Apply finish to the headlight, allow to dry and then glue the headlight lens (a pearl button) into the headlight with epoxy.

To rout the windows in the side walls, reference the centerline on the template to the centerline on the window. Note the entry hole for the router bit.

With the template clamped to the workpiece, rout the window opening.

Mary's Ferry Boat

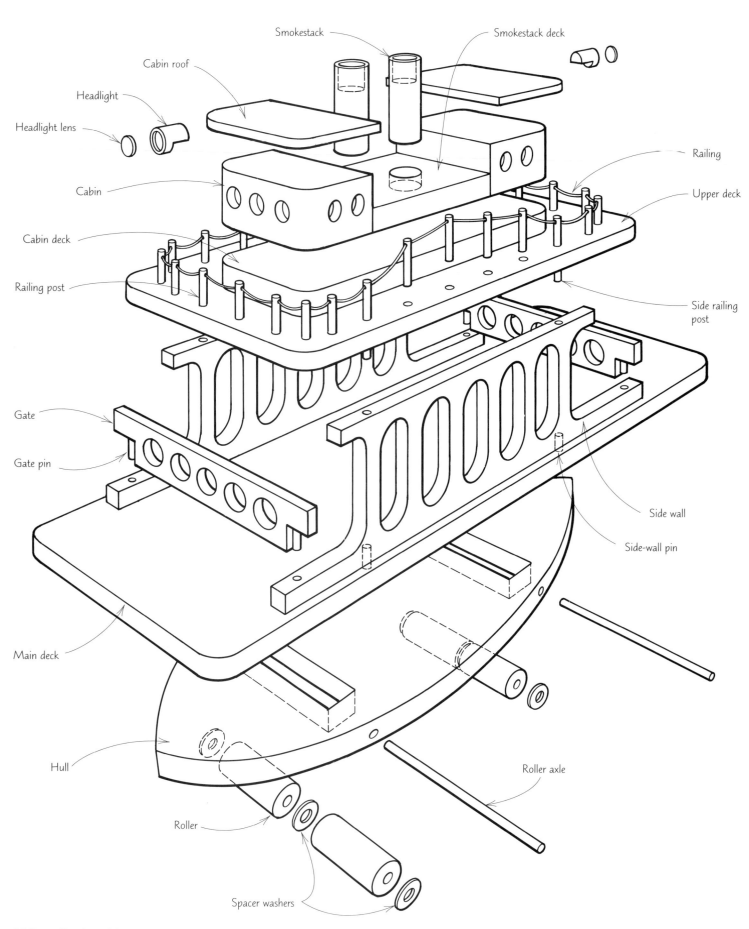

Smokestack

Smokestack deck

Cabin roof

Headlight

Headlight lens

Cabin

Railing

Upper deck

Cabin deck

Railing post

Side railing post

Gate

Gate pin

Side wall

Side-wall pin

Main deck

Hull

Roller axle

Roller

Spacer washers

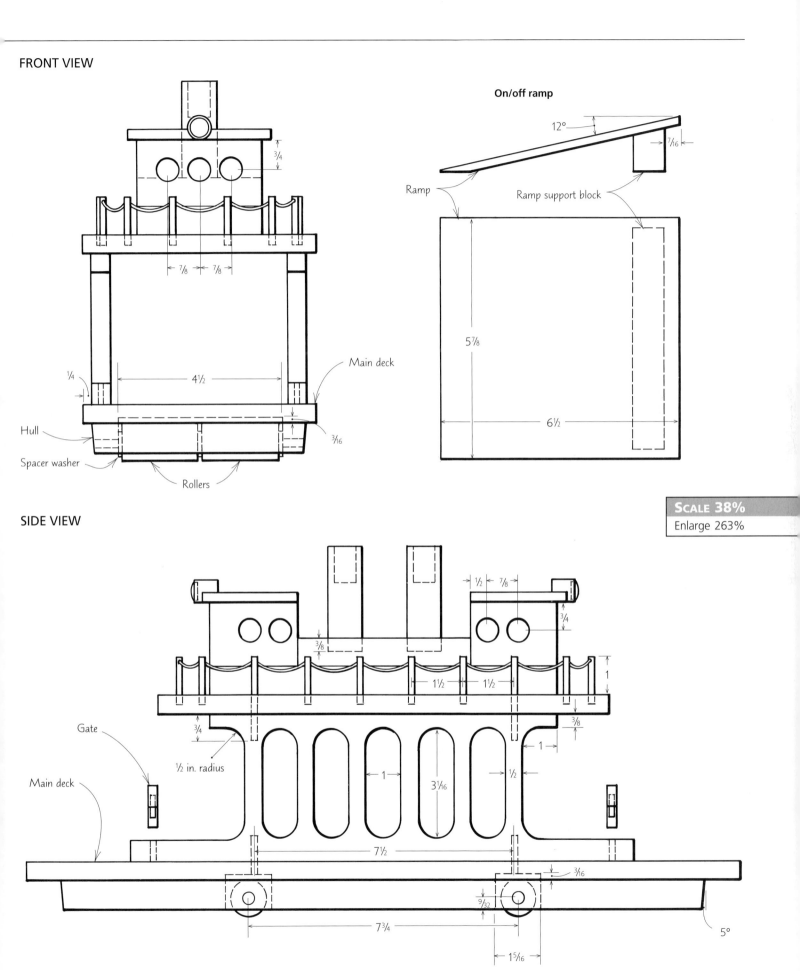

On/off ramp

12°

7/16

Ramp

Ramp support block

5 7/8

6 1/2

3/4

7/8 7/8

1/4

4 1/2

Main deck

Hull

Spacer washer

Rollers

3/16

SCALE 38%
Enlarge 263%

SIDE VIEW

1/2 7/8

3/4

3/8

1

1 1/2 1 1/2

3/8

Gate

3/4

1

1/2 in. radius

1

Main deck

3 1/16

1/2

7 1/2

3/16

9/32

7 3/4

5°

1 5/16

Assembly

Finish all parts as described on pp. 16-18. To keep the ferry boat from rolling around during assembly, install the rollers, axles and spacer washers as the last step.

1. Center and glue the hull to the underside of the main deck.

2. Glue the side walls to the main deck. Re-drill the holes for the side-wall pins; glue in the pins.

3. Center the six-piece cabin/deck unit and glue it onto the upper deck.

4. Center and glue the upper deck onto the side walls.

5. Using the two post holes in the upper deck that fall over the ends of the side walls as a guide, drill into the top edge of the side walls $\frac{3}{4}$ in. deep. The railing posts for these holes will extend into the side walls to create a doweled joint.

6. Adjust the length of the railing posts so that the holes for the string railing are all at the same height, and then glue the posts in place, making sure all the holes align.

7. Glue the headlights to the cabin roofs with epoxy.

8. Glue the smokestacks to the smokestack deck.

9. Thread nylon string through the railing posts.

10. Insert the rollers into the roller wells with a spacer washer on either side and one in between the rollers. Slide the axle dowels into the axle holes and spot-glue the exit hole and trailing end of the dowel. Check the rollers for free movement. Trim the dowel ends, and then sand to match the taper of the hull.

11. Cut the steel gate pins to length and insert them in their holes in the side walls. Press the gate down on top of the pins to mark their location. Drill the pin holes in the gates and epoxy the pins in place.

12. Make the on/off ramp as shown in the drawing on p. 129 and you'll be able to load and unload the fleet of vehicles presented in the next project.

Parts List

Quantity	Description	Finished Dimensions	Material
HULL ASSEMBLY			
1	Hull	$\frac{13}{16}$ x 6 x $18\frac{1}{2}$	Birch
4	Rollers	1-in.-dia. dowel by $2\frac{1}{8}$ in. long	Birch
6	Spacer washers	$\frac{5}{16}$ in.	Steel
2	Axles	$\frac{3}{8}$-in.-dia. dowel by $5\frac{1}{2}$ in. long	Birch
MAIN DECK			
1	Deck	$\frac{1}{2}$ x $6\frac{1}{2}$ x $20\frac{1}{2}$	Maple
2	Side walls	$\frac{1}{2}$ x 4 x $14\frac{1}{2}$	Baltic birch plywood
4	Side-wall pins	$\frac{3}{16}$-in.-dia. dowels by $1\frac{1}{8}$ in. long	Birch
UPPER-DECK ASSEMBLY			
1	Upper deck	$\frac{1}{2}$ x $6\frac{1}{2}$ x 13	Maple
1	Cabin deck	$\frac{3}{4}$ x $3\frac{1}{2}$ x 10	Maple
1	Smokestack deck	$\frac{3}{4}$ x $3\frac{1}{2}$ x 5	Maple
2	Smokestacks	1-in.-dia. dowel by $2\frac{7}{8}$ in. long	Birch
2	Cabins	$1\frac{3}{4}$ x $2\frac{1}{2}$ x $3\frac{1}{2}$	Maple
2	Cabin roofs	$\frac{1}{4}$ x $2\frac{3}{4}$ x 4	Walnut
2	Headlights	$\frac{5}{8}$-in.-dia. dowels by $\frac{11}{16}$ in. long	Birch
2	Headlight lenses	$\frac{9}{16}$-in.-dia. pearl button	Plastic
20	Railing posts	$\frac{3}{16}$-in.-dia. dowels by $1\frac{5}{16}$ in. long	Birch
4	Railing posts (sides)	$\frac{3}{16}$-in.-dia. dowels by $2\frac{1}{16}$ in. long	Birch
1	Railing	40-in.-long string	Nylon
GATES			
2	Gates	$\frac{1}{4}$ x $1\frac{1}{8}$ x $6\frac{1}{2}$	Baltic birch plywood
4	Gate pins	$\frac{1}{8}$ in. dia. by $\frac{3}{4}$ in. long	Steel
ON/OFF RAMP			
1	Ramp	$\frac{1}{4}$ x $6\frac{1}{2}$ x $5\frac{7}{8}$	Baltic birch plywood
1	Support block	$\frac{13}{16}$ x $1\frac{1}{8}$ x $5\frac{3}{4}$	Birch

FULL-SIZE PATTERN

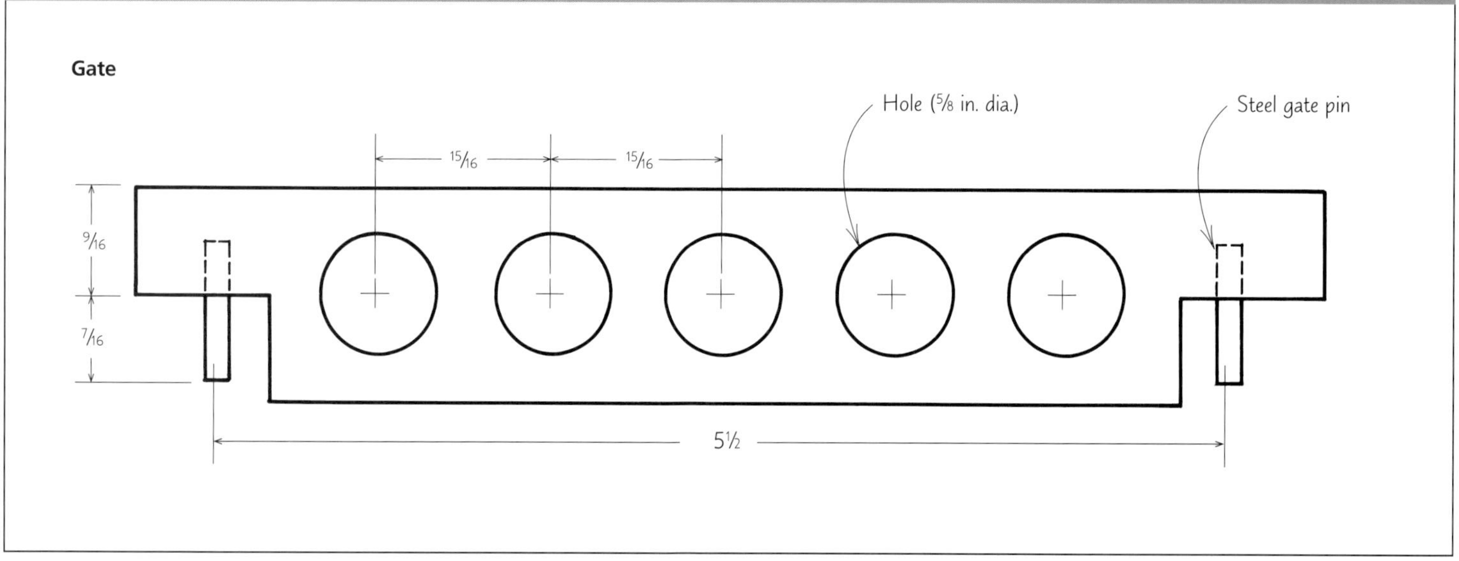
Gate
Hole (5/8 in. dia.)
Steel gate pin
15/16
15/16
9/16
7/16
5 1/2

TOP VIEW (half-section)

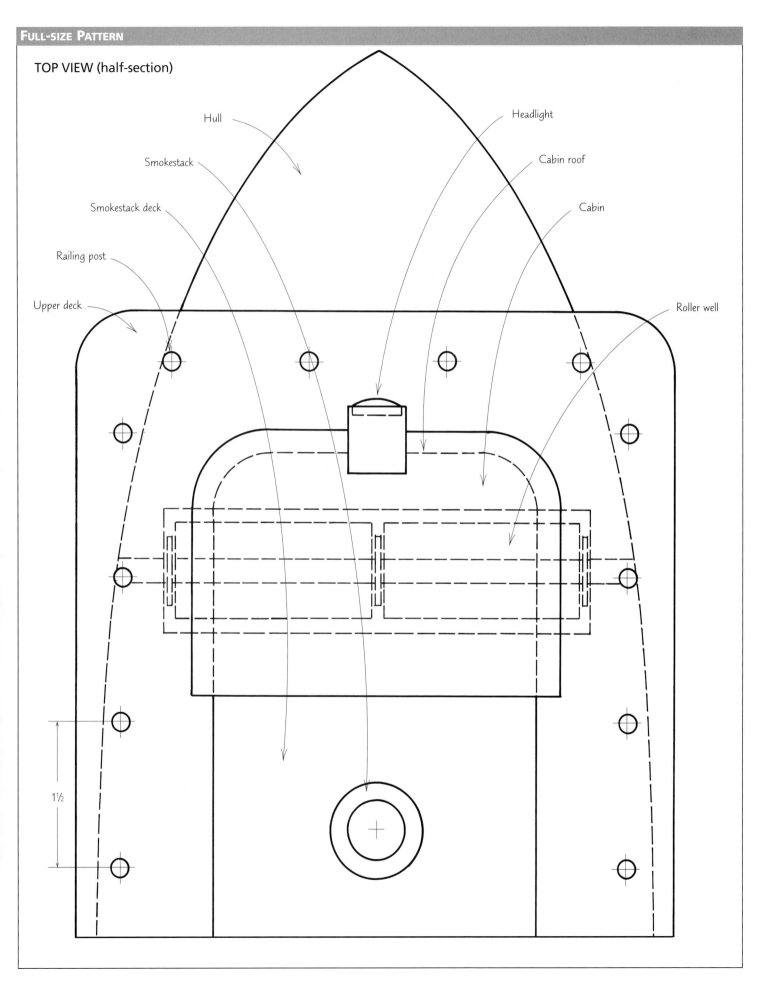

Hull

Headlight

Smokestack

Cabin roof

Smokestack deck

Cabin

Railing post

Upper deck

Roller well

1½

Four Ferry-Boat Vehicles

Although I originally designed these four vehicles to ride the ferry boat (Project 20), they also travel well on imagined roads in the playroom and backyard. The small parts in the vehicles present some interesting challenges, so be sure to review the techniques outlined on pp. 3-14. The most difficult job in making the cars is cutting and fitting the fenders. For a detailed, step-by-step guide to the process, see the sidebar on pp. 138-139.

Pick-up Truck

Sedan

Woodie Wagon

Coupe

General Construction

Except for cutting the fragile fenders, the construction of each of these four vehicles is fairly straightforward. Use the parts list at right and the drawings on pp. 134-137 to prepare the parts, and then sand and finish the parts as described on pp. 16-18. Assemble the vehicles by starting with the main body and gluing parts to it one at a time. Specific instructions are included with the drawing for each toy, but first here are some general tips on construction.

• Use a 1 3/8-in.-dia. hole saw to cut out the wheels for all the vehicles. Trim the wheels to the correct diameter (1 1/8 in.) on a lathe.

• Turn the rounded back end of the headlights on a lathe, using a simple press-fit wooden collet, as shown in the photo below. The wooden collet is a 3/4-in.-dia. dowel, end-drilled to accept the 3/8-in.-dia. headlight stock. Drill a small hole from the back side of the collet so you can push the headlights out once the lights are turned. The collet is held in a standard three-jaw lathe chuck.

• To make the headlights sit securely on the top of the fenders, sand a small groove at the appropriate spot with sandpaper wrapped around a 3/8-in.-dia. dowel.

• Use epoxy for all small parts. Because there's always a chance that small pieces will come loose, I don't recommend these toys for children under three years of age.

• Cut the thin tapered roofs on the Sedan, the Woodie and the Coupe on the table saw.

(text continues on p. 138)

Use a wooden collet to hold the headlight while you shape the back end.

Parts List

Quantity	Description	Finished Dimensions	Material
SEDAN			
1	Body	1 5/16 x 2 1/8 x 5 3/16	Cherry
1	Roof	5/16 x 1 5/16 x 3 1/2	Cherry
1	Windshield	1/4 x 1 5/16 x 7/8	Cherry
4	Window posts	1/4 x 1/4 x 7/8	Cherry
2	Fenders	3/8 x 1 3/16 x 5 1/2	Cherry
1	Radiator	1/8 x 1 3/8 x 1 15/32	Cherry
2	Headlights	3/8-in.-dia. dowel by 1/2 in. long	Birch
4	Wheels	1 1/8 in. dia. by 3/8 in. thick	Maple
4	Spacer washers	1/4 in.	Steel
2	Axles	1/4-in.-dia. dowel by 2 1/4 in. long	Birch
PICK-UP TRUCK			
1	Body	1 1/4 x 1 9/16 x 5 7/16	Poplar
1	Cab	1 3/8 x 1 15/16 x 1 13/16	Poplar
2	Fenders	1/2 x 1 1/8 x 2 5/8	Poplar
4	Wheels	1 1/8 in. dia. by 3/8 in. thick	Walnut
4	Spacer washers	1/4 in.	Steel
2	Axles	1/4-in.-dia. dowel by 2 1/4 in. long	Birch
1	Bed floor	1/8 x 1 9/16 x 2 7/8	Cherry
1	Bed front panel	1/4 x 1 1/2 x 1 9/16	Cherry
2	Bed side panels	1/4 x 1 1/2 x 3	Cherry
WOODIE WAGON			
1	Body	1 1/4 x 1 3/8 x 4 1/8	Birch
1	Hood	1 1/4 x 1 1/2 x 1 1/2	Birch
1	Roof	5/16 x 1 3/8 x 4 1/2	Birch
1	Windshield	1/4 x 1 3/8 x 1	Birch
1	Back window	1/4 x 1 3/8 x 1	Birch
1	Inside window	1/4 x 1 3/8 x 1	Birch
2	Window posts	1/4 x 1/4 x 1	Birch
2	Fenders	1/2 x 1 3/32 x 5 9/16	Walnut
2	Headlights	3/8 in. dia. by 7/16 in. long	Birch
4	Wheels	1 1/8 in. dia. by 3/8 in. thick	Maple
2	Front wheel spacers	1/2-in.-dia. dowel by 3/16 in. long	Birch
2	Spacer washers	1/4 in.	Steel
2	Axles	1/4-in.-dia. dowel by 2 1/4 in. long	Birch
COUPE			
1	Body	1 5/16 x 1 1/2 x 3 3/8	Poplar
1	Hood	1 5/16 x 1 3/8 x 1 3/4	Poplar
1	Roof	5/16 x 1 5/16 x 1 3/4	Birch
1	Windshield	3/16 x 1 5/16 x 13/16	Poplar
1	Rear window	3/16 x 1 5/16 x 13/16	Poplar
2	Window trim	3/16 x 3/16 x 1 1/4	Birch
1	Radiator	1/8 x 1 1/8 x 13/16	Poplar
2	Fenders	1/2 x 1 1/8 x 5 7/16	Poplar
2	Headlights	3/8 in. dia. by 3/8 in. long	Birch
4	Wheels	1 1/8 in. dia. by 3/8 in. thick	Walnut
2	Front wheel spacers	1/2 in. dia. by 3/16 in. long	Birch
2	Spacer washers	1/4 in.	Steel
2	Axles	1/4-in.-dia. dowel by 2 1/4 in. long	Birch

Sedan

The body of the Sedan is cut from a solid block (see the pattern at the bottom of the page). To help strengthen the short grain in the back wall, drill a hole and insert a dowel pin vertically into the back.

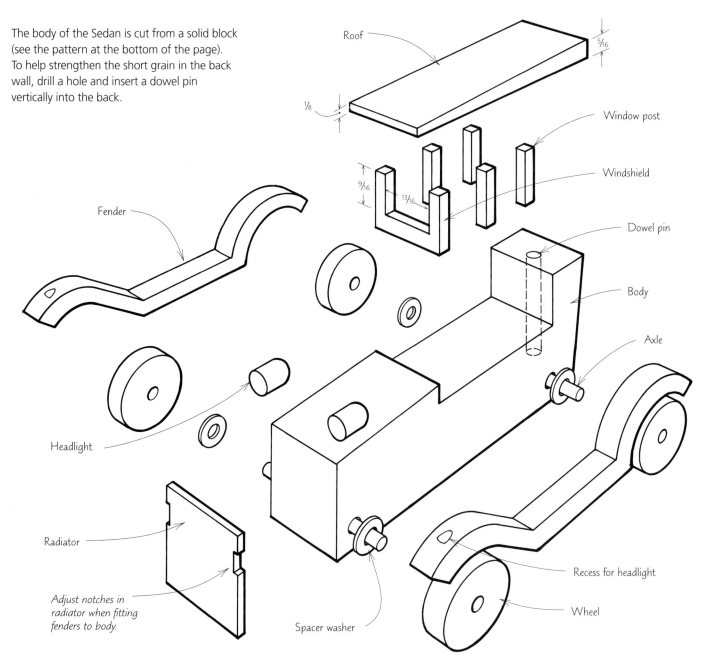

Roof

5/16

1/8

Window post

Windshield

9/16

13/16

Fender

Dowel pin

Body

Axle

Headlight

Radiator

Adjust notches in radiator when fitting fenders to body.

Spacer washer

Recess for headlight

Wheel

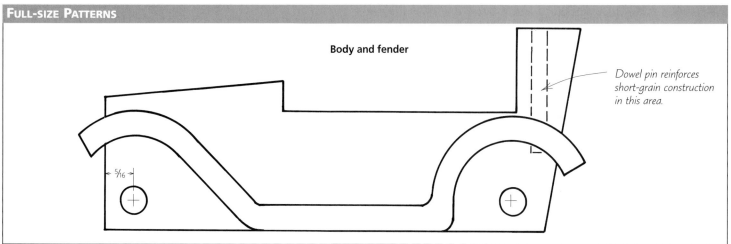

Body and fender

Dowel pin reinforces short-grain construction in this area.

5/16

Pick-up Truck

The main body can be made in two sections; the location of the joint is indicated in the drawing. Glue these sections together before adding the Pick-up's bed.

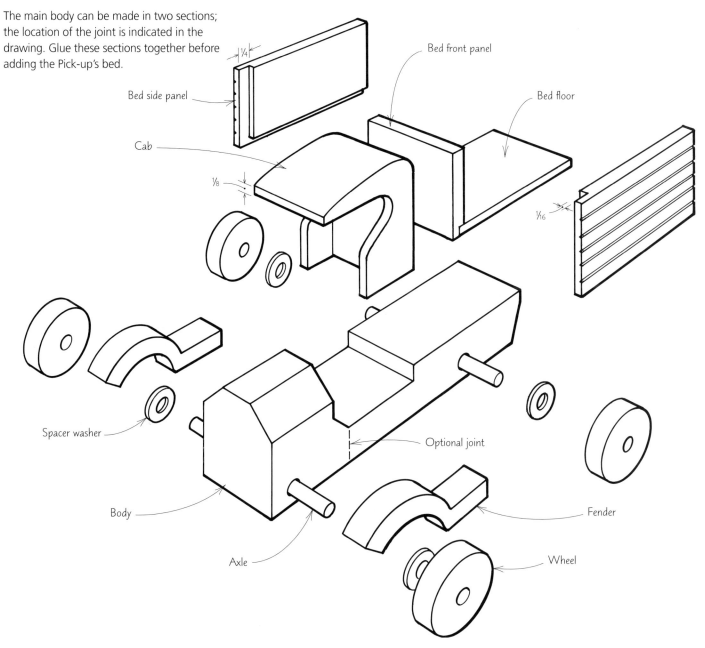

Body and fender

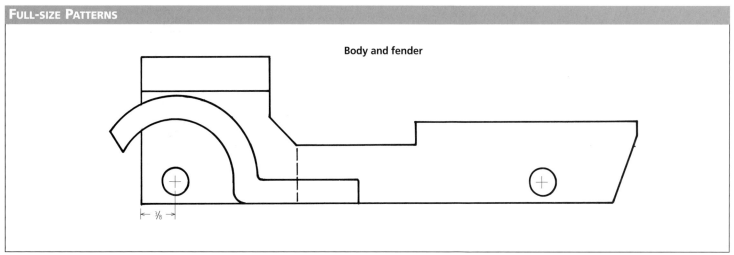

Woodie Wagon

This vehicle can be made with or without the recess for the passenger compartment. If you want to include this detail, cut the workpiece oversize and use an overhead router to hollow out the recess.

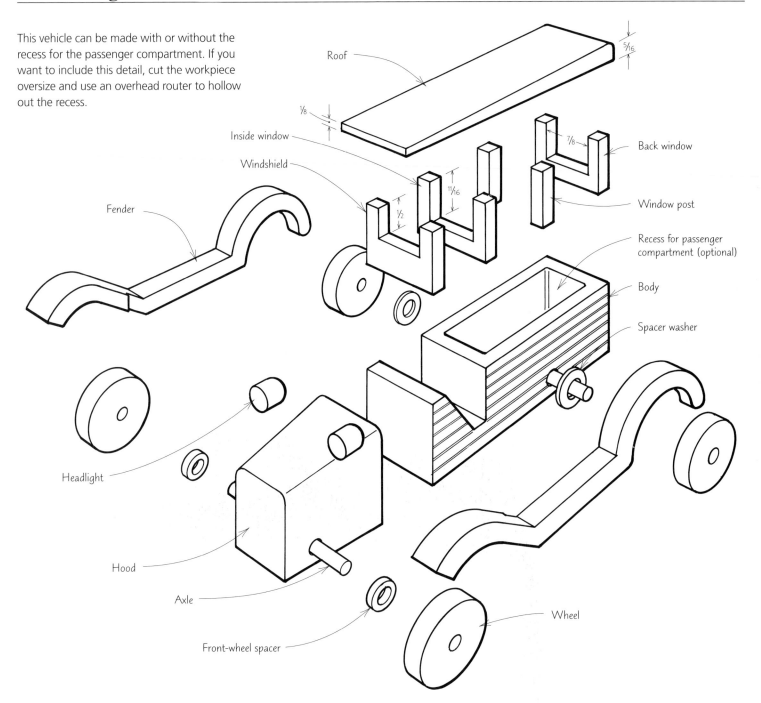

Roof

5/16

1/8

Inside window

Windshield

Fender

Back window

7/8

Window post

11/16

1/2

Recess for passenger compartment (optional)

Body

Spacer washer

Headlight

Hood

Axle

Front-wheel spacer

Wheel

FULL-SIZE PATTERNS

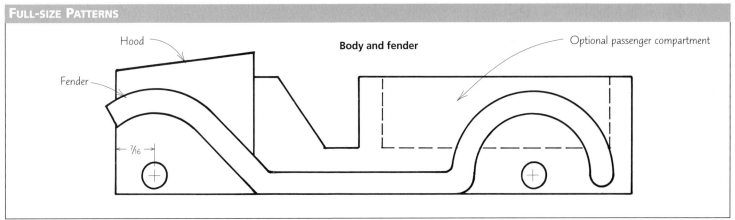

Hood

Fender

Body and fender

Optional passenger compartment

7/16

Coupe

To make it easier to match the radiator to the front profile of the hood, shape the hood before cutting the radiator. Adjust the notches in the sides of the radiator when fitting the fenders to the body of the car (alternatively, notch the fenders to fit the radiator).

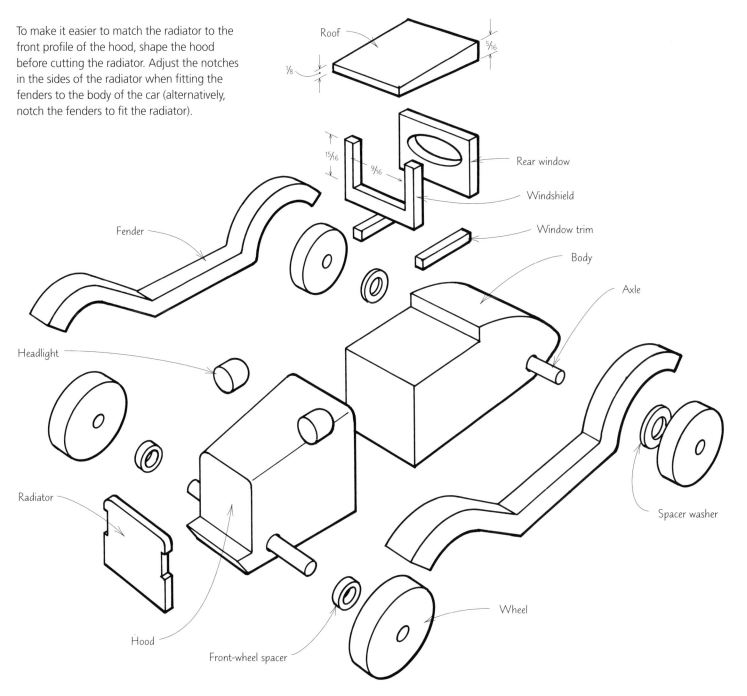

Roof

⁵⁄₁₆

¹⁄₈

Rear window

Windshield

¹⁵⁄₁₆

⁹⁄₁₆

Window trim

Body

Axle

Fender

Headlight

Radiator

Spacer washer

Hood

Front-wheel spacer

Wheel

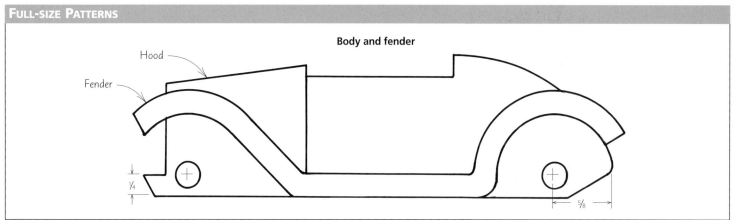

FULL-SIZE PATTERNS

Body and fender

Hood

Fender

¼

⅝

General Construction (continued)

Cut the tapered roof for the Woodie Wagon using an angle block to guide the workpiece.

Secure the blank with double-sided tape to a simple angle block (you need to make a separate angle block for each roof). Slide the block against the table-saw fence (see the photo at left).

• The bed of the Pick-up Truck and the sides of the Woodie Wagon have equally spaced parallel grooves to simulate planking. Use the spacer-block technique and a rip-fence stop (see p. 8) to cut these grooves on the table saw. (I used a thin-kerf blade for this operation.)

• Use an angle jig to help cut the 5° angle on the sides of the hood for the Woodie Wagon and the Coupe.

• Cut the wooden wheel spacers for the front ends of the Woodie and the Coupe from a length of end-drilled ½-in.-dia. dowel.

MISCELLANEOUS FULL-SIZE PATTERNS

Sedan radiator

Notch for fender

Pick-up cab

Interior cutout is optional.

Coupe back window

Coupe radiator

Making the Fenders

Making the one-piece fenders can seem like a bit of a challenge, but it's really not too difficult if you follow the correct sequence of steps. The left and right fender for each vehicle are mirror images, so you can fabricate them as a single unit using two oversized blanks fastened together with double-sided tape.

The fenders for the Pick-up Truck and Sedan are somewhat simpler than those for the Wagon and Coupe because they do not require any angled cuts. These fenders can be fabricated from blanks of the correct thickness, but the blanks must be oversize in width to allow for the full profile layout. The fenders for the Wagon are the trickiest to make—they have a 1⁄16-in. shoulder as well as the front-end angle cut—so I'll take you step-by-step through the process of making these fenders, as shown in the drawings on the facing page. The same basic techniques can be used to make the fenders for the other vehicles.

1. Cut the fender blanks to 13⁄16 x 17⁄8 x 59⁄16. Fasten the blanks together with double-sided tape and lay out the top view on the blanks.

2. Lay out the side view on the blanks, and then drill 1¼-in.-dia. through holes for the wheel clearance and 5⁄16-in.-dia. through holes to create the inside radius where the fenders blend into the running boards. I use a Forstner bit for a clean cut.

3. Using a tenoning attachment on the table saw, make the angled cuts at the front of the fender and the straight cuts to about 2¼ in. deep at the back of the fender. Do not connect the cuts yet.

4. Bandsaw the top profile of the fender, and then sand this surface smooth while it still has some support from the blank. Handle the piece with care because the short grain on the fender curves is fragile.

5. Finish cutting the bottom profile and carefully sand the underside.

6. Connect the cuts made in Step 3, creating a 1⁄16-in. shoulder where the straight cut meets the angle cut. (If the hood is the same width as the body, as on the Coupe, you don't have to deal with the shoulder.) Gently sand any rough spots, and then carefully separate the two fenders with an X-Acto knife.

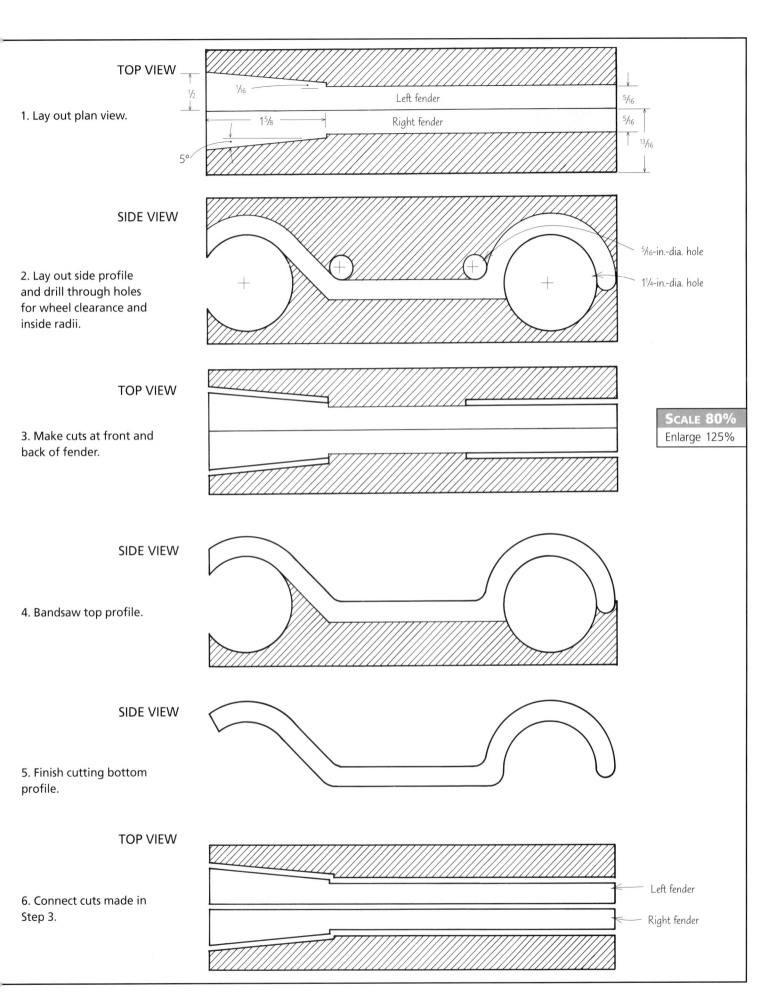

TOP VIEW

1. Lay out plan view.

Left fender

Right fender

SIDE VIEW

2. Lay out side profile and drill through holes for wheel clearance and inside radii.

$\frac{5}{16}$-in.-dia. hole

$1\frac{1}{4}$-in.-dia. hole

TOP VIEW

SCALE 80%
Enlarge 125%

3. Make cuts at front and back of fender.

SIDE VIEW

4. Bandsaw top profile.

SIDE VIEW

5. Finish cutting bottom profile.

TOP VIEW

6. Connect cuts made in Step 3.

Left fender

Right fender

U-Fly-It Plane

The original design for this toy grew out of my curiosity and fascination with flying as a young child. During World War II, I would often badger my uncle, a lieutenant commander in the U.S. Navy, about the workings of his airplane. He would draw sketches as he explained the series of cables and pulleys that controlled the wings and tail movement, much like a marionette is controlled by pulling its strings. Thus was planted the seed for the U-Fly-It Plane.

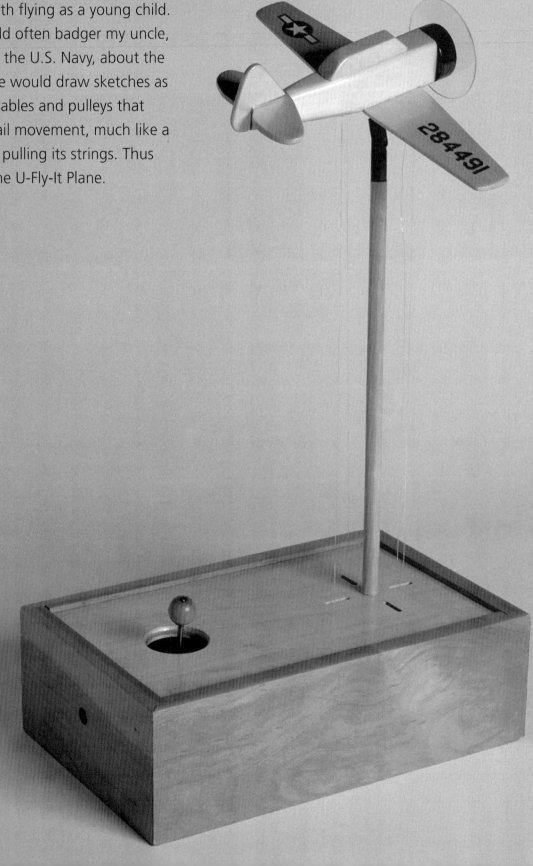

Parts Preparation

Like a flight simulator, the U-Fly-It Plane, mounted on a universal joint on top of a post, duplicates the stick-controlled movements of early training planes: forward to dive, back to climb and left or right to bank or turn. The joystick, connected to a parallelogram-shaped bracket inside the control box, manipulates the plane through a set of strings tied from the bracket to the underside of the plane, as shown in the photo below and the drawing on p. 142.

The most difficult part in making this toy was fabricating the universal joint that would allow the plane to swivel in all four directions in response to the controlling cables. My first effort was a cobbled-together affair made of pieces of tin can, strings and a wooden cigar box. The current version represents the state of the art in tabletop aviation. All the flight controls are directly under the aircraft for greatest movement with the least frictional interference. An engineering challenge for the craftsman, this project promises fun for all ages when completed.

Because this is a fairly complex project, it's a good idea to make a mock-up model first so you can evaluate the stability of the plane and the control mechanism.

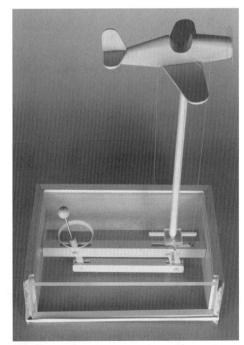

For illustrative purposes, the author cut the deck of this mocked-up control box from Plexiglas so that the control mechanism would be clearly visible.

Parts List

Quantity	Description	Finished Dimensions	Material
CONTROL-BOX MECHANISM			
1	Roll bar	⅝ x ⅝ x 9	Birch
2	Roll-bar axles	⅜ in. dia. by 1¹/₁₆ in. long	Birch
1	Dive/climb bar	½ x ½ x 6¼	Birch
1	Dive/climb swivel T	¼ x 1⅞ x 2⅛	Baltic birch plywood
1	Roll arm	³/₁₆-in.-dia. dowel by 2⅛ in. long	Birch
1	Joystick housing	⅜-in.-dia. dowel by 2⅜ in. long	Birch
1	Joystick	⅛-in.-dia. rod by 2⅝ in. long	Steel
1	Joystick knob	⅝-in.-dia. bead	Birch
2	Pivot pins	³/₁₆-in.-dia. dowel by ½ in. long	Birch
1	Pivot pin	³/₁₆-in.-dia. dowel by ⅝ in. long	Birch
4	Escutcheon pins	#16	Brass
4	Control lines	Thin fishing line, approx. 18 in. long	Clear nylon
CONTROL BOX			
2	Sides	½ x 3¼ x 10⅛	Pine
2	Ends	½ x 3¼ x 6½	Pine
1	Deck	¼ x 6 x 9⅝	Baltic birch plywood
1	Post-hole mounting block	¼ x 1 x 1	Baltic birch plywood
AIRCRAFT			
1	Fuselage	⅞ x 1⅛ x 4⅞	Pine
1	Wing	³/₁₆ x 1⅝ x 8	Pine
1	Stabilizer	⅛ x 1³/₁₆ x 2¾	Pine
1	Rudder	⅛ x 1⁵/₁₆ x 1⁷/₁₆	Pine
1	Cockpit	⅜ x ½ x 2¼	Pine
1	Cowl	1³/₁₆ in. dia. by ⁷/₁₆ in. thick	Walnut
1	Propeller	2¼ in. dia. by ¹/₁₆ in. thick	Plexiglas
1	Propeller spinner	#8/32 screw with acorn nut	Brass
4	Screweyes	Miniature	Steel
MOUNTING POST AND UNIVERSAL JOINT			
1	Post	⅜-in.-dia. dowel by 10 in. long	Birch
1	Connector	⅜-in.-dia. dowel by 1⅛ in. long*	Birch
1	Plane mount	⅜-in.-dia. dowel by ⅞ in. long*	Birch
2	Pins	4d finishing nail	Steel

*Reducing the length of these pieces will improve the stability of the universal joint (but will require greater skill in cutting).

CONTROL-BOX MECHANISM

The control box contains the working mechanism that controls the plane, as shown in the drawing on p. 142. The joystick poking out the top of the box passes through and is attached to a roll bar that pivots as the stick is moved left or right. The pivoting roll bar causes the attached roll arm, which is parallel to the plane's wing, to tilt from left to right. The roll arm is attached to the wing with nylon strings so that as one end of the roll arm dips, the corresponding end of the plane's wing is pulled down with it.

The end of the joystick is attached to one end of the dive/climb bar. Pushing or pulling on the joystick moves the dive/climb bar back and forth inside the control box and causes the dive/climb swivel T to pivot on its axis (the roll arm serves as the axis for the swivel T). The swivel T is parallel to and connected to the

U-Fly-It Plane

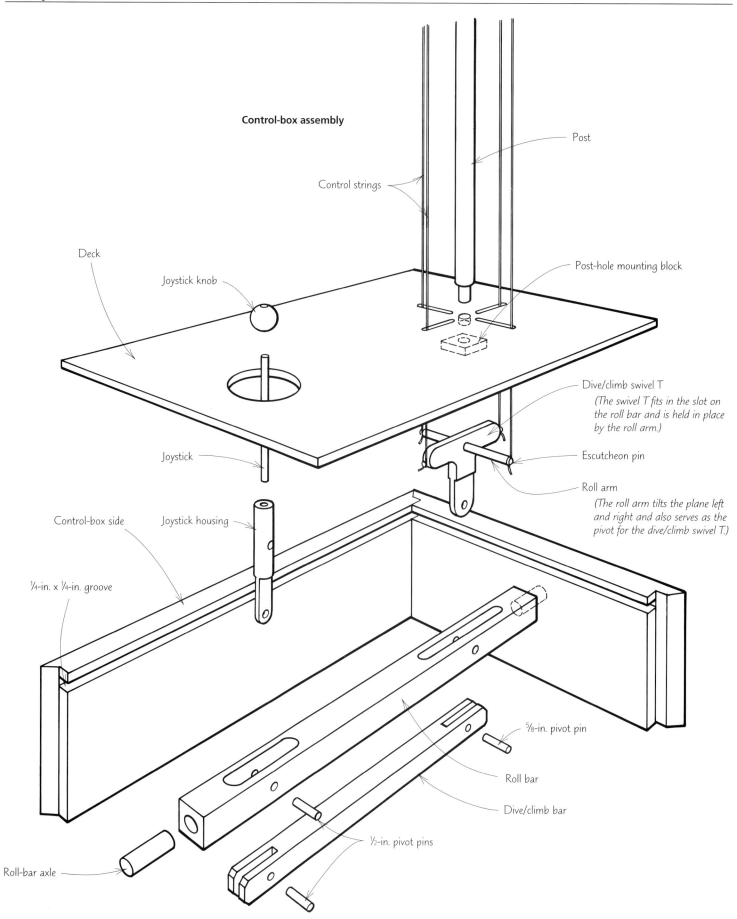

Control-box assembly

Post

Control strings

Deck

Joystick knob

Post-hole mounting block

Dive/climb swivel T
*(The swivel T fits in the slot on
the roll bar and is held in place
by the roll arm.)*

Escutcheon pin

Joystick

Roll arm
*(The roll arm tilts the plane left
and right and also serves as the
pivot for the dive/climb swivel T.)*

Control-box side   Joystick housing

¼-in. x ¼-in. groove

⅝-in. pivot pin

Roll bar

Dive/climb bar

½-in. pivot pins

Roll-bar axle

Parts Preparation (continued)

fuselage of the plane. As the back end of the T goes down, it pulls down the back of the plane causing the plane to climb, and vice versa.

I suggest you make the internal mechanism first, because it is more critical than its housing, and then make the control box to fit the mechanism.

1. Cut the roll bar to size, and then drill the two holes in the side as shown in the drawing below. Rout the slots to receive the swivel T and the joystick housing, and then drill the axle holes at the end of the bar, being careful not to drill into the slots.

2. Cut the dowels for the roll-bar axles slightly long; they will be trimmed to length when fitting the mechanism to the control box.

3. Cut the dive/climb bar to size, drill the $\frac{3}{16}$-in.-dia. pivot-pin holes and slot the ends.

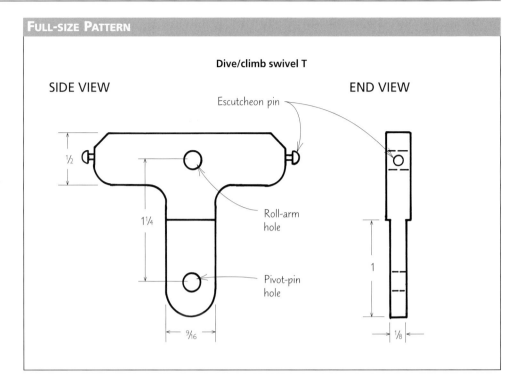

FULL-SIZE PATTERN

Dive/climb swivel T

SIDE VIEW

END VIEW

Escutcheon pin

Roll-arm hole

Pivot-pin hole

$\frac{1}{2}$

$1\frac{1}{4}$

$\frac{9}{16}$

1

$\frac{1}{8}$

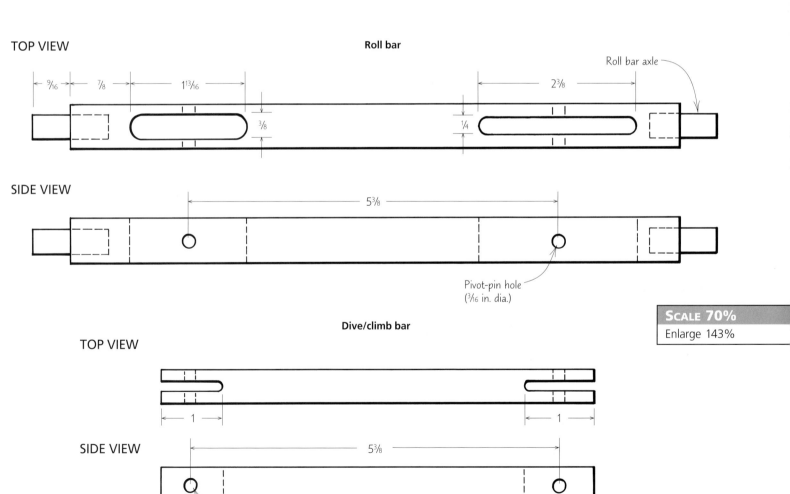

TOP VIEW

Roll bar

Roll bar axle

$\frac{9}{16}$ $\frac{7}{8}$ $1\frac{13}{16}$ $\frac{3}{8}$ $\frac{1}{4}$ $2\frac{3}{8}$

SIDE VIEW

$5\frac{3}{8}$

Pivot-pin hole
($\frac{3}{16}$ in. dia.)

SCALE 70%
Enlarge 143%

Dive/climb bar

TOP VIEW

1 1

SIDE VIEW

$5\frac{3}{8}$

Pivot-pin hole
($\frac{3}{16}$ in. dia.)

4. Trim the bottom of the dive/climb swivel-T blank to ⅛ in. thickness by fastening the blank to an auxiliary board with double-sided tape and cutting each side on the table saw. Cut the dive/climb swivel T to shape, and then drill the ³⁄₁₆-in.-dia. holes for the roll arm and pivot pin, as shown in the full-size drawing on p. 143.

5. Cut the roll arm to length, and then drill a hole into each end to receive the #16 brass escutcheon pins (which the control strings are tied to). I drilled these holes on the lathe.

6. I made the joystick in three pieces, although you could make it from a single piece of dowel about 4½ in. long. I used a short piece of dowel for the joystick housing that connects to the parallelogram-shaped bracket. The joystick is a short length of steel rod with a wooden bead epoxied to its end for a knob.

Use the simple wooden jig shown in the drawing at right to cut the ⅛-in.-thick flat area on the end of the joystick housing. Insert the joystick housing into the through hole in the top of the jig; make sure that the dowel fits snugly so it won't rotate. Set the rip fence, and then run the jig through the table saw with one side against the fence. Flip the jig end for end and run it through the saw again.

7. Drill the two ³⁄₁₆-in.-dia. holes in the joystick housing. Use the bottom hole to pivot the stick against a belt sander to create the bottom end radius (see p. 14).

Use a simple slotted jig to cut the flat section on the end of the joystick housing.

Cutting Jig for Joystick Housing

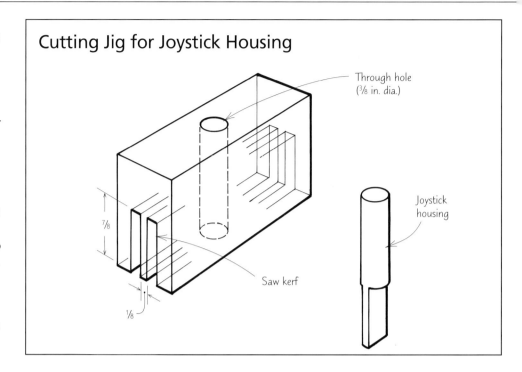

Through hole (³⁄₈ in. dia.)

Joystick housing

Saw kerf

⅞

⅛

Joystick assembly

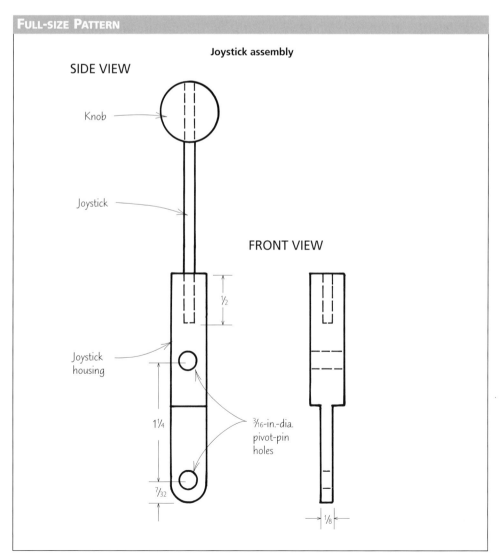

SIDE VIEW

Knob

Joystick

FRONT VIEW

Joystick housing

½

1¼

⁷⁄₃₂

³⁄₁₆-in.-dia. pivot-pin holes

⅛

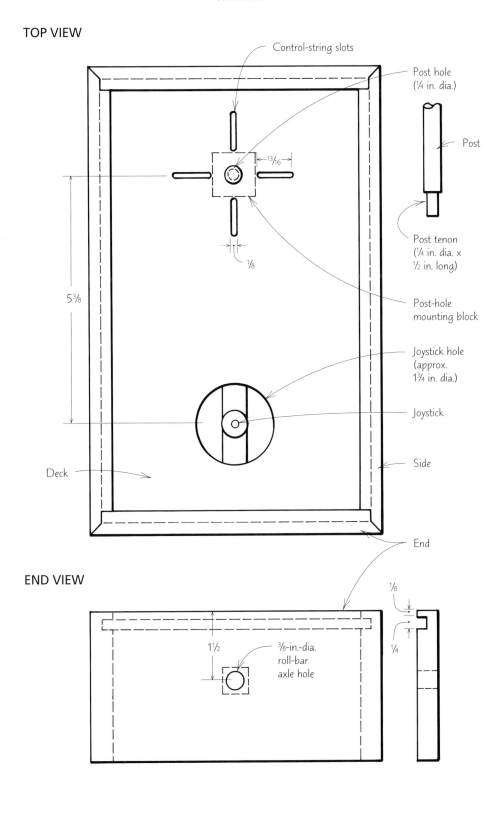

Control box

TOP VIEW

Control-string slots

Post hole
(¼ in. dia.)

Post

13/16

1/8

Post tenon
(¼ in. dia. x
½ in. long)

Post-hole
mounting block

5⅜

Joystick hole
(approx.
1¾ in. dia.)

Joystick

Deck

Side

End

END VIEW

1½

⅜-in.-dia.
roll-bar
axle hole

1/8

¼

CONTROL BOX

I made my control box with a mitered rabbet joint, but any joint will do, even a simple butt joint. The only critical dimension is the interior length, which should be 9 1/16 in. to accommodate the roll bar specified in the parts list. (You could, of course, change the length, as long as you adjust the length of the roll bar.)

1. Cut the sides and ends of the box to size, and then cut a groove for the deck in all four pieces.

2. Drill ⅜-in.-dia. holes in the end walls to receive the roll-bar axles.

3. Cut the deck to fit the box. Glue the post-hole mounting block to the underside of the deck, and then drill and slot the top, as shown in the drawing at left. Cut the hole for the joystick.

THE AIRCRAFT

The aircraft shown in the photo on p. 140 is a modified version of an AT-6 Texan, a trainer plane that was used extensively during World War II in the U.S. Army Air Corps, the U.S. Navy and the Royal Air Force. If you want to make this plane, follow the parts list on p.141 and the full-size drawings on p. 146. However, feel free to use your own design; you might also consider building a smaller version of the biplane in Project 11, which would make a beautiful display piece. Whatever design you choose, I recommend using pine to simplify fabrication.

1. Shape the fuselage using the same techniques as for the biplane (see pp. 78-79).

2. Cut the wing, stabilizer, rudder, cockpit and cowl to shape per the full-size drawings.

3. Cut a clear Plexiglas disc for the propeller.

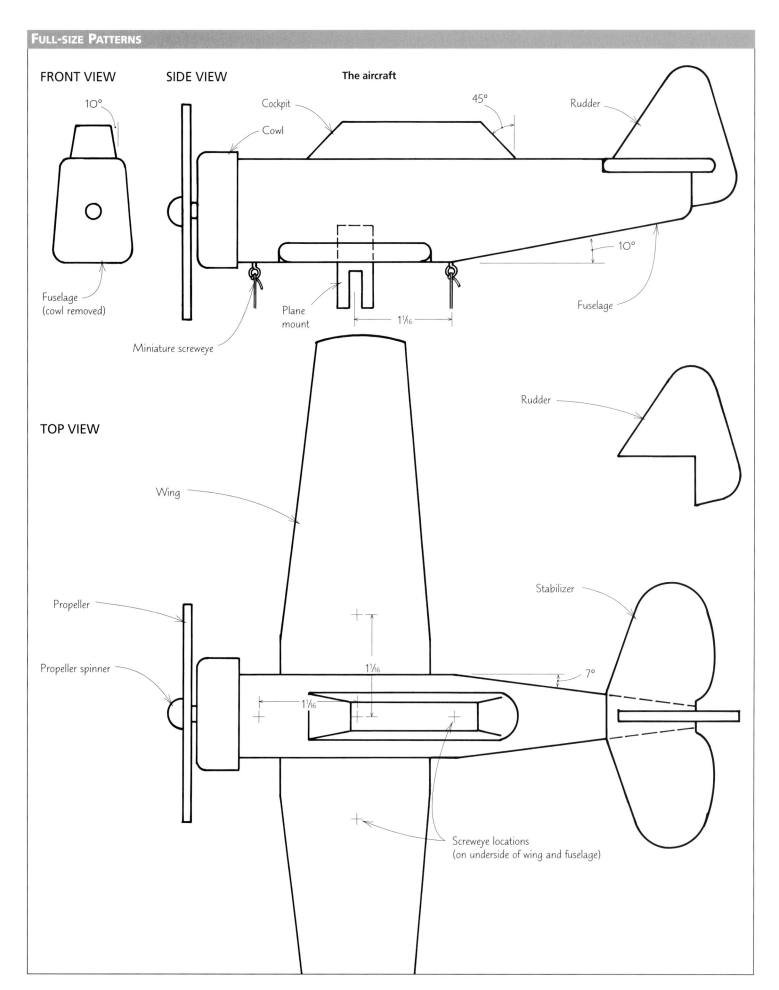

FRONT VIEW

10°

Fuselage
(cow removed)

SIDE VIEW

The aircraft

Cockpit

Cowl

45°

Rudder

10°

Fuselage

Plane
mount

1 1/16

Miniature screweye

TOP VIEW

Wing

Rudder

Propeller

Propeller spinner

Stabilizer

7°

1 1/16

1 1/16

Screweye locations
(on underside of wing and fuselage)

Parts Preparation (continued)

MOUNTING POST AND UNIVERSAL JOINT

The key to the success of this toy is the pivoting universal joint that connects the plane to the mounting post. I've tried a number of different solutions, ranging from a simple rounded-end metal rod inserted into the mounting post to the more challenging universal-joint pivot assembly presented here. If you want to take the easy way out, you can substitute a universal joint (or a ball joint) from a ¼-in.-drive socket set, available in most hardware stores. Another simple alternative is presented in the sidebar on p. 148.

The universal-joint assembly requires patience and precision to produce a smooth-working joint with no play. I've made the joint using both plastic rod and dowel stock; I prefer the plastic rod for its superior strength, although I've not yet had any failures with the dowel stock. All cuts for the universal joint were made on the table saw using the jig shown in the drawing at right.

1. Cut the plane mount, connector and post to length.

2. To cut the slot in the end of the plane mount, insert the dowel into the center hole of the jig and run the jig through the saw with face A down. The blade should be centered on the dowel.

3. To cut the tongue on the end of the mounting post, insert the dowel into the center hole of the jig and run the jig through the saw with face B down and side 1 against the fence. Flip the jig end for end and run it

through the saw again with side 2 against the fence.

4. To make the connector piece, cut a slot as described in Step 2. Without removing the piece, flip the jig over and cut the tongue as described in Step 3.

5. After cutting the plane mount, connector and post, drill the holes for the pins that hold

the universal joint together (see the drawing on p. 148). I used 4d finishing nails for pins; drill the holes to match the pins you'll be using.

6. Radius the ends of each piece using the holes as pivot points (see p. 14).

7. Turn a tenon on the bottom end of the post to fit the mounting hole in the deck.

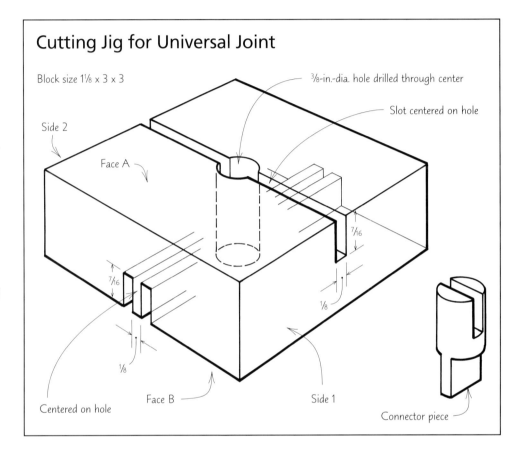

Cutting Jig for Universal Joint

Block size 1⅛ x 3 x 3

⅜-in.-dia. hole drilled through center

Slot centered on hole

Side 2

Face A

⁷⁄₁₆

⅛

⁷⁄₁₆

⅛

Centered on hole

Face B

Side 1

Connector piece

Cut a slot in the end of the plane mount using the universal joint-cutting jig.

With the jig turned over, make two cuts to form the tongue on the end of the mounting post.

The connector piece requires a slot on one end and a tongue on the other.

ENLARGED DETAIL

Universal mounting joint

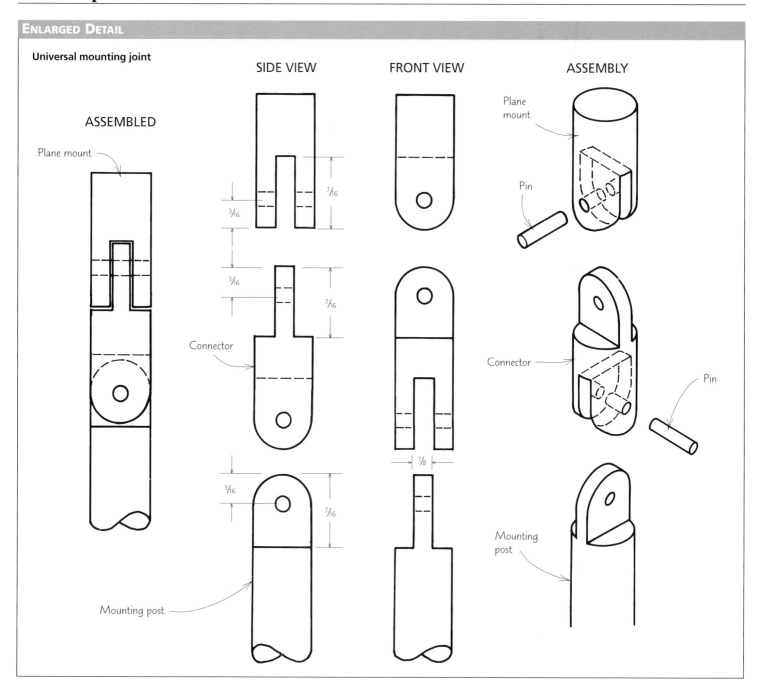

ASSEMBLED

Plane mount

Mounting post

SIDE VIEW

7/16

3/16

3/16

7/16

Connector

3/16

7/16

FRONT VIEW

1/8

ASSEMBLY

Plane mount

Pin

Connector

Pin

Mounting post

A Simple Ball-Joint Connection

I'm always on the lookout for ways to improve the design of my toys, and the connection between the fuselage of the plane and the mounting post is one area that's been through several revisions over the years.

While I was writing this book, I came across a ball joint that's used on a desk-pen set (I found it in the Cherry Tree

catalog, item #3025 and 3009; see Sources of Supply on p. 151). The ball joint fits perfectly between the fuselage and the post and allows you to pivot and roll the plane a little farther in all directions than the universal joint described in the text. The joint was a little tight at first, but using a little WD-40 helped loosen it up.

Assembly

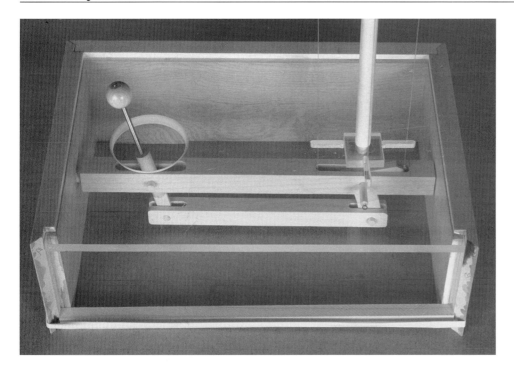

Finish all parts as described on pp. 16-18.

CONTROL-BOX MECHANISM

1. Assemble the parallelogram-shaped bracket first. Position the swivel T in the longer slot in the roll bar, and then slide the roll arm through the roll bar and into the swivel T. If necessary, re-drill the holes in the roll bar so that the roll arm can rotate freely. The roll arm should be a press-fit in the swivel T. You may need to pin the roll arm onto the T to prevent it from slipping (pin through the top center of the T).

2. Insert the joystick housing into the short slot in the roll bar, and then pin it in place with a pivot pin. The pivot pin should be a press-fit in the roll bar, and the joystick housing should swing freely on the pin. Glue the pivot pin to the roll bar if necessary, but be sure the joystick housing moves freely.

3. Attach the swivel T and the joystick housing to the dive/climb bar with two pivot pins, as shown in the drawing on p. 142. Double-check all mechanical movements, and then put this assembly aside.

CONTROL BOX

1. Glue the box sides and ends together, sliding the deck into the groove before gluing the last side into place.

2. Position the pre-assembled parallelogram-shaped bracket into the box. From each end, insert the roll-bar axles and check the mechanism's movement. Mark the axles for cutting flush with the ends, and then remove the axles.

3. Tie the control lines to the two brass pins on the roll arm and the two pins on the swivel T. Leave the lines long and trim them to length after tying to the aircraft.

4. Thread the lines through the corresponding deck slots, reposition the parallelogram-shaped bracket in the box and glue the axles (cut to the correct length) in place. Check the roll bar for free movement.

AIRCRAFT

1. Glue the plane parts together with epoxy, following the drawing on p. 146.

2. Find the center point on the underside of the wing and mark out the screweye locations.

3. Drill a $\frac{3}{8}$-in.-dia. hole for the plane mount and pilot holes for the screweyes.

4. Coat the threads of the screweyes liberally with epoxy, and then screw them into the wing and the fuselage.

MOUNTING POST AND UNIVERSAL JOINT

1. Assemble the universal joint, and then pin together with pieces of a 4d finishing nail cut to length.

2. Epoxy the plane mount into the center hole in the underside of the wing.

3. Insert the tenoned end of the post into its hole in the deck.

4. Epoxy the joystick to the joystick housing, but don't glue the knob in place yet.

5. Cut a boxboard or cardboard disc that will fit snugly into the joystick hole in the deck (the disc will hold the joystick in the centered position while you tie the control strings to the aircraft). Punch a $\frac{1}{8}$-in.-dia. hole in the center of the disc. Slide the disc onto the joystick and position it in the hole in the deck. Tape the disc in place.

6. Have someone hold the plane level in all directions while you tie the control lines. Try to tie them all to the same tension, which sounds a lot easier than it is (inserting a needle into each knot while tightening the lines will allow you to make minor adjustments to the tension). Once the plane is tied down, remove the disc, epoxy the knob onto the joystick and prepare for takeoff.

If you find that you need to improve the stability of the control mechanism, there are a couple of things you can do. One is to make the swivel T a little wider and the roll arm a little longer, which will allow you to space the control strings slightly farther apart. Make sure to reposition the screweyes on the underside of the plane. The second way to improve stability is to reduce the length of the top two pieces of the universal joint (the plane mount and the connector). Building a mock-up version first will help you evaluate the stability of the control mechanism.

Sources of Supply

Books

- Dover Publications, 31 East 2nd St., Mineola, NY 11501; (516) 294-7000
  A complete line of books on collectibles and things of the past—ideal for design inspiration.

Toy parts

- Casey's Wood Products, 15½ School St., Freeport, ME 04032; (800) 452-2739, (207) 882-6554; FAX (207) 882-6554
  All-wood products such as wheels, pegs, people, cargo drums.

- Cherry Tree Toys, P.O. Box 369, Belmont, OH 43718; (800) 848-4363
  All-wood products (as above); toy plans.

- Streamline Industries, 845 Stewart Ave., Garden City, NY 11530
  Headlight buttons (⁹/₁₆ in. dia. and ¹¹/₁₆ in. dia.); pearl buttons for headlights may also be available from local sewing stores or fabric stores.

- Woodworks, 4521 Anderson Blvd., Fort Worth, TX 76117; (800) 722-0311, (817) 581-5230; FAX (817) 581-5235
  Outstanding selection of dowels, people, wheels and other turnings.

Hardware

- Hillman Fastener, 10590 Hamilton Ave., Cincinnati, OH 45231; (800) 800-4901
  Push nuts are usually available from hardware stores or homebuilding centers, but if you can't find any locally, you can mail-order them from the above source.

  Check local hardware stores, hobby shops and home centers for steel axles, plastic rod, flat-head rivets, aluminum tubing and brass tubing.

General woodworking supplies

- Constantine's, 2050 Eastchester Rd., Bronx, NY 10461; (800) 223-8087; FAX (800) 253-9663
  Dowels, wood, veneers, finishing supplies, drums, pegs, wheels.

- General Hardware Manufacturing Co., 80 White St., New York, NY 10013; (212) 431-6100; FAX (212) 431-6499
  "Wiggler" center finder (item #S-389-4).

- The Woodworkers' Store, 21801 Industrial Blvd., Rogers, MN 55374-9514; (800) 279-4441; FAX (612) 428-8668
  Tools, hardware, wood products.

- Woodworker's Supply, 1108 North Glenn Rd., Casper, WY 82601; (800) 645-9292
  Tools, dowels and miscellaneous wood parts.

Safe finishes

- Garrett Wade, 161 Avenue of the Americas, New York, NY 10013; (800) 221-2942
  Behlen's Salad Bowl Finishes, shellac flakes, alcohol and brushes.

- Livos Plantchemistry, The Natural Choice, 1365 Rufina Circle, Santa Fe, NM 87501; (800) 621-2591, (505) 438-3448; FAX (505) 438-0199
  Citrus-based, non-toxic finishes.

- Peterson Chemical Corp., 710 Forest Ave., P.O. Box 102, Sheboygan Falls, WI 53085-0102; (800) 558-7596
  #100 clear gloss epoxy.

- Woodfinishing Enterprises, 1729 N. 68th St., Wauwatosa, WI 53213; (414) 774-1724
  Non-toxic finishes.

For information on full-sized plans for the toys presented in this book, please send a self-addressed stamped envelope to Jim Makowicki, P.O. Box 7, Sandy Hook, CT 06482-0007.

Publisher: *James P. Chiavelli*
Acquisitions Editor: *Rick Peters*
Publishing Coordinator: *Joanne Renna*

Editor: *Peter Chapman*
Production Editor: *Diane Sinitsky*
Designer/Layout Artist: *Christopher Casey*
Illustrator: *Vincent Babak*
Photographers: *Susan Kahn, Boyd Hagen; assistant, Scott Phillips*

Typeface: *Frutiger Light*
Paper: *Warren Patina Matte, 70 lb., neutral pH*
Printer: *Quebecor Printing/Kingsport, Kingsport, Tennessee*